AF608149

CHINA'S GLOBAL IDENTITY

Other Titles of Interest from Georgetown University Press

Bridging Troubled Waters: China, Japan, and Maritime Order in the East China Sea
James Manicom

The China-India Rivalry in the Globalization Era
T.V. Paul, Editor

China in the Era of Xi Jinping: Domestic and Foreign Policy Challenges
Robert S. Ross and Jo Inge Bekkevold, Editors

Meeting China Halfway: How to Defuse the Emerging US-China Rivalry
Lyle J. Goldstein

Middle Powers and the Rise of China
Bruce Gilley and Andrew O'Neil, Editors

CHINA'S GLOBAL IDENTITY

Considering the Responsibilities of Great Power

HOO TIANG BOON

Georgetown University Press / Washington, DC

Library of Congress Cataloging-in-Publication Data

Names: Tiang Boon, Hoo, 1977- author.
Title: China's Global Identity : Considering the Responsibilities of Great Power / Hoo Tiang Boon.
Description: Washington, DC : Georgetown University Press, 2018. | Includes bibliographical references and index.
Identifiers: LCCN 2018002795 (print) | LCCN 2018017536 (ebook) | ISBN 9781626166158 (ebook) | ISBN 9781626166141 (pbk. : alk. paper) | ISBN 9781626166134 (hardcover : alk. paper)
Subjects: LCSH: China—Foreign relations—20th century. | China—Foreign relations—21st century. | China—Foreign relations—United States. | United States—Foreign relations—China.
Classification: LCC DS775.8 (ebook) | LCC DS775.8 .H67 2018 (print) | DDC 327.51—dc23
LC record available at https://lccn.loc.gov/2018002795

∞ This book is printed on acid-free paper meeting the requirements of the American National Standard for Permanence in Paper for Printed Library Materials.

19 18 9 8 7 6 5 4 3 2 First printing

Printed in the United States of America.

Cover design by Martyn Schmoll.

CONTENTS

ILLUSTRATIONS

Tables

Figures

ACKNOWLEDGMENTS

Many intellectual, professional, and personal debts have been incurred over the long course of writing this book. Initial research for the book would not have been possible without the generous financial support of Nuffield College, Oxford, and funding from the Oxford University Contemporary China Studies Program. Oxford has been ideal as a stimulating testbed for many of the book's early ideas, and the project gained much from the critiques of fellow Oxanians as well as feedback from presentations at the Department of Politics and International Relations and Nuffield College. Insights reaped at other venues have also greatly aided the development of this work. I am particularly appreciative of the comments to my presentations at Harvard University and the US Council on Foreign Relations.

In China, I was fortunate to spend time as a visiting scholar at the China Foreign Affairs University, Shanghai Institutes for International Studies, and Shanghai Academy of Social Sciences. These institutions provided not only exceptional hospitality and support; they also facilitated numerous opportunities for me to meet Chinese analysts and, on occasions, former and current officials. During my several trips to China over the years I also had opportunities to visit other academic/policy institutions, including Peking University, Renmin University, Tsinghua University, Fudan University, Communication University of China, the China Institutes of Contemporary International Relations, the China Institute for International Strategic Studies, the Academy of Military Science, the National Defense University, and the National Institute for South China Sea Studies. The discussions and interviews I have had with my Chinese interlocutors have been invaluable to this book.

At my home ground, faculty colleagues at the S. Rajaratnam School of International Studies (RSIS) in Nanyang Technological University have been exceedingly supportive. I am grateful to Ambassadors Ong Keng Yong and Barry Desker for their support and confidence. I also thank Joseph Liow, Ralf Emmers, Tan See Seng, Ang Cheng Guan, Bhubhindar Singh, and Kumar Ramakrishna for their intellectual comradeship and encouragement. I am especially indebted to my dean, Joseph, for his counsel and support at a crucial stage of the project.

Outside of RSIS, many colleagues and friends have also been generous with their time and talents. I extend my gratitude and thanks to Evelyn Goh, Thomas Christensen, Peter Katzenstein, Richard Bush, Rana Mitter, Jia Qingguo, John Garver, Brian Job, Andrew Hurrell, Zhang Yongjin, Bob Carr, Gerald Chan, Shi Yinhong, Katherine Morton, He Kai, Sarah Percy, Chen Zhimin, Laurence Whitehead, Shaun Breslin, Pang Zhongying, James Reilly, Robin Markwica, Amy King, Nicola Leveringhaus, and John Ciorciari—all of whom either read segments of the manuscript in its various stages and provided helpful suggestions, shared their expertise and knowledge, or asked interesting questions that made a difference to my work.

Working with the team at Georgetown University Press has been a joy. The book's publication owes much to the expertise and dedication of Don Jacobs, Glenn Saltzman, Virginia Bryant, and Ann Baker. I am especially beholden to Don, who provided expert advice and guidance throughout the publication process and was always incredibly patient and understanding. My profuse thanks also go to the two anonymous reviewers whose careful attention and perceptive comments helped refine the manuscript further.

I wish to acknowledge the special role of Rosemary Foot, Khong Yuen Foong, and David Shambaugh in my journey of writing this book. This note cannot do justice to Rosemary's impact in my scholarly life, but if I were to highlight two things I have learned (or hope to have learned) from her, they are, one, the art of the nuance. Things are seldom black or white in international politics; they are more shades of gray. It behooves the careful scholar to capture this nuance in his or her work. Two, academic stamina and discipline. Rosemary taught me the importance of staying focused and doing regular writing even when inspiration seems distant. The maxim is to write in the best of times, the worst of times. Another major scholarly influence is Yuen Foong. I was unaware at that time, but the seeds of this book were planted the day I stepped into his legendary seminar, "Analysis of Defence and Security Policies," more than a decade ago. Being taught by and, over the years, mentored by Yuen Foong opened my mind to a whole new level of intellectual imagination and thinking I never thought possible. A third influential figure in my book journey is David Shambaugh, whom I have had the tremendous fortune of being informally tutored by. I had no right to receive the attention and generosity of the world's preeminent China expert, but David not only read my manuscript several times and gave indispensable advice to improve the book, he also spent significant time sharing his wise counsel on being a better scholar on China. I am truly indebted to all three individuals for their mentorship and friendship.

My greatest debt is to May Lin. It is often said that writing is a lonely process, but this has not been my experience with this book. May Lin walked together with me in its voyage and did so with a curious mix of jovial forbearance. Despite her illness she read much of the manuscript numerous times, scrutinized my interpretations and arguments, and offered many valuable suggestions to improve the work. Last, but not least, Olivia and Sophia have been exceedingly understanding in accepting why I have had to be away from them on many occasions. I dedicate this book to them.

INTRODUCTION

In a scene from Sam Raimi's film *Spiderman*, Uncle Ben speaks to Peter Parker after the latter, with his newfound superhuman strength, gives the school bully a severe thrashing. Dispensing advice, Uncle Ben admonishes Peter gently, telling him that just because "he can do so [beat up the bully], it doesn't mean he has to." After all, Uncle Ben counsels, "with great power comes great responsibility."

The reel world is obviously different, but Uncle Ben's words bring to mind a concept that has been very real in the world of great-power politics. For the past two decades the concept of the responsibility of power has been central to American engagement with the aspiring superpower of the People's Republic of China (PRC). Even as President Bill Clinton assured China's leaders that the United States "welcomes China to the great-power table," he reminded them that "great powers also have great responsibilities."[1] The George W. Bush administration promulgated a similar message, urging China to move beyond membership in the international system to become a "responsible stakeholder."[2] And when President Barack Obama met Xi Jinping during the Chinese president's first state visit to the US in 2015, the crux of Obama's message was that China's rise comes with expanded responsibilities. In response to the growth in Chinese power and influence, it has been a consistent American policy belief that China should contribute more to the management of global issues because it has a duty to sustain the international system that enabled its rise.

Yet this call for China to assume greater responsibilities has not been incongruent with messages emanating from Beijing. The message has squared with a Chinese global identity evolution premised on the idea of China as a "responsible great power" (*fuzeren daguo*, or RGP for brevity). For some time now, Chinese political elites have been characterizing—and debating—China's role as a responsible power in international society. In fact, this is a Chinese role imagination that has been formalized at the highest political levels. *The Eighteenth Party Congress Report* states that China will "exhibit the function of a responsible great power."[3] The *2016 Report on the Work of the Government* avers

China as a "responsible major country."[4] The RGP identity has become a key motif in Chinese foreign policy lexicon and discourse.

It is a significant development that requires explanation. How has the responsible great-power identity been produced in China? What factors animate its origins and evolution? What is its content? And to what extent have external actors such as the US played a role in shaping this identity? To date, virtually no focused studies have addressed these questions. This lack of an in-depth examination of China's RGP identity has been lamented by Alastair Iain Johnston. In his book *Social States* Johnston notes: "Explaining the evolution of the [RGP] identity at this particular time in history is obviously an important question," one for which he wished he had a "definitive answer."[5]

This book embarks on the first sustained study of China's great-power identity. Mobilizing the concept of global identity, it tells the story of how and why China has come to pursue a role imagination as a responsible power. The book traces the evolution of the RGP identity and uncovers the politics, history, events, and ideas behind its emergence and development.

Why is it important that we study China's responsible-power identity? Or, alternatively put, what is the significance of this particular face of China to world politics? First, there exists a growing perspective among scholars and policymakers that China is basically non–status quo or revisionist in orientation and trajectory. Indeed, this perspective has become increasingly persuasive in recent years (especially with Xi's China), and many analysts see a "more confident, assertive . . . anti-status quo [China that] is pushing back against the West, promoting its own alternative norms and policies . . . and generally seeking to test the leadership capacity of the United States." Observers cite, in particular, China's actions in the territorial disputes of the East and South China Seas as epitomizing a new, more belligerent foreign policy. The idea of an assertive, "post-responsible" China has become increasingly prevalent.[6]

Yet such views present a one-dimensional portrait of China's diplomacy. Its full complexity should be taken into account, including those occasions when Beijing has acted in more cooperative and beneficent ways or reacted with restraint and compromise. For example, Beijing is implementing the One Belt, One Road initiative, with funding support of at least US$40 billion, to enhance infrastructure connectivity and economic integration among countries straddling the spaces between Asia and Europe. It reached a surprising pact on climate change with the US, pledging to cap its carbon dioxide emissions by 2030. It played a constructive part in facilitating the historic nuclear deal between the P5+1 UN group and Iran, a role that garnered "appreciation" from the Obama administration.[7] How do we square these apparent contradictions, so to speak?

It is important to emphasize that I am *not* arguing that China is becoming a more "responsible" stakeholder or is fundamentally a benign power. I argue, however, that many existing interpretations are insufficiently attentive to the evolution and complexity of Chinese thinking on the PRC's great-power role and responsibility. Unpacking the dimensions and content of this particular identity space is important because these ideas shape the parameters of China's conduct as a great power. In other words, understanding how Chinese elites have perceived the role and obligations of Chinese power will shed insights into why China has behaved (or not behaved) in certain ways in global affairs. As this book shows, there is a vibrant epistemic terrain related to the RGP identity within China. For some time now Chinese elites have been debating intensely the kind of responsible power that China should be. That these identity debates take place frequently, away from the attention of most of the world, suggests the Chinese regard the idea of big-power responsibility far more seriously than had it been purely a convenient propaganda tool.

Second, and more than that, these identity discussions may well hold clues to the larger questions about the implications of China's ascendancy: how it might use its power as this power grows and the impact on the global order. Will this rise lead to John Mearsheimer's tragedy of great-power politics or Hugh White's great-power concert in global governance, or neither? China's evolving ideas of its identity and obligations as a great power can help us better understand the answers.

Beyond providing a more complete story to the complexities of China's big-power behavior and the consequences of its power ascent, this book also speaks to a number of gaps in the existing international relations (IR) literature. For one, scholarship that brings together the motifs of China's responsibility and its great-power role is scant. To be sure, these themes have been referenced in several IR studies (including, but not limited to, accounts on China), but most works go no further than to merely note the RGP identity without providing a focused examination or explanation of the phenomenon. But even among those few studies that focus on the subjects of Chinese power and responsibility, at least three areas require addressing. First, the majority of them focus overwhelmingly on questions of Chinese conduct, particularly in terms of assessing whether Beijing has behaved more or less "responsibly" in international society.[8] These studies appear less interested in making sense of China's perspectives of global responsibility or unpacking the emerging RGP identity, endeavors that could provide fuller insights to the motivations that drive China's behavior. This book eavesdrops on that neglected internal dialogue and process.

Second, among those who have discerned China's RGP character, there is a tendency to interpret this role imagination as nothing more than for external image-building and propaganda purposes.[9] This is an incomplete understanding. As my book shows, a mosaic of factors—not only image concerns—has had a shaping effect on the RGP identity, including contingent events, the role of the US, strategic instrumentality, domestic ideational influences, and Chinese social aspirations in international society. All of these elements are important in weaving together the story of China's identity as a responsible power.

Third, most accounts appear unsure about when the RGP identity discourse started to emerge, with most believing that such narratives began surfacing only after the 2005 American call on China to be a "responsible stakeholder." The findings of my research indicate otherwise and show that there was already a nascent discussion of the RGP concept within China beginning in the early 1990s and that such conversations have been taking place for a while now.

In tracing the evolution of the RGP identity, a further contribution of the book is that its findings shed light on the origins of China's sense of self as a great power. China's impressive economic ascendancy in the past three decades is often cited as the prime reason underpinning the rise of its great-power confidence and self-perception. This is a partial explanation at best. It is commonly overlooked that Chinese self-awareness as a great power has had longer and deeper antecedents. Here the book argues that three earlier "cognitive priors" in China's identity makeup have been particularly salient[10]: a civilizational complex of a "great central kingdom"; a perception of "suppressed greatness" in the late Qing and Republican eras; and a post-1949 Maoist outlook of a "great power awakening."

This book also adds new insights to the evolving dynamics of the most consequential major power relationship today: US-China relations. A considerable amount of this literature focuses on three core interrelated issues: whether or to what extent China is displacing the United States as the preeminent global power; the consequences (in particular, the dangers) of power transition between the two countries; and American policy responses to China's rise. These themes are the subject of focus of a research project led by Graham Allison at the Harvard

Belfer Center for Science and International Affairs. Allison has suggested that unless "painful adjustments" are made by the two sides, both the PRC and the US are headed for a Thucydides Trap where "war is more likely than not."[11] I engage this conversation by looking from the relatively different angle of the American role in molding China's great-power identity. The centrality of the US in Chinese deliberations is often underestimated, and this book highlights the various ways in which the world's prevailing hegemon has, directly or indirectly, shaped identity discussions in Beijing. The findings suggest the United States has had a bigger impact on China's sense of its place in the world than most people realize.

Global Identity and Its Formation

This study engages the concept of global identity to analyze China as a great power. By global identity I am referring to the structure of ideas of political elites that relate to their country's role in the international system. This is a conception of identity that is essentially statist. It follows Lowell Dittmer and Samuel Kim's characterization of a country's identity as an ideational structure stratified by the interdependent tiers of state and society. At the top of this structure are state elements, such as "policies, principles, basic lines, and world views" of governing or policy elites, while the lower and broader tier embodies the collective perspectives and beliefs of the larger societal body.[12] Global identity, as interpreted in this study, is primarily produced at the top of this structure—that is, the level of the state. Hence it does not correspond to some national or cultural solidarity group per se and is not a characterization centered at the societal level. This relates to the fact that, "to the extent that only a small elite is actively involved in national and foreign affairs," the identity of a country—especially one pertaining to the international domain—is primarily mediated or directed by its elites.[13] This is not to imply that global identity stands in isolation from societal forces. Depending on the political context, the views of elites can often reflect the sentiments of the broader society. Elites' perceptions and societal sentiments are not mutually exclusive, and in various issues of national concern they are often congruent or overlapping.[14]

How does a state's global identity develop? Here I draw on the logic of "the self" and "the other" to conceptually organize thinking about the RGP identity's formation. The self-other dialectic has been theorized and used widely in various social science disciplines, so this study is applying an identity framework that has substantial intellectual foundations.

The framework proposes that in the construction of an identity, there are basically two key sources of role ideas: self and other.[15] The self refers to the owner of the identity in question; in our case it is the state. However, equating the state as a unitary actor in the context of identity formation is not without its problems. One issue lies in the fact that much of the empirical evidence in identity studies focuses on individuals or small groups and that to apply these findings to international politics, where the principal actors are states, requires some degree of theoretical extrapolation. Yet this is an extrapolation that is not entirely unjustified. States, after all, are "peopled" too, which means it is arguably plausible to project findings in identity studies to IR.[16] In this sense a state is analogous to a "group Self, capable of group-level cognition."[17] Additionally, anthropomorphizing the state—that is, humanizing "phenomena that are, in reality, collections of [individuals]"—is commonly applied in studies of collective identity and nationalism.[18] These studies have comprehensively shown that it is plausible for agency to be scaled to the level of large groups and, by extension, of the state in a way that would not overly prejudice the overall research. A related point is that collective agency does not preclude the presence of contesting identity views within a state. Moreover, there can be different degrees or layers of contestation. To connect to our case of China, Chinese elites may agree on the overall shape of an international identity (e.g., China is X) but they may dispute its content or the ways to fulfill it (i.e., What kind of X is China? How should China become X?).

The other represents the external source of role ideas that contribute to the self's definition and learning. Some scholars write of a historical or cultural other where a particular past or culture is a source of identity learning, but in global identity this typically refers to other states.[19] This book focuses on the United States as the primary relevant other in China's RGP identity. There is undoubtedly more than one state that can assume the role of an other in Chinese identity. Japan, for example, is seen as a "victimizing" other in the production and sustenance of China's victim self-perception, while North Korea is an important connection in contemporary Chinese socialist identity.[20] Overall, however, in relation to China's place in the global order, the United States is arguably the most critical other. One study finds that almost 80 percent of new research in the Chinese Academy of Social Sciences (CASS), a state-affiliated network of Chinese think tanks, focuses on topics related to the United States.[21]

My field interviews with PRC analysts in Beijing and Shanghai also corroborate the centrality of the US in Chinese strategic estimations.[22] This centrality is underpinned by a number of reasons, of which the most evident is that Beijing perceives the US as the key "constraint" or "enabler" of its rise, especially after the dissolution of the Soviet Union.[23] Moreover, as the predominant power in international society, the United States is effectively the gatekeeper to China's aspirations for great-power status. Whether Washington recognizes Chinese power has an inexorable impact in the capitals of the world, a social reality that is not lost on Beijing. This recognition extends to the notion of China's "accountability" to international society, where America has essentially acted as the main adjudicator of the PRC's global responsibility.

It is worth further clarifying two aspects about the role of the other. First, it can be both a source of affirming difference and/or of similarity, "from conceiving the other as anathema to the self to conceiving it as an extension of the self."[24] In the case of the United States it is both a different and a similar other to China. While American democratic identity is dissonant with the socialist face of Chinese identity, American identity as the leading member of the great-power club is a position that China evidently aspires to and seeks to identify with. Second, while this study focuses on the US as the key significant other, this does not mean it is always the only external source of role learning in China's great-power evolution. Where relevant, the book will look at how other foreign actors have also complemented the US in informing Chinese great-power perceptions.

Taken together, role ideas of the self and other interact in a mutually constitutive process to impart shape and content to an actor's identity. Relating to international politics, this means that a state's identity is an evolving product of its self-perception (internal collective cognition) and social learning from other states (external learning) about its role in international society.

The sociological premise of the self-other model should not be taken to imply an absence of instrumentality in global identity formation. In other words, why a state categorizes itself in certain ways within the international system or why it filters out certain interpretations of external role messages can be linked to functional reasons or particular strategic interests. As Amitav Acharya's work on constitutive localization shows, states are not passive heirs of external ideas and norms.[25] They have the capacity to adjudicate their role preferences even as these preferences are subjected to external influences. Accordingly, there is no reason why identity formation cannot be "rationalistic"—that is, constructed on the basis of interests or purposes as deliberated by the state. Such a position references what some scholars have called "pragmatic constructivism" and reflects a synthesis of sociological and rationalist approaches in IR.[26] There are indeed robust theoretical antecedents to substantiate the view that identity construction can be pragmatic. Ernst Haas's work on neofunctionalism shows that, other than a normative dimension, a collective identity can equally be informed by a "logic of consequences."[27] James Fearon and David Laitin's study on ethnic identity finds that identity construction (even one commonly understood as primordial) can in fact be manipulated by elites for strategic ends.[28] My account of identity formation stands on the shoulders of these scholars, highlighting the volition in identity construction that strict sociological accounts tend to take for granted.

Other Possible Identities

A nontrivial clarification is that there can be more than one face to a state's global persona. States can have multiple global identities. For China, the RGP role is one out of at least five mutually nonexclusive Chinese identifications in the international system that also conceive the country as a socialist state, third-world country, developing nation, and victim of history. It is useful to briefly review these other Chinese identities so as to provide alternative reference points for our discussion of the RGP identity.

The socialist face of China (*shehui zhuyi guojia*) has traditionally been a prominent aspect of its identity in the international milieu, but this has receded in relative importance with the end of the Cold War. Such an identity still holds significance within the domestic political context, with the Chinese Communist Party (CCP) government deliberately seeking to conflate national identification with "identification with the Communist leadership."[29] Many aspects of Chinese society are also still organized around Marxist-Leninist principles, even as the PRC has embraced economic capitalism.[30] Nevertheless, in foreign policy this identity has diminished in relevance. Since the 1990s Chinese leaders have appeared reluctant to identify China in socialist terms on the international stage other than in reference to its relationship with specific countries, particularly North Korea, Vietnam, Cuba, and Laos.[31]

Like its socialist profile, China's third-world identity (*disan shijie guojia*) has seen a general decline. In the 1960s, in part because of the Sino-Soviet split,

Maoist China sought political solidarity with nations of the Third World—putatively countries in Asia, Africa, and Latin America. This identification was predicated on a supposed connection with the "have-nots" and oppressed former colonies of the world, but it also had strategic rewards in the form of garnering a potential support constituency for China in its struggle against the global status quo.[32] It persisted in the 1970s, as shown by the official announcement of Mao's Three Worlds theory at the UN General Assembly Sixth Special Session in 1974.[33] But with the passing of Maoist China by the late 1970s, the third-world identity became increasingly nonviable to Beijing. It raised inevitable tensions with Chinese strategies of reform, which emphasized accommodation with the international status quo in order to join the ranks of those outside of the Third World. China's sense of pride in its civilizational greatness also continued to weaken any imagined association with the unglamorous category of the Third World. Unsurprisingly, Peter Van Ness notes that since the 1980s, China has wanted to "escape from being Third World."[34] That said, China's third-world identity has not followed a linear path to irrelevance. Although its relative importance has waned, Beijing has not been averse to the identity's strategic invocation on select occasions. For example, in the wake of international sanctions after the 1989 Tiananmen crackdown, Beijing was quick to articulate an identification with the Third World, depicting itself as a target of oppression by Western "neo-imperialism."[35] Beijing has also been keen to promote a third-world identity centered on "non-Westernness" in its diplomacy with Africa, in part to boost its growing economic and energy agenda there and in part to cultivate a support constituency potentially valuable in multilateral settings.[36]

China as a developing nation (*fazhan guojia*) is a profile that has been comparatively more consistent in Chinese identity discourses. Objective reality informs this profile: despite its rapid economic growth, the PRC is still lagging behind in a number of international development measures (e.g., gross national income per capita, degree of urbanization, level of poverty), while the 2015 UN Human Development Index ranked China 90 out of 188 countries.[37] It is often the case that the "developing nation" identity is conflated with China's third-world characterization, but ideationally they are not entirely coterminous. Increasingly, the developing-nation discourse is often more about China's level of economic development than an imagined solidarity based on bloc politics. Of course, all third-world countries are also developing nations, but when China's developing-nation identity is evoked these days it is not necessarily implying a political connection with the Third World and refers more to the fact that China is not yet a fully prosperous country.[38] This distinction should not be ignored.

The victim self-perception (*shouhaizhe*) draws from China's historical memory of suffering and humiliation at the hands of imperialist powers during the nineteenth and early twentieth centuries. Central to this identity is the national narrative that China had been treated unfairly and badly by outsiders in the past. As William Callahan's work on Chinese national humiliation (*guochi*) discourses and Peter Hays Gries's study of Chinese defensive nationalism show, the victim persona has been a frequently invoked side of China.[39] When the G7 group of developed countries imposed collective sanctions on the PRC in the aftermath of Tiananmen, Deng Xiaoping, the paramount leader, immediately saw these sanctions as reminiscent of the eight-country allied invasion of China at the turn of the nineteenth century.[40] When the Chinese embassy in Belgrade was accidentally bombed by American forces in 1999, an opinion-editorial in *Renmin Ribao* (*People's Daily*) instinctively compared the incident to past instances of foreign aggression, declaring that the PRC is not "1899 China" and that "the Chinese people are not to be bullied."[41] When Chinese premier Wen Jiabao gave his first press interview as head of the State Council in 2003, one of the first things he said was that "the [war] suffering of Old China had left an indelible imprint" on him.[42] These are just some examples of how a particular understanding of history—the victimized China—has continued to color contemporary Chinese worldviews.

In highlighting these other Chinese identities on the global stage, it is worth emphasizing that my focus is on unpacking a specific face of China: its identity as a responsible great power. As with Callahan's, Gries's, and others' explorations of the victim self of China, my aim is to illuminate its RGP side. Yet in seeking to do so there is a need to be mindful that the various faces of China do not exist in isolation: to varying degrees they are interrelated and linked. To understand China's RGP identity we need to understand its points of intersection with other Chinese identities. For instance, the relationship between the responsible great power and victim identities is not entirely contradictory. Some Chinese scholars see the RGP identity as a response to the victim role, arguing that because of China's experience as a victim of hegemonic forces, it would never seek to be a hegemonic force itself; it would be "harmonious" and responsible.[43] A similar dynamic is also reflected in the common Chinese "victim" slogan "*Wuwang guochi*" (Never forget national humiliation). The slogan is typically followed by the statement "*Zhenxing Zhonghua*" (Rejuvenate the Chinese nation), which implies a revival of Chinese great-power identity.[44]

Elite Perceptions

Identity is physically unobservable but is given form and content by the identity discourses that concretize it. For this study's context, the relevant discourses are those that relate to domestic elites' narratives and debates about China's global role or place, including their assessments about American role expectations of China. By paying close attention to when, how, and why such identity discourses are produced, it is possible to recover collectively held perceptions of China's self as a responsible great power.

An unavoidable question at this point is, *Whose* discourse? In particular, who are the domestic elites whose identity discourses this study should track? There are basically two levels of examination. The first is the obvious choice of leaders and officials in the Chinese foreign policymaking system. The second category is Chinese intellectuals outside of the formal bureaucracy but working within the state-affiliated or state-funded epistemic setup. While Chinese intellectuals do not represent the state per se, their views and writings are often reflective of the spectrum of opinion in Beijing; they bespeak a "microcosm of wider thinking in the Chinese leadership."[45] At the same time, Chinese intellectuals are becoming increasingly influential in their own right, giving rise to what has been described as the growing "pluralistic elitism" within China.[46]

This ideational influence and relevance can be seen in the ways by which Chinese intellectuals play important contributory roles in the foreign policy system. For one, they directly influence policy when they are asked to collaborate with or provide inputs to the Chinese government. Such consultancy roles could be ad hoc, where, depending on the international political situation, relevant specialists are invited to brief or submit reports to senior government officials and party leaders.[47] One notable instance of such specialist work is the research report, submitted by Zheng Bijian to then-president Hu Jintao, advocating the idea of the "development path of China's peaceful rise." The recommendations of Zheng, the former vice president of the Central Party School, eventually culminated in the formulation of China's peaceful rise doctrine.[48] Consultancy work can also come on a more official basis, such as when scholars are appointed to national advisory roles or take part in state policy projects. Scholars at the China Institute of International Studies and the China Institutes of Contemporary International Relations, for example, are frequently involved in research work for their "patrons," the Ministry of Foreign Affairs (MFA) and the Ministry of State Security, respectively.[49] Meanwhile, there is a growing trend of cross-pollination of individuals in the scholarly and bureaucratic spheres. Former senior officials are often appointed as leaders of think tanks or as honorary deans at university departments, while academics occasionally move to state ministries or party organs to do formal policy work.

Meanwhile, Chinese intellectuals exert indirect policy influence when their publications offer policy ideas. This is not to say that these ideas will eventually become policy, but such writings in journals, policy-oriented reports, and books constitute a nontrivial part of the terrain of information on which policymakers and party officials draw. Articles in the Chinese IR journal *Guoji Zhanwang (Global Review)* have notably been reproduced in the People's Daily Internal Reference, an internal report consulted by Chinese policymakers.[50] Another type of indirect policy contribution relates to the unofficial information collection/dissemination role played by think-tank analysts. Think-tank scholars often participate in "Track-II" policy conferences, they receive diplomatic guests from abroad, and they travel overseas for study trips. These exchanges are a source of intelligence for the Chinese policymaking system and they act as an unofficial channel for disseminating information or conveying specific messages to external audiences.[51] Finally, as media pundits and authors of popular books, Chinese intellectuals can influence the direction and scope of public debate on national issues.

Having established the analytical relevance of the two types of discourse to examine—official and intellectual—the final question is, Where should one look for these discourses? Put differently, what are the sources of Chinese identity discourse? To this end, the book taps into an extensive range of primary Chinese documentary sources that include: (i) leadership accounts; (ii) party publications and government reports; (iii) party and state newspapers and news networks; (iv) international relations journals; and (v) international relations books. Many of these writings are produced primarily for domestic audiences. They reflect the active debate within China about the "roles, opportunities, dangers, risks, and responsibilities" of being a great power.[52] I have also supplemented these documentary sources by conducting field interviews and discussions in China on several occasions between 2011 and 2015. A more detailed outline of these primary accounts and sources is provided in the Note on Sources.

Structure of the Book

"China's identity in relation to international society," writes Qin Yaqing, one of China's foremost IR thinkers and an advisor to the Chinese leadership, "constitutes the century-puzzle of the Chinese since 1840."[53] One wonders whether this question will ever be comprehensively resolved. But it is becoming clear that one of the more prominent answers to have emerged, particularly in the post–Cold War era, is the identity notion of China as a responsible great power.

Yet China's great-power story did not begin at that time. Certainly by the 1990s it had become evident that China was emerging as a global power and would become the most plausible challenger to American global preeminence, but Chinese self-awareness and self-confidence as a great power goes back much further. Chapter 1 traces this important backstory. Engaging this history is crucial because before we can even discuss China's consciousness of the obligations that bear on a great power, we must first understand how and why China sees itself as a great power. Chapter 1 shows that this great-power self-perception has had longer and deeper antecedents. It teases out three historical narratives that have been particularly salient in the evolution of this big-power mind-set: (i) a premodern "great Central Kingdom" complex; (ii) a notion of "suppressed greatness" in the late Qing and republican eras; and (iii) a post-1949 Maoist perspective of a "great-power awakening." The chapter also surveys early Chinese ideas of the responsibilities of power and provides a historical contextualization to the book's subsequent discussion of Chinese understandings of global obligations.

The remaining chapters start the book on a more contemporary examination of China's responsible great-power identity. This investigation is chronicled in four time frames: 1978–1996; 1997–2004; 2005–2012; and post-2013. Chapter 2 focuses on the period from 1978 to 1996. It argues that the start of China's identification as a responsible great power can basically be traced to the period between the early to mid-1990s, when Chinese leaders began to officially pursue the RGP narrative and draw linkages between China's responsibility and its global-power role. This RGP narrative, however, did not emerge out of an ideational vacuum. The fact is that since 1978 and the promotion of reform and opening-up policies by Deng Xiaoping, there has been a radical shift in China's global orientation. Given that the creation of identity is an evolutionary process, it is negligent to delineate an understanding of the RGP identity without at least some reference to preceding events. This explains why chapter 2 unfolds from 1978 onward.

Chapters 3 and 4 chart and explain the development of the RGP identity in the periods 1997–2004 and 2005–2012, respectively. The years 1997 and 2005 stand out as distinctive points in China's RGP trajectory because these are the junctures that have been observed to be particularly consequential in terms of the subsequent expansion of the RGP discourse, both inside and outside of

China. The year 1997 marked the onset of the Asian financial crisis, an event that led to palpably increased self-justification and regional appreciation of China as a responsible power due to its actions to eschew currency devaluation, a surprising move seen to be stabilizing for neighboring economies. Subsequent Chinese support for America's War on Terror from 2001 onward also played a nontrivial role in shaping discussion of the RGP identity. Taken as a whole, chapter 3 demonstrates that the period from 1997 to 2004 can be considered the second distinctive phase of China's self-identification as a responsible power.

From 2005 onward there has been a further widening and deepening of the RGP discourse in China, in part as a response to the responsible stakeholder discourse promulgated by American officials. Notably, over this period (2005–2012) there had been a sharpening of the key intellectual positions in the domestic conversation on China's responsibilities, a debate that came to be shaped by three "responsibility" schools of thought—what I have labeled as the internationalist, developmental, and skeptics' positions. Chapter 4 unpacks these standpoints.

The penultimate chapter tracks the calibrations and continuities in the RGP identity since Xi Jinping's ascension to power in China. Analytically, this period (2013 to present) warrants a specific examination for the reason that under Xi's stewardship, Chinese diplomacy has clearly adjusted—toward what has been described as a more assertive foreign policy approach that seems intent to renegotiate China's relationship with the global order in greater favor of Chinese interests.[54] These shifts have led some scholars to speak of the "fall" of the responsible power, with the assumption that China has now "abandoned" that role reference.[55] I suggest such arguments oversimplify the actual situation. In fact, a deconstruction of the RGP identity in the Xi era can help throw some light on (and provide an alternative explanation of) why Chinese diplomacy is changing in the way it has in global affairs.

Chapters 2, 3, 4, and 5, as well as parts of chapter 1, all devote discussion to the role of the United States in contouring China's great-power identity. On that score, at least since the mid-1990s the message from successive US administrations has been remarkably consistent: while the US welcomes China to the great-power table, this ascendancy should be matched by the latter's willingness to shoulder the responsibilities that come with its increasing power. This represents, in effect, a conditional American affirmation of China's great-power identity. There is considerable evidence to suggest that American narratives have had an influence on spurring further internal reflection on and contestation of the PRC's role as a great power.

In summary, the book seeks to provide an original account of how and why China has come to pursue a role imagination as a responsible power. The conclusion reviews the key aspects and insights of this evolutionary story, drawing together our conceptual framework of the self-other logic to make sense of the answers. The ending sections discuss what these answers mean in the larger context of China's rise, its potential trajectory, and the impact on the global order.

Notes

1. Joseph Nye, "The 'Nye Report': Six Years Later," *International Relations of the Asia-Pacific* 1, no. 1 (2001): 98.
2. Robert B. Zoellick, "Whither China: From Membership to Responsibility?," Remarks to the National Committee on US-China Relations, September 21, 2005, https://2001-2009.state .gov/s/d/former/zoellick /rem/53682.htm.
3. *Hu Jintao Zai Zhongguo Gongchan Dang Di Shiba Ci Quanguo Daibiao Da Huishang De Baogao (Report of Hu Jintao to the Eighteenth National Congress of the Communist Party of China)*, available at http://cpc.people.com.cn/n/2012/1118 /c64094-19612151-1.html.
4. *Zhengfu Gongzuo Baogao* (*Work Report of the Government*) (2016), available at http://www.mofcom.gov.cn/article/i/jyjl/l/201603/20160301282908.shtml.
5. Alastair Iain Johnston, *Social States: China in International Institutions, 1980–2000* (Princeton, NJ: Princeton University Press, 2008), 149n156.
6. See, for example, Michael Swaine, "Perceptions of an Assertive China," *China Leadership Monitor* 32 (2010): 1; Michael Yahuda, "China's New Assertiveness in the South China Sea," *Journal of Contemporary China* 22, no. 81 (2013): 446–59; "Discord: China's Tough New Attitude Is Both Dangerous and Counterproductive," *Economist*, January 13, 2011; Yong Deng, "China: The Post-Responsible Power," *Washington Quarterly* 37, no. 4 (2015): 117–32.
7. Read-Out of the President's Call with President Xi Jinping, Office of the White House Press Secretary, July 21, 2015, https://obamawhitehouse.archives.gov/the -press-office/2015/07/21/readout-president%E2%80%99s-call-chinese-president -xi-jinping.
8. They include Rosemary Foot, "Chinese Power and the Idea of a Responsible State," *China Journal* 45 (2001): 1–19; Beverley Loke, "Between Interest and Responsibility: Assessing China's Foreign Policy and Burgeoning Global Role," *Asian Security* 5, no. 3 (2009): 205–12; and Susan Shirk, *China: Fragile Superpower* (Oxford, UK: Oxford University Press, 2008), chap. 5. Some related studies do not probe China's "level of responsibility" per se; they assess its "compliance" levels with

international regimes or the extent to which it is a "status quo" state. See Ann Kent, *Beyond Compliance: China, International Organizations, and Global Security* (Stanford, CA: Stanford University Press, 2007); Alastair Iain Johnston, "Is China a Status Quo Power?," *International Security* 27, no. 4 (2003): 5–56.

9. Hongying Wang, "National Image Building and Chinese Foreign Policy," *China: An International Journal* 1, no. 1 (2003): 46–72.
10. Amitav Acharya, *Whose Ideas Matter? Agency and Power in Asian Regionalism* (Ithaca, NY: Cornell University Press, 2009).
11. Graham Allison, "The Thucydides Trap: Are the U.S. and China Headed for War?," *The Atlantic*, September 24, 2015.
12. Lowell Dittmer and Samuel Kim, "In Search of a Theory of National Identity," in *China's Quest for National Identity*, ed. Lowell Dittmer and Samuel Kim (Ithaca, NY: Cornell University Press, 1993), 24–27. Rodney Bruce Hall critiques mainstream IR theories for failing to "delineate [the state] from the nation." See Rodney Bruce Hall, *National Collective Identity* (New York: Columbia University Press, 1999), 4.
13. Michael Ng-Quinn, "National Identity in Premodern China: Formation and Role Enactment," in *China's Quest for National Identity*, ed. Lowell Dittmer and Samuel S. Kim (Ithaca, NY: Cornell University Press, 1993), 32–33.
14. In fact, as Robert Putnam's "two-level games" show, elite perceptions are often beholden to societal pressures, especially in liberal democracies. See Robert D. Putnam, "Diplomacy and Domestic Politics: The Logic of Two-Level Games," *International Organization* 42, no. 3 (1988): 427–60.
15. George H. Mead, *Mind, Self, and Society: From the Standpoint of a Social Behaviorist*, vol. 1 (Chicago: University of Chicago Press, 1934).
16. Alexander Wendt, *Social Theory of International Politics* (Cambridge, UK: Cambridge University Press, 2008), 215.
17. Ibid., 225.
18. Johnston, *Social States*, 95. See also Katherine Verdery, "Whither 'Nation' and 'Nationalism'?," *Daedalus* 122, no. 3 (1993): 37–46.
19. See, for example, Edward E. Sampson, *Celebrating the Other: A Dialogic Account of Human Nature* (Taos Institute Publications, 2008), 106; and Thomas Diez, "Europe's Others and the Return of Geopolitics," *Cambridge Review of International Affairs* 17, no. 2 (2004): 319–35.
20. Shogo Suzuki, "The Importance of 'Othering' in China's National Identity: Sino-Japanese Relations as a Stage of Identity Conflicts," *Pacific Review* 20, no. 1 (2007): 23–47.
21. John Lee, "China's America Obsession," *Foreign Policy*, May 6, 2011, http://www.foreignpolicy.com/articles/2011/05/06/china_s_america_obsession.
22. Interviews with Chinese scholars, Beijing and Shanghai, April–June 2011.
23. Rosemary Foot and Andrew Walter, *China, the United States, and Global Order* (Cambridge, UK: Cambridge University Press, 2011), 19.
24. Alexander Wendt, "Collective Identity Formation and the International State," *American Political Science Review* 88, no. 2 (1994): 386.
25. Acharya, *Whose Ideas Matter?*

26. Ernst B. Haas and Peter M. Haas, "Pragmatic Constructivism and the Study of International Institutions," *Millennium* 31, no. 3 (2002): 573–601.
27. Ernst B. Haas, *Beyond the Nation-State: Functionalism and International Organization* (Stanford, CA: Stanford University Press, 1964); Thomas Risse, "Neofunctionalism, European Identity, and the Puzzles of European Integration," *Journal of European Public Policy* 12, no. 2 (April 2008): 291–309; and John Gerard Ruggie, Peter J. Katzenstein, Robert O. Keohane, and Philippe C. Schmitter, "Transformations in World Politics: The Intellectual Contributions of Ernst B. Haas," *Annual Review of Political Science* 8 (2005): 271–96.
28. James D. Fearon and David D. Laitin, "Violence and the Social Construction of Ethnic Identity," *International Organization* 54, no. 4 (2000): 845–77. Another study that notes the instrumental nature of identity construction is David Laitin's *Identity in Formation: The Russian-Speaking Populations in the New Abroad* (Ithaca, NY: Cornell University Press, 1998).
29. Guoguang Wu, "Identity, Sovereignty, and Economic Penetration: Beijing's Responses to Offshore Chinese Democracies," *Journal of Contemporary China* 16, no. 51 (2007): 295–313.
30. Interview with Chinese scholar, Beijing, May 2011.
31. See "Zhuchaoxian Dashi Liu Hongcai Juxing Qingzhu Jiandang Jiushi Zhounian Zhaodaihui" (Ambassador to North Korea Liu Hongcai hosts ninetieth anniversary celebration of CCP's founding), Ministry of Foreign Affairs, China, June 30, 2011, http://www.fmprc.gov.cn/mfa_chn//zwbd_602255/wshd_602258/t835593.shtml; "Xi Jinping Huijian Laowo Renmin Gemingdang Zhongyang Zong Shuji, Guojia Zhuxi Zhumali" (Xi Jinping meets the general secretary of the Lao people's revolutionary party and Laos president Choummaly Sayasone), Renmin Wang (People's Daily Network), June 16, 2010, http://politics.people.com.cn/GB/1024/11887650.html; "Jia Qinglin Huijian Yuenan Guojia Zhuxi Chen Deliang" (Jia Qinglin meets Vietnam's president Tran Duc Luong), Ministry of Foreign Affairs, China, March 23, 2006, http://www.fmprc.gov.cn/web/gjhdq_676201/gj_676203/yz_676205/1206_677292/xgxw_677298/t241881.shtml; and "Meng Jianzhu Huijian Guba Guowu Weiyuan Hui Fuzhuxi Jian Neizheng Buzhang" (Meng Jianzhu meets Cuban State Council Vice-Chairman and Interior Minister), Renmin Wang (People's Daily Network), August 30, 2010, http://politics.people.com.cn/GB/1026/12596837.html.
32. Peter Van Ness, *Revolution and Chinese Foreign Policy: Peking's Support for Wars of National Liberation* (Berkeley: University of California Press, 1970), 15–18; Alaba Ogunsanwo, *China's Policy in Africa, 1958–1971* (Cambridge, UK: Cambridge University Press, 1974), 71.
33. Xie Yixian, *Zhongguo Dangdai Waijiao Shi, 1949–2001 (Contemporary Chinese Diplomatic History, 1949–2001)* (Beijing: Zhongguo Qingnian Chubanshe, 2002), 290–91.
34. Peter Van Ness, "China as a Third World State: Foreign Policy and Official National Identity," in *China's Quest for National Identity*, ed. Lowell Dittmer and Samuel Kim (Ithaca, NY: Cornell University Press, 1993), 212.

35. Ibid., 211–12.
36. Scarlett Cornelissen and Ian Taylor, "The Political Economy of China and Japan's Relationship with Africa: A Comparative Perspective," *Pacific Review* 13, no. 4 (2000): 615–33.
37. United Nations Development Programme, *Human Development Report 2015,* 209.
38. As former foreign minister Qian Qichen described it, to say that a country is a developing nation is to point out that "its economy is less developed and is in the process of moving from a traditional economy to a modern one." Qian, cited in Qi Pengfei, *Zhongguo Gong Chandang Yu Dangdai Zhongguo Waijiao, 1949–2001 (Chinese Communist Party and Contemporary China's Diplomacy, 1949–2009)* (Beijing: Zhonggong Dangshi Chubanshe, 2010), 252. Xiao Huanrong similarly notes the distinction between the developing-nation identity and the third-world nation concept. See Xiao Huanrong, "Zhongguo De Daguo Zeren Yu Diqu Zhuyi Zhanlue" (China's great-power responsibility and strategy of regionalism), *Shijie Jingji Yu Zhengzhi (World Economics and Politics)* 1 (2003): 46.
39. William A. Callahan, *China: The Pessoptimist Nation* (Oxford, UK: Oxford University Press, 2010); Peter Hays Gries, *China's New Nationalism: Pride, Politics, and Diplomacy* (Berkeley: University of California Press, 2005).
40. Deng Xiaoping, "Zhenxing Zhongguo Mingzhu" (Rejuvenate the Chinese nation), in *Deng Xiaoping Wenxuan Disanjuan (Selected Works of Deng Xiaoping),* vol. 3 (Beijing: Renmin Chubanshe, 1993), 357.
41. Han Zhongkun, "Zhongguo, Bushi Yibajiujiu" (China, this is not 1899), *Renmin Ribao (People's Daily)*, May 12, 1999.
42. "Guowu Yuan Zongli Yu Zhongwai Jizhe Jianmian Hui" (State council premier's press conference with Chinese and foreign reporters), Xinhua, March 18, 2003.
43. For example, Jin Canrong argues that one key idea underpinning China's RGP identity is the notion of "independent diplomacy," which is especially "precious" in view of "Chinese historical experience of foreign encroachment and slavery." See Jin Canrong, *Daguo De Zeren (Big Power's Responsibility)* (Beijing: Zhongguo Renmin Daxue Chubanshe, 2011), 24–25.
44. Callahan, *China*, 14–16.
45. Rana Mitter, "An Uneasy Engagement: Chinese Ideas of Global Order and Justice in Historical Perspective," in *Order and Justice in International Relations*, ed. Rosemary Foot, John Lewis Gaddis, and Andrew Hurrell (Oxford, UK: Oxford University Press, 2004), 225.
46. See Xuanli Liao, *Chinese Foreign Policy Think Tanks and China's Policy Towards Japan* (Hong Kong: Chinese University Press, 2006), 15–52; Merle Goldman, "Politically-Engaged Intellectuals in the 1990s," *China Quarterly* 159 (1999): 700–711. See also Yongjin Zhang, "Politics, Culture, and Scholarly Responsibility in China: Toward a Cultural Sensitive Analytical Approach," *Asian Perspective* 31, no. 3 (2007): 103–24.
47. Interviews with Chinese scholars from Beijing and Shanghai in May 2011 and November 2011, respectively.

48. Bonnie S. Glaser and Evan S. Medeiros, "The Changing Ecology of Foreign Policy-Making in China: The Ascension and Demise of the Theory of 'Peaceful Rise,'" *China Quarterly* 190 (2007): 291–310.
49. The China Institute of International Studies (CIIS) is affiliated with the Ministry of Foreign Affairs, while the China Institutes of Contemporary International Relations (CICIR) is bureaucratically linked to the Central Committee Foreign Affairs Office and the Ministry of State Security. Hence, it is not surprising to find that these institutions have collaborative projects with the government and party. See David Shambaugh, "China's International Relations Think Tanks: Evolving Structures and Process," *China Quarterly* 171 (2002): 575–96.
50. *Shanghai Guoji Wenti Yanjiu Yuan 2010 Niandu Baogao (Shanghai Institutes for International Studies 2010 Annual Report)* (Shanghai: Shanghai Guoji Wenti Yanjiu Yuan), 15.
51. Shambaugh, "China's International Relations Think Tanks," 576.
52. David Shambaugh, *China Goes Global: The Partial Power* (Oxford, UK: Oxford University Press, 2013), 14.
53. Qin Yaqing, "International Society as a Process: Institutions, Identities, and China's Peaceful Rise," *Chinese Journal of International Politics* 3, no. 2 (2010): 130.
54. Hoo Tiang Boon, ed., *Chinese Foreign Policy under Xi* (London and New York: Routledge, 2017), chap. 1.
55. Deng, "China."

1

THE ORIGINS OF CHINA'S GREAT-POWER IDENTITY

This chapter sketches the historical antecedents of China's identity as a responsible great power. The discussion spans the imperial epoch to the end of the Maoist era. It also examines Chinese elites' perceptions of their nation's great-power identity and the idea of responsibility, both as separate phenomena and in terms of their potential linkages. I begin with a historical survey of the great-power aspects of the RGP identity, while in the second part I focus on the idea of responsibility.

There are two important caveats to state up front. First, even as this chapter seeks to locate the historical facets of the RGP identity, it does not attempt or pretend to be an in-depth historical review. This is neither the intent nor the scope. As pointed out in the introduction, the main intention here is to provide a contextualization of China's RGP identity from a historical perspective, which will serve as the basis for a more informed discussion of the RGP identity thereafter. Second, my focus is on the great-power and responsibility elements of China's identity and not on China's identity writ large. This is not to suggest the exclusion of potentially contradictory identity discourses (such as a "weak China" complex). To the extent that such discourses are contextually relevant and share linkages with Chinese great power perceptions, they are necessarily discussed.

Imperial China: Great Central Kingdom

For considerable periods in Chinese traditional history, Chinese ruling classes and elites tended to perceive their nation as the "great central kingdom."[1] This was the so-called Central Kingdom complex, predicated on a sinocentric understanding of China as "all [realms] under heaven" (*tianxia*).[2] China, according to this conception, was not just a glorious and powerful civilization—it was essentially the only veritable civilization around, since it was geographically convergent with "heaven," and it was difficult to think of any civilized equivalents existing outside of this boundary.[3] As a corollary, the Chinese emperor was also the "son of Heaven" (*tianzi*) and had the supposed celestial right to preside over "all of human affairs."[4] The *Book of Odes* would thus write, "Under the wide heaven, there is no land that is not the Emperor's" (*putian zhixia, mofei wangtu*).[5]

Imperial China from the Central Kingdom perspective was thus more than just a great power. It was the world's greatest power, a "world empire"—to borrow the words of Immanuel Wallerstein—in which the sense of the Chinese polity overlapped with the idea of the world.[6] In other words, in the Central Kingdom outlook China is essentially coterminous with the world. As for peoples who fall outside of this world, they are typically tarred with the inferior civilizational label of "barbarians" (*yi*). This denigration of foreigners as *yi* means that in the Chinese imperial order there is little justification or need for an institution that performs a dedicated, interstate-style foreign affairs function.[7] The authoritative Confucian *Book of Rites*, in fact, explicitly instructed that "the officials of the Empire shall have no intercourse with foreigners."[8]

It is important to recognize that the Central Kingdom conception should be understood with a certain degree of abstraction and generalization. For a start, it would be facile to characterize the Central Kingdom outlook as being uniform or prevalent across all dynastic periods. There were various instances in Chinese history when China was less than politically unified and was segmented into various feudal states (e.g., the Warring States period of 476–221 BC or the Three Kingdoms era of AD 220–264). Ironically, the idea of the Central Kingdom was said to have originated during the period of the Zhou dynasty, when China had a nominal central government and was effectively a collection of feudal states along the Yellow River.[9] Moreover, China, even when politically unified, waxed and waned in territory and power throughout the course of its premodern history: from around its peak, during the Han, Tang, and early Qing dynasties, to approximately its smallest, during the Northern and Southern Song times.[10]

Second, the sinocentricity implied in the Central Kingdom perspective was, on numerous occasions, more form than substance. As Rana Mitter writes, "There is a great deal of evidence which shows that pre-modern Chinese in reality regarded themselves as being part of a much flatter hierarchical system than their own rhetoric suggests."[11] Tang China, for example, pursued considerable trading relations with foreigners, while during this period Chinese external trade extended across the Indian Ocean to as far as the African coast.[12] Early Qing China also did not hesitate to sign the Treaty of Nerchinsk with the Russians in 1689, a diplomatic démarche that basically denotes tacit recognition of Russian equality.[13] These two historical exemplars are even more striking if one considers that Tang and early Qing China represent arguably the height of Chinese prestige and power when, presumably, sinocentrism was at its corresponding acme. Meanwhile, during periods when Chinese power declined or when strategic priorities shifted, it was also not uncommon to find the imperial government initiating a policy of "matrimonial alliances and sending of gifts" to appease truculent foreign tribes along its northern and western fronts.[14] The historical account of the "political bride" Wang Zhaojun marrying a tribal warlord in 33 BC in order to secure peace along the Han borders is one classical case.[15] Lastly, even the tributary system—frequently cited as evidence of a sinocentric Chinese worldview—was in reality more symbolic and titular than commonly assumed.[16] This is not to imply that tributary relations did not represent a sense of Chinese civilizational superiority; they certainly did and, as Samuel Kim points out, such tributary relations were often maintained at some financial cost to the imperial court in order to burnish a Chinese image of preeminence.[17] Rather, the point is that the Chinese suzerain-vassal dynamic was underpinned by much ritualism and symbolism and that beneath the euphemistic veneer of tributary relations, the substantive arrangement that existed was one that served mainly to regulate trading relationships. To a considerable extent, therefore, the tributary practice was essentially an indirect mode by which the imperial court imposed tariffs on foreigners keen on trading with and in China.[18] Indeed, many of these so-called vassals maintained de facto political autonomy vis-à-vis the Central Kingdom, even if some of them had been ostensibly "subjugated" in the first instance by Chinese military power.[19]

The third point relates to the fact that there were periods during which Imperial China was in effect governed by "barbarians" from the north, notably the Mongols during the Yuan dynasty (1279–1367) and the Manchus during the Qing dynasty (1644–1911). Given the sinocentricism and the "othering" of foreign peoples as inferiors, "alien" rule of China suggested potential complications for the Central Kingdom perception. Yet, this was hardly the case. Not only did the Central Kingdom outlook continue to persist, it was in fact reinforced and perpetuated during the Mongol and Manchu reigns.[20] Especially for the latter, the embrace of the Central Kingdom narrative was not difficult. In the course of Manchu rule over China, described by John Fairbank as a "synarchic" regime, the Manchus had become strongly sinicized, to the extent that they became "staunch champions" of Chinese cultural heritage and political tradition.[21] In that sense the Manchus, in ruling the Central Kingdom, essentially came to be included within the Chinese civilizational world.[22]

What were some of the factors that helped engender the Central Kingdom outlook? For one, the material power (both economic might and military strength) wielded by the Chinese empire fostered a strong endogenous sense of self-primacy and preeminence.[23] Certainly, Chinese power declined and rose at various points, but there were significant periods when Imperial China's power was prominent and sustained, such as during the Han, Tang, Ming, and early Qing eras. According to Yan Xuetong, China enjoyed "superpower" status during these phases of Chinese "high noon."[24] The material power retained by the Chinese empire for considerable parts of its history made it natural for ruling elites to conceive of or assume China as the most significant political force.

Yet, this impression of the centrality and universality of the Chinese state would not have prospered without a "missing" peer other—or, more precisely, the perceived lack of a civilizational equivalent that could rival China. This is not to suggest that the Chinese were unaware of other centers of civilization, such as the Byzantine and Persian empires. There was certainly some level of awareness. But, constrained by geographical barriers, such cross-civilizational contacts were usually limited or irregular.[25] In any event, when such contacts did take place, they seemed to the Chinese only to affirm the superiority of their sinocentric model. As Kim argues, "The absence of a rival civilization became a potent factor in the development of the Chinese image of world order."[26] Finally, although the tributary system characterized in many ways the Chinese approach toward commercial relations with neighboring states, the symbolism of creating prima facie appearance of Chinese superiority was at least helpful for sustaining the psychology of Imperial China's preeminent position.[27]

In sum, the Central Kingdom complex was the embodiment of premodern China's sense of its great-power status, an outlook that emphasized the primacy of Chinese power. Of course, the Central Kingdom complex was not a constant or uniform phenomenon and was certainly contextually nuanced. Still, notwithstanding these qualifications, the Central Kingdom complex was a largely recurring theme in premodern Chinese state identity and positioned China as the principal political force and hegemon.

Late Qing and Republican China: "Weak China, Suppressed Greatness"

Moving to the late Qing era, China's belief in the superiority of its own model was fundamentally shaken. Technologically advanced foreign powers from Europe, America, and Japan dominated and humiliated China at will, making a mockery of the notion of the "great central kingdom."[28] Indeed, this period, beginning with the Anglo-Chinese Opium War (1839–1842), marked the start of the so-called century of shame (*bainian guochi*), and the label of "great victim" rather than "great power" seemed a far more apt description of China.[29]

The encounters with alien forces, clearly stronger and more developed than the stagnant Qing empire, proved to be a powerful experience for the Chinese, albeit one that was largely traumatic. These encounters were cognitively and emotionally distressing for the Chinese: not only was the idea of the Central Kingdom comprehensively overturned; they illustrated China's swift metamorphosis from "power to pupil," and it was not even seen or treated as an equal.[30] The arrival of foreign imperialism meant that the Chinese self-perception of the Central Kingdom was to be forcibly reevaluated and China had little choice but to "learn" its new international role—as prescribed by external others—as a pupil. As Michael Hunt notes, "much of the impetus" for Chinese self-reflection was the consequence of "repeated blows struck by foreign powers."[31]

By the late nineteenth century there was a growing sentiment among reformist Chinese elites that China had to "self-strengthen" (*ziqiang*).[32] This advocacy represented a tacit admission by these elites that China had become moribund and that in order to arrest the slide, reform measures were unavoidable. The call for reforms clearly exemplified the Chinese sense of weakness at that time.[33] Yet there was also a second, more revisionist dimension to the *ziqiang* discourse: that China's weak position was basically anomalous and its tradition of being a strong centralized state demanded a return to its former status. For Qing reformists like Feng Guifen, *ziqiang* was not merely about rectifying China's problems; more than that, it was about restoring China to its original strength, surpassing foreigners and becoming again the "leading power in the world" and "the greatest country on earth."[34] Even among anti-Qing revolutionaries such as Qiu Jin and Song Jiaoren there existed a sense of a Chinese claim to national greatness. Song, for example, exhorted the Chinese to live up to "the mighty accomplishments of [their] ancestors over the past five thousand years—in conquest, administration, expansion of national territory, and the elevation of national prestige."[35] Memories of China's greatness endured among many Chinese political elites even as they were coming to terms with the unwelcome reality of an anemic China.

This broad perceptual tenor of a weak China with its greatness suppressed was to continue into the Republican era (1912 onward), by which time Chinese elites were becoming increasingly radical in their political outlook. The emerging view among many nationalists (such as Sun Yatsen) was that only fundamental "political renovation" would suffice.[36] In fact, for many of those associated with the momentous May Fourth Movement of 1919, political transformation was not enough; a sweeping societal makeover was also required where, in particular, Confucian tradition, ostensibly representing the cultural and ideological evil responsible for China's decline, had to be jettisoned.[37] At the same time, the growing iconoclastic mood also underscored the fact that Chinese perceptions of a weak China were becoming acute. Sun would describe China as a "hypo-colony" (*ci zhimingdi*), which was apparently worse than a semi-colony since it was a "slave to many countries."[38] This burgeoning sense of China in crisis meant that for many Chinese nationalists, their immediate concern was to "save China" (*jiu zhongguo*) and avert national ruin. The closely related, restorative theme of "rejuvenating China" (*zhenxing zhongguo*) to "regain its lost international status" was also important but secondary, compared to the more exigent aim of national salvation.[39]

In 1928 Chiang Kai-shek established the nationalist government in Nanjing. While Chiang's regime managed to achieve some degree of political unification and gained diplomatic recognition fairly swiftly, internal conditions remained fundamentally bad. China was still gripped by civil conflict and remained effectively a "de facto federation."[40] On the external horizon, moreover, the threat of Japan loomed ominously. A perception (both domestic and foreign) of Chinese vulnerability persisted. Chiang certainly shared this view as well, but, like many of his peers, Chiang's image of China also encompassed visions of reviving its greatness. Hence, among the various reasons underpinning the generalissimo's pursuit of a strong state solution to "restore unity and order, end foreign humiliation, abolish unequal treaties, regain lost territory," a prime motivation for Chiang was to "ultimately restore China's lost grandeur."[41]

Interestingly, this sense of grandeur appeared to show some signs of recovery by the time of the Second World War, when nationalist China aligned itself with the Allied camp. Great-power aspiration was, of course, not the main reason for Chiang to side with the Allies. Rather, it was strategic pragmatism as well as a common enemy in Japan that drove Chiang's government to throw in its lot with the Allies.[42] Indeed, China's contribution to the Allied cause remained limited. Although China was strategically vital to "keeping Japan divided in a two-front war," its material weakness vis-à-vis its major Western allies was clear, and many American analysts lamented China's "dubious military value" to the war effort.[43] Considerable military and financial aid from the United States was needed "just to keep [the Chiang regime] afloat."[44]

Yet, as the war wore on, China's patent material shortcomings did not deter the Americans from taking the lead in symbolically inducting China into the great-power club. Indeed, this appeared to be a key US policy. As Secretary of State Cordell Hull would later relate in his memoirs, it was a US foreign policy objective to recognize and build China "as a major power entitled to equal rank with the three big Western Allies, Russia, Britain, and the United States."[45] China was thus able to take part in the Washington and Quebec "great power" conferences of May and August 1943, respectively, and two months later, in October 1943, it was "formally acknowledged as one of the Big Four" in the Declaration of the Moscow Conference. By the end of World War II in 1945, de jure recognition of nationalist China as a great power seemed to be acquired when it became one of the five permanent members of the new United Nations (UN) Security Council.[46]

Formal external recognition of China's big-power status contributed to some degree to a restoration of Chinese great-power beliefs. Yet, the impact of this recognition should not be overstated. First, there had been conscious efforts by the nationalist government to elevate China's international status. John Garver has shown that China's great-power status was not simply bestowed on it by the Big Three; it was also, to a considerable extent, a "hard-won diplomatic achievement" by Chiang's government.[47] Second, the great-power status accorded to China was, in reality, more nominal than substantial. Privately both Winston Churchill and Josef Stalin did not share much optimism about China's great-power potential. Churchill in particular had been hugely skeptical. As he bluntly put it, treating China as "one of the world's four great powers [was] an absolute farce."[48] At the same time, American estimations of Chinese power were more circumscribed than commonly assumed. True, among the three, the US did project a more sanguine view of Chinese power than the Soviet Union or Great Britain. But the primary rationale for doing so, as Warren Cohen has suggested, might have had less to do with genuine American belief in China's potential and more to do with the assumption that a "grateful" China would be largely acquiescent to the US.[49] Thus Cohen notes that, ultimately, "Roosevelt, no less than Churchill or Stalin, denied Chiang an equal role in the process of making strategic or logistical decisions."[50] Indeed, the US had been quick to sign away Chinese sovereign interests in Outer Mongolia during the 1945 Yalta Conference, an Allied big-power meeting at which China was conspicuously left out.

The nineteenth to the early mid-twentieth century represented an intense period of national shock, angst, and reflection for the Chinese. Once sure of its own primacy during considerable parts of its history, China's "great central kingdom" identity was brutally exposed as a myth and severely questioned by superior Western and Japanese forces. Consequently, these foreign examinations led to a deep sense of Chinese self-doubt and vulnerability; a disconcerting self-image of a weak China was to form an uncomfortable association with enduring perceptions of China's former grandeur. In some ways, perhaps, it is flawed to assume that China's great-power outlook had ceased to exist totally during this period. It is more accurate to say that Chinese perceptions of national greatness had been forcibly suppressed, were latent rather than active, and were more an expectation than a reality. This may partly explain why, after the Second World War, the nationalist government repeatedly underlined China's regained status of a great power, even though such a status was largely nominal and lacked substance.[51]

Maoist China: "Great Power Awakening"

The emergence of communist China in 1949 marked the beginning of a period of a more substantial revival of China's great-power identity. Territorially, save for Outer Mongolia, the communists inherited a China that was approximately the size of the Qing empire at its peak. But, more significant, the founding of the People's Republic of China represented, for the first time since 1911, a concentration of the resources of China in the hands of a single authority that had the trappings of a modern state rather than a collapsing dynastic polity. This was a bona fide unified China compared to the nationalists's 1928 quasi-version. Several analysts came to conclude that the PRC's establishment had fundamentally altered the global balance of power.[52]

Mao Zedong and his colleagues, like the nationalists, shared a common and enduring vision of China fulfilling its "rightful" place as a great power. This was in some ways reflected in Mao's well-known speech, "The Chinese People Have Stood Up," of September 21, 1949. Underlining that China was "a great, courageous and industrious nation" that possessed, at base, "very favorable conditions" of population and territorial size, Mao asserted that it was inevitable that the Chinese would "emerge in the world as a nation with an advanced culture," own a "powerful" military force, and "win [a] speedy victory on the economic front."[53] Mao, of course, was under no illusion that China had become overnight a modern power comparable to that of the US and USSR; in the same speech he readily admitted that the Chinese had "fallen behind."[54] That said, Mao appeared to harbor considerable optimism regarding the PRC's future, noting that it was "infinitely bright."[55]

Events in the early 1950s seemed to indicate that Mao's early confidence was well placed. During this period the recognition of China's potential for great-power status was considerably enhanced. Two factors were particularly influential. First, in February 1950 China operationalized its policy of "leaning to one side" (*xiangyi biandao*) and entered into a formal alliance with the Soviet Union. While this was in the apparent capacity of a subordinate ally that acknowledged the primacy of Moscow as the leader of the global socialist movement and implied that China was not an equal of the USSR, the Sino-Soviet alliance nonetheless entailed appreciable benefits for Chinese great-power aspirations: (i) it greatly improved Chinese security vis-à-vis the main perceived enemy—the US; and (ii) it promised an augmentation of China's conventional-power capabilities. Indeed, during the alliance's early stages, Washington developed a perception of China as "a land of burgeoning power . . . with enormous potential that was on the verge of being realized with Soviet help."[56]

Second, China unexpectedly and impressively fought American-led UN forces to a standstill in the 1950–53 Korean War. Although the Soviet factor had been crucial to China's military success in Korea, it was still a hugely competent Chinese performance.[57] After all, the Chinese had taken on an established great power, the United States (which was, in their words, "an enemy wielding weapons many times superior to ours") and had stood its ground.[58] Consequently, the war result translated to more positive assessments, both internally and externally, of China's major-power credentials.[59] As Michael Yahuda notes, the Korean War brought about "a significant change in China's self-confidence and international image" and "earned the PRC the great power status for which the Chinese have long yearned."[60] The Americans, in particular, acquired what was described as "a deep respect" for Chinese military power in the aftermath of the war, a perceptual consequence that would later have ramifications for US strategy in Vietnam (the so-called ghost of the "Yalu debacle").[61]

By 1954 it seemed that the Chinese were confident enough to publicly declare themselves as a major power. Shortly after the 1954 Geneva Conference on Korea and Indo-China, the *People's Daily (Renmin Ribao)* proclaimed:

> For the first time as one of the Big Powers, the People's Republic of China joined the other major powers in negotiations on vital international problems and made a contribution of its own that won acclaim of wide sections of world opinion. The international status of the People's Republic of China as one of the big powers has gained universal recognition. Its international prestige has been greatly enhanced. The Chinese people take the greatest joy and pride in the efforts and achievements of their delegation at Geneva.[62]

This "big power" declaration was, of course, propaganda in many respects, but at the same time it is worth noting that the North Vietnamese success at the battle of Dien Bien Phu in 1954 represented a clear proxy victory for the PRC—and for communism in general—and was hence encouraging to Chinese esteem and great-power aspirations.

Further hints of China's great-power aspirations came at the Afro-Asia Bandung Conference in 1955. Although the PRC identified itself with the newly decolonized states in Africa and Asia, it also openly attempted to claim a leadership role among these countries and did so with "considerable success."[63] And, as if to suggest the Chinese brand of leadership would be a benevolent one, Mao went on in 1956 to issue statements on the nature of the PRC's great powerhood: it would eschew "great-power chauvinism" (*daguo zhuyi*) and behave as a "modest" great power.[64] The mid-1950s also saw a continuation of the broader international recognition of China's power that had grown since the PRC's formation. A considerable impression in Asia during this period was that China was a "dynamic, permanent, and not unfriendly world power" and that communism represented the inexorable "wave of the future." Even Moscow, as the PRC's patron, began to revise its estimation of

Beijing and treat it more as a peer than a junior ally. Stalin's death in 1953 was, of course, an important factor in the shifting Sino-Soviet dynamic, but it was still a testimony to China's growing clout in 1956 that the Kremlin felt compelled to openly turn to Beijing for counsel and assistance in the wake of upheavals in Eastern Europe.[65] These positive external assessments were affirming to Chinese great-power imaginings.

Nevertheless, against this backdrop of a seeming rise in China's big-power stature and ambition, there were discernable indications that Beijing itself recognized its material inadequacies vis-à-vis the developed world. One clear example was the mid-1950s "catching up" discourse, a direct admission that China was still in many ways underdeveloped and far from being a complete world power.[66] In fact, in 1956 Mao described China as a "poor" and "blank" country. As the chairman put it, "By 'poor,' I mean we do not have much industry and our agriculture is underdeveloped. By 'blank,' I mean we are like a blank sheet of paper and our cultural and scientific level is not high."[67]

Beijing's perception of its material shortcomings was linked to the need to "catch up" with the developed world—the US, in particular—and this desire would prove to be an important motivation behind the ultimately disastrous 1958 policy of the Great Leap Forward (GLF). The Chinese leadership evidently felt that unless China attained greater material muscle, it would "never be taken seriously by imperialists," a conclusion it seems to have arrived at when the 1955–1957 US-Sino ambassadorial dialogues failed to produce any tangible results. Consequently, Mao drew the link between economic parity and international respect, declaring that once the PRC had achieved its targets in the "three great commanders of grain, steel, and machinery," Beijing would be able "to negotiate with the Americans with a bit more spirit."[68]

By the early 1960s, however, it had become clear that, instead of "catching up," the Chinese had only succeeded in widening their economic disparity with most of the developed world. The GLF program had turned out to be a complete economic disaster, triggering a nationwide famine in China that resulted in approximately thirty million deaths.[69] Unsurprisingly, this trail of devastation severely undermined Chinese big-power hopes. Indeed, there were signs that during this time—the "bitter years" (specifically, 1959–1962)—Beijing felt somewhat vulnerable and insecure. This was illustrated to some extent by the unconventional consideration among some of its leaders for a more conciliatory policy, termed the "Three Reconciliations and the One Reduction" (*sanhe yishao*) toward the US, the USSR, and India.[70]

The early 1960s was also the period when the growing Sino-Soviet divide, which started to brew in the late 1950s, erupted into open antagonism between Moscow and Beijing. From a strategic perspective, the rupture of the Sino-Soviet alliance was hardly propitious for China; not only did it signify a weakening of the PRC's strategic position, it meant that Beijing now faced two superpower adversaries concurrently as well as the disconcerting prospect of superpower collusion at China's expense.

The emergence of a China unconstrained by Soviet influence reflected, to some extent, a determination by Beijing to be regarded as an equal to the US and USSR (even if it was materially out of its depth). In this respect freedom from the Soviet orbit represented an opportunity for China to further consolidate its own sphere of influence and reinvent itself as a "third force" in world politics. Thus, by 1963 not only had China refuted the Marxist-Leninist credentials of the Soviets, it attempted to cast itself as the one "true source" of Marxist-Leninism, the "epicenter of world revolution."[71] Beijing, in effect, was openly challenging Moscow's position as the leader of the international communist camp. At the same time, and building on the earlier prestige gains from the 1955 Bandung Conference, Beijing also attempted to further advance its claims to leadership of the Third World. While the Chinese rhetoric emphasized China's common identification with the former "oppressed" colonies, it was evident that the Chinese leaders (Mao, in particular) turned to the Third World because they saw it as representing a fertile base of support—"the area of greatest political opportunity," as was claimed—for China to build an alternative front against the global status quo.[72] Peter Van Ness notes: "Mao was prepared to incur the risk of opposing both superpowers at the same time because, in his view, the opportunity to take a leadership role in global politics and to enhance China's power was so great."[73]

To be sure, the roles as the "thought center" of the socialist bloc and as the leader of the Third World overlapped. They were also, on various occasions, evoked in terms of China's "victim" identity, where the primary argument was that because China had been a "victim" of foreign imperialism, it made sense to align with the socialist and anticolonial worlds that supposedly shared similar historical experiences. But regardless of the permutations, these two conceptions essentially embodied the channels by which China asserted its global leadership claims from a position of weakness.

In 1964 China's great-power aspirations were boosted with the successful development of nuclear weapon capability. After all, the PRC had: (i) acquired one of the more vivid symbols of great power status; (ii) broken the "nuclear monopoly" of the other major powers; and (iii) crucially demonstrated Chinese determination and indigenous ability to master a sophisticated technology with minimal external assistance.[74] Earlier, in 1958, Mao also stated that if the Chinese did not possess the bomb, "others [would not] think what we say [can] carry weight."[75] Hence, in terms of Chinese prestige and the development of China's great-power outlook, the acquisition of nuclear weapons clearly had positive implications. However, the impact of these implications should not be overstated. First, there is considerable evidence that the Chinese leadership had approached the nuclear issue from the standpoint of a vulnerable power—that is, from a position of weakness rather than strength. Thus, in a vein similar to the 1950s "catching up" discourse, Mao argued in 1956 that "if we are not to be bullied in the present day world, we cannot do without the Bomb."[76] Others referred to the role of nuclear status in helping China shed the label of the "sick man of the east." This suggests a strong link between the acquisition of nuclear weapons and the goal of averting victimization rather than as a conscious effort to achieve great-power status as such.[77] Second, the development of nuclear weapon capability did not dramatically improve China's military strength vis-à-vis the military power of the US or USSR. True, China had entered the nuclear club, but it was virtually a nuclear infant compared to the more established members. So, even as China's nuclear explosion had altered the extant nuclear order in considerable ways, there was still a huge asymmetry between Chinese nuclear capacity and that of the Americans and the Soviets.[78]

With the advent of the most radical phase of the Cultural Revolution in the late 1960s (1966–1969), matters of foreign affairs took a backseat compared to those of domestic concerns. Yet, even as Beijing became embroiled in a no-holds-barred, intraparty power struggle, Chinese foreign policy in this period still encompassed "profound internationalist content."[79] The CCP leadership (or, more accurately, those who still retained influence in steering Chinese foreign policy, such as Mao, Zhou Enlai, and Lin Biao) continued to articulate the dual, globalist images of China as the "center of world revolution" and leader of the Third World. But, compared to the early and mid-1960s, the emphasis shifted more to the former than the latter, where the version of international socialism promulgated by Beijing assumed a more radical, more revolutionary, and more deterministic shape.[80]

Given the more radical flavor of China's foreign policy discourse during the Cultural Revolution period, it seems that ideological interests took precedence over big-power considerations. To be sure, China still asserted global leadership claims through its dual conceptions as the mentor of the socialist camp and mentor of the Third World. Plus, in 1967 it managed to successfully develop a thermonuclear capability. Nevertheless, the evidence suggests that, on balance, because of the fixation with ideology as well as the upheavals in Chinese society and state, the Cultural Revolution period represented a time when a certain degree of stasis and introspection marked China's big-power outlook.

This situation changed dramatically, however, in the early 1970s with the dawn of the Sino-American rapprochement when China effectively became a "tacit ally" of the US.[81] During this period, in part due to the external validation that the rapprochement gave, China's sense of itself as a global power was appreciably strengthened. Broadly, the rapprochement enhanced China's great-power identity in two key ways. First, the Richard Nixon administration took substantial steps to court the Chinese, which signified, to a considerable extent, an acknowledgment by the world's most powerful country of China's big-power qualities and potential. China was perceived by the US, a significant other, to possess enough strategic leverage to justify a major policy volte-face. This American perception, in turn, heightened the Chinese sense of its own significance in global politics. Gilbert Rozman has described Beijing as being "enamored" with the great-power triangle and that it "increasingly measured its importance as one of the three global powers capable of shifting the global balance of world power."[82] Second, the rapprochement eased the PRC's entry into the UN since the US no longer actively sought to block Chinese representation.[83] The UN seat thus allowed the PRC to finally secure one of the most basic markers of great-power status: a formal place in the UN Security Council as one of the Permanent Five, at the expense of the nationalist government in Taiwan.

The rapprochement clearly played a substantial role in imbuing a stronger sense of Chinese great-power identity in the 1970s. But it should be pointed out that, even though the Nixon administration recognized the strategic weight of Chinese power, it was not oblivious to the fact that, objectively, China was still economically and militarily backward. Nixon himself drew attention to this reality in his second State of the World Report in 1971.[84] Moreover, the Chinese leadership recognized and readily admitted China's material weaknesses. Zhou stated in 1975 that China remained a "poverty-stricken and backward country" and that it would take around two decades or more before China reached the "front ranks in the world."[85] In addition, the rapprochement was underpinned by a confluence of factors beyond China's perceived strategic value in the great-power triangle; they included, inter alia, Beijing's assessment that the Soviets (in the form of "socialist imperialism") represented the greatest threat to Chinese interests, US strategic considerations in Indochina, and Nixon's grand strategic doctrine of détente.[86] In fact, inasmuch as the rapprochement was about American courting of the Chinese, it was equally about Chinese wooing of the Americans. For these reasons American recognition of China's big-power credentials should not be exaggerated.

Responsibility in Chinese History

Having sketched out the broad contours of China's great-power identity (until the end of Mao's era), we now turn to a survey of Chinese notions of responsibility, paying particular attention to the extent to which this idea had been evoked as part of a Chinese great-power outlook.

The concept of responsibility in premodern China can be traced to the philosophical influence of Confucius and his disciples. To be precise, the literal equivalent of responsibility in Chinese language—*zeren*—featured little in classical Confucian discourse. The phrase that was used was *yiwu* (the character *yi* implies righteousness, while *wu* means task), which roughly corresponds to the meaning of duty or burden.[87] But what determined the allocation of duty within Chinese society? For the Confucians the idea is to employ a functional understanding of social distinctions as the mediating paradigm. As the leading Confucian Xun Zi put it in his "Rich Country" essay, it would be difficult for "proper" conduct to be established "when the duties of office and the tasks of the occupations lack clear [social] distinctions."[88] As such, in the Confucian conception social distinctions are an inevitable aspect of human life whereby one's distinct position within society (*dingwei*) dictates one's commensurate duties or obligations.[89] The role of the son entails corresponding duties of filial piety toward the parents. The ruler has the duty to govern the subjects with kindness and wisdom, while the subjects have the reciprocal duty of serving the ruler with unquestioned loyalty. There are other examples, of course, but the key point is that Confucian discourses of responsibility are framed mainly in terms of socially defined duties within a communitarian setting and are largely domestic in character and scope.

This is not meant to imply that there were no external dimensions to premodern Chinese conceptions of responsibility. The Central Kingdom worldview of the Imperial era meant the internal Confucian social order manifested itself to some degree beyond the borders of China.[90] In other words, just as social distinctions were needed to regulate relations in Chinese society, social distinctions were needed to regulate the Central Kingdom's relations with foreign nations.[91] As an extension of Confucian thought, this implies that a relationship of duty also existed between the Chinese civilization and outsiders. However, unlike the more reciprocal sense of obligations that functioned within Chinese society, on the external front the moral equation was asymmetric and the burden of duty rested primarily with outsiders. Foreign peoples (whether "barbarians" or "vassals") had a supposed duty to show reverence to the Chinese monarch, but the latter, as the "son of Heaven" with apparent powers of authority over all mankind, was not necessarily beholden to the obligation of demonstrating "virtuosity" to foreign peoples.[92] Such an outlook could clearly be seen in the Qianlong emperor's condescending reply to King George III during the Macartney Mission to China in 1793. Qianlong decreed that it was the "bounden duty of [George III] to reverently appreciate [the Chinese emperor's] feelings and to obey [the Chinese emperor's] instructions henceforward for all time, so that [George III] may enjoy the blessings of perpetual peace."[93] Of course, such a skewed understanding of responsibility, couched in terms of foreigners' duties to the Chinese throne, existed only in Chinese minds. One would be hard pressed to find among foreign nations, vassals included, a place where a concrete sense of duty toward the imperial court existed.

In republican China, political discourses of responsibility moved noticeably away from the traditional Confucian conception. That said, the level of discussion of the responsibility concept could hardly be described as substantial or extensive; it was certainly not among the key themes or ideas that concerned the Chinese political elites at the time.[94] Still, Sun Yatsen had considered the concept of responsibility to be significant enough to be included in his blueprint for rejuvenating China.

Sun essentially conceived two forms of responsibility for the Chinese nation. The first related to the notion of "internal" responsibility (*duinei zeren*), whose primary claim was that it was the responsibility of "four hundred million" Chinese people to "liberate all oppressed Chinese," "revive nationalism and recover [China's] national status." The second pertained to the notion of "external" responsibility (*duiwai zeren*) and this related to expectations of China's big-power obligations to the world. According to Sun:

> There was a common phrase in ancient China: "Help the weak, lift up the fallen [*jiruo fuqing*]." Because of this strategy, China was strong for a few thousand years . . . if China becomes strong again, not only must we restore our national standing, we must also assume a great responsibility towards the world. If China cannot assume that responsibility, even when she becomes strong again, she will be a great disadvantage, not an advantage, to the world. . . .What is China's responsibility to the world? . . . We must aid the weaker nations and oppose the imperialist powers of the world.[95]

Sun added that in order to effectively oppose imperialist powers and to "liberate those nations who equally suffered from imperialism," it was beholden upon China to work with an "international united front of both oppressed and free nations."[96] In doing so, Sun envisioned, China would "unify the world on the foundations of morality and peace" and "bring about a great harmony of equality and fraternity."[97] Sun emphasized that the goal of "safeguarding world peace" constituted the "divine duty" (*tianze)* of the Chinese nation. Sun later would codify the tenet of "safeguarding world peace" into the Kuomintang Party program and the Chinese Revolutionary Party Premier's Oath in 1912 and 1914, respectively.[98]

What were the salient features of Sun's discussion of the responsibility idea? First, responsibility was a moral imperative that concerned the entire Chinese nation; there was a nationalistic quality to it. Second, China had inescapable obligations to the global community that were centered on fighting imperialism and helping weaker nations similarly oppressed by imperialism. Third, China's responsibility—both internal and external—was inexorably linked to its self-image as a "suppressed" great power: it was the internal responsibility of the Chinese nation to reestablish China's great-power standing so that China could better fulfill its external obligations to the world.

Interestingly, and perhaps as a result of Sun's influence, Chiang Kai-shek articulated and advanced a formulation of responsibility that was broadly similar to Sun's ideas. In his widely circulated 1943 manifesto, "China's Destiny," Chiang argued that it was the responsibility of all Chinese people to rebuild China into a "completely free and independent state that can fulfill its duty to the peoples of the world."[99] This "world" duty, in Chiang's view, obliged China to stand "shoulder to shoulder" with other nations, sharing with them "the responsibilities for the maintenance of permanent world peace and the liberation of mankind."

Indeed, Chiang had claimed that it was precisely because of this sense of duty and responsibility that compelled China to seek "independence and strength." The generalissimo also took the opportunity in "China's Destiny" to remind the international community that China had effectively taken on "one of the heaviest responsibilities of all the Allied nations" in its War of Resistance with Japan; he described this as "a foreign policy of not shirking its own responsibility."[100] In sum, although Sun's and Chiang's evocations of responsibility appear somewhat quixotic and were certainly propagandistic, it could be argued that, given both men's central place in Chinese political history, the discussions of China's "world" obligations represented some of the earliest antecedents of a connection between Chinese ideas of responsibility and its great-power identity.[101]

During the Maoist period, like the republican years, the subject of responsibility was not a prominent aspect of Chinese political discourse. Nevertheless, from time to time the PRC leaders engaged in a language of responsibility in their political rhetoric, although it seems that the precise Chinese phrase for responsibility, *zeren*, was rarely used.

The PRC leadership's interpretation of responsibility had both domestic and foreign dimensions. On the domestic front, the responsibility concept was primarily given expression in the 1950s political line of "central" or "basic duty" (*zhongxin* or *jiben renwu*); its key emphasis was the economic construction of China.[102] In the lexicon of Mao, "Economic construction is the center of all duties" (*yi jingji jianshe wei yiqie renwu de zhongxin*).[103] To be sure, the linking of China's "central duty" with economic development was first made by Mao in 1933, when the CCP had yet to win power. But in 1949, with the victory of the CCP in the Chinese civil war, Mao again urged his comrades not to forget the central duty of China's economic construction, further exhorting them to master "techniques and management methods of productivity."[104] Three months after the PRC's establishment, Zhou Enlai made a similar argument, noting that economic productivity was "the basic duty of new China."[105] By 1956 the central duty–economic construction nexus had gained formal endorsement at the Eighth National Congress of the CCP, where Liu Shaoqi, representing the central committee, announced that the central duty of China was to ensure the growth of its productivity levels.[106] In the 1960s, however, it seemed that this narrative of central duty increasingly fell out of favor with the Chinese leadership. As the political emphasis shifted from economic construction to the imperative of class struggle, Mao chose instead to characterize Chinese domestic obligations in terms of class and revolutionary duties.[107]

Concerning the external elements of Maoist China's outlook on responsibility, Yongjin Zhang has argued that the 1954 Geneva Conference could be considered the beginning of the PRC's understanding of the idea that being a great power within the postwar world "carried with it the heavy burden of responsibility bestowed upon great powers."[108] While Zhang did not cite any supporting Chinese statements, there appears to be some later rhetorical evidence in corroboration of this claim. In November 1956, in a major speech commemorating (incidentally) Sun Yatsen, Mao stated: "China is a land with an area of 9.6 million square kilometers and a population of 600 million people, and she ought to have made a greater contribution to humanity. Her contribution over a long period has been far too small. For this we are regretful."[109] Here the language of responsibility was not explicitly evoked by Mao; the term used was "contribution" (*gongxian*). That said, it appears that Mao intended to evoke a connection between this "contribution" and China's great-power identity. Although Mao did not mention great power directly, he nonetheless drew attention to China's big-power attributes of population and territorial size.

Interestingly, from 1954 onward China started to render aid to some Third World countries despite the fact that, economically, China was barely in a better position than many it supported. This aid, from 1954 to around the time of Mao's death in 1976, amounted to almost US$5 billion.[110] Certainly there were various motivations behind the Chinese aid calculus, but one potential consideration was that because the Chinese were claiming a leading role in world politics (albeit through leadership in the Third World), they needed to demonstrate a certain degree of big-power "magnanimity." As Yahuda has argued, "Although China's economic aid has been less tied and more disinterested than most, the idealism which inspired it was linked to Chinese aspirations to 'greatness.'"[111] Third World aid thus could be seen in some ways as one example of China's big-power contribution.

The other way in which the PRC's responsibility was externalized relates to its ideological commitments—specifically, China's international revolutionary duty. Here the argument is that since China had succeeded its own revolution and had become the center of world revolution, it was to some extent responsible to its fellow "oppressed" brethren in their respective revolutionary struggles. Hence, in 1963 at a meeting with African leaders, Mao declared, "The people who have triumphed in their own revolution should help those still struggling for liberation. This is our internationalist duty."[112] In 1965 Lin Biao made a similar exhortation, asserting that "socialist countries [like China] should regard it as their internationalist duty to support the people's revolutionary struggles in Asia, Africa and Latin America."[113] Given that China's big-power outlook was in some ways exemplified by its revolutionary center role, it could be argued that this internationalist duty, as defined by Beijing, was an expression of Chinese noblesse oblige but couched in ideological terms.

To be sure, Chinese claims of revolutionary responsibility were often more form than substance, and Chinese contributions to the international revolutionary cause were usually limited to ideological inspiration or broad rhetorical guidance.[114] Nevertheless, during the Vietnam War China did extend substantial material and logistical support to North Vietnam in the form of large quantities of military equipment as well as the deployment of Chinese engineering troops. There was also a considerable level of Chinese operational assistance: from 1965 to 1969 some sixteen divisions of Chinese anti-aircraft artillery units, with an overall strength of over 150,000 men, were deployed in Vietnam.[115] While there were various reasons underlying China's substantial involvement in the Vietnam War, one explanation pertained to the fact that Beijing was essentially enacting its revolutionary "big brother" persona and was hence "obliged" to render help that measured up to its "center of world revolution" status.[116] In that sense, more than just an "internationalist duty," China's military assistance to the North Vietnamese was also partially an indication of a big-power mind-set.

Conclusion

This chapter has provided a contextualization of China's RGP identity from a historical perspective. This is not a history of China's state identity as such. Rather, it is a history of evolving Chinese perceptions of its great-power identity and the idea of responsibility, and the extent to which these two aspects were linked.

During the premodern era the Central Kingdom complex was the exemplification of traditional China's sense of its great-power status, an outlook that projected the Chinese state as the principal political force in the world. However, by the nineteenth century Chinese belief in the superiority of its own model was fundamentally shaken and the Central Kingdom conception was brutally exposed as a myth. Consequently, a "weak China" complex emerged, but it was one that resided in tension with suppressed perceptions of China's national greatness. In the Maoist period there was a more substantive sense of China's revival as a great power, though the Chinese leadership was also keenly aware of the PRC's material inadequacies and on various occasions sought to project the country as an impoverished country. Concerning the dimension of responsibility, the historical record suggests that there were only moderate doses of this facet in Chinese political narratives. While some of the narratives on responsibility connected to Chinese perceptions of a great-power identity, these linkages were generally limited and, when evoked, were either circumstantial or indirect.

Notes

1. Zi Zhongyun, "The Impact and Clash of Ideologies: Sino-US Relations from a Historical Perspective," *Journal of Contemporary China* 6, no. 16 (1997): 531–36.
2. While the term "Middle Kingdom" is commonly used, I use the transliteration that scholars such as Zhang Tiejun and Zi Zhongyun have adopted: "Central Kingdom."
3. The concept of *tianxia* gained further expression and content in the form of the *wufu* (five areas) theory of the Han dynasty. Based on the *wufu* theory, the Central Kingdom was basically divided into five realms: the center came under the emperor's direct control, while the remaining four were mainly administered by the imperial court. See Zhang Tiejun, "Self-Identity Construction of the Present China," *Comparative Strategy* 23, no. 3 (2004): 281–301; Yongjin Zhang, "System, Empire, and State in Chinese International Relations," *Review of International Studies* 27, no. 5 (2001): 53.
4. Samuel Kim, *China, the United Nations, and World Order* (Princeton, NJ: Princeton University Press, 1979), 20.
5. Immanuel Hsu, *The Rise of Modern China* (New York: Oxford University Press, 1975), 6.
6. Immanuel Wallerstein, *The Modern World System: Capitalist Agriculture and the Origins of the European World Economy in the Sixteenth Century* (London: Academic Press, 1974); Warren Cohen, "China's Rise in Historical Perspective," *Journal of Strategic Studies* 30, nos. 4–5 (2007): 683–87.
7. Kim, *China, the United Nations, and World Order*, 24; Zhang, "System, Empire, and State," 55.
8. Werner Levi, *Modern China's Foreign Policy* (Minneapolis: University of Minnesota Press, 1953), 4.
9. Kim, *China, the United Nations, and World Order*, 21.
10. Ong Siew Chey, *China Condensed: Five Thousand Years of History and Culture* (Singapore: Marshall Cavendish International, 2005), 1–82.

11. Rana Mitter, "An Uneasy Engagement: Chinese Ideas of Global Order and Justice in Historical Perspective," in *Order and Justice in International Relations*, ed. Rosemary Foot, John Lewis Gaddis, and Andrew Hurrell (Oxford, UK: Oxford University Press, 2003), 209.
12. Historically the Tang dynasty was known for its "extroverted" and cosmopolitan nature. Michael Hunt, "Chinese Foreign Relations in Historical Perspective," in *China's Foreign Relations in the 1980s*, ed. Harry Harding (New Haven, CT: Yale University Press, 1984), 6–7; Ong, *China Condensed*, 60.
13. Mitter, "Uneasy Engagement."
14. Michael Ng-Quinn, "National Identity in Premodern China: Formation and Role Enactment," in *China's Quest for National Identity*, ed. Lowell Dittmer and Samuel Kim (Ithaca, NY: Cornell University Press, 1993), 56.
15. Ong, *China Condensed*, 22.
16. Michael Hunt, for example, describes the tributary system as instantiating "unshakeable sinocentrism." See Hunt, "Chinese Foreign Relations in Historical Perspective," 6.
17. In fact, the imperial court paid for all expenditures relating to a tributary envoy's trip to "pay homage" to the Chinese emperor. See Kim, *China, the United Nations, and World Order*, 25.
18. Mitter, "Uneasy Engagement."
19. Ng-Quinn, "National Identity in Premodern China." Yongjin Zhang and Barry Buzan argue that the tributary system could be considered a form of historical East Asian international society. See Yongjin Zhang and Barry Buzan, "The Tributary System as International Society in Theory and Practice," *Chinese Journal of International Politics* 5 (2012): 3–36.
20. Kim, *China, the United Nations, and World Order*, 22.
21. The term "synarchy" is used to describe the "joint Sino-Foreign administration" of China. See John Fairbank, "Synarchy under the Treaties," in *Chinese Thought and Institutions*, ed. John Fairbank (Chicago: University of Chicago Press, 1957), 204–31.
22. As Lyman Miller writes, "the ruling Manchu house became so submerged in Chinese traditions of governance as to have lost any distinctive identity apart from the Han Chinese they governed." See Lyman Miller, "The Late Imperial Chinese State," in *The Modern Chinese State*, ed. David Shambaugh (Cambridge, UK: Cambridge University Press, 2000), 24.
23. Wang Gungwu, *China and the World since 1949: The Impact of Independence, Modernity, and Revolution* (London: Macmillan, 1977), 3.
24. It is also asserted that China accounted for as much as 30 percent of the world's gross domestic product during the early nineteenth century. See Yan Xuetong, "The Rise of China in Chinese Eyes," *Journal of Contemporary China* 10, no. 26 (2001): 33.
25. Li Zhaojie, "Traditional Chinese World Order," *Chinese Journal of International Law* 1, no. 1 (2002): 20.
26. Kim, *China, the United Nations, and World Order*, 22.

27. As Michael Ng-Quinn puts it, the Chinese need to "play the role of the suzerain was more psychological than material." Ng-Quinn, "National Identity in Pre-modern China," 55–56. On the socialization effects of the tributary system, see Zhang and Buzan, "Tributary System as International Society," 18–27.
28. Cohen, "China's Rise in Historical Perspective," 687–91.
29. Other labels of China then included the "sick man of Asia" (*dongya bingfu*) or "a heap of loose sand" (*yipan sansa*).
30. William Kirby, "The Internationalization of China: Foreign Relations at Home and Abroad in the Republican Era," *China Quarterly* 150 (1997): 433.
31. Michael Hunt, "Chinese National Identity and the Strong State: The Late Qing-Republican Crisis," in *China's Quest for National Identity*, ed. Lowell Dittmer and Samuel Kim (Ithaca, NY: Cornell University Press, 1993), 63–64.
32. Kim, *China, the United Nations, and World Order*, 38–39.
33. By 1898 several reformers, led by the late Qing official Kang Youwei, insisted that China's situation of debility needed more than just "self-strengthening"; China needed to "dismantle the building and build anew" and implement a radical and thorough shake-up of the system. See Hunt, "Chinese National Identity and the Strong State," 60.
34. William Theodore De Bary, Wing-Tsit Chan, and Burton Watson, *Sources of Chinese Tradition* (New York: Columbia University Press, 1960), 708–10.
35. Don Price, *Russia and the Roots of the Chinese Revolution, 1896–1911* (Cambridge, MA: Harvard University Press, 1974), 181.
36. Hunt, "Chinese National Identity and the Strong State," 68–70.
37. To be sure, there were prominent intellectuals such as Zou Taofen who argued that Confucianism should be adapted rather than cast aside. See Rana Mitter, *A Bitter Revolution: China's Struggle with the Modern World* (Oxford, UK: Oxford University Press, 2004), 14–15, 110–17.
38. De Bary, Chan, and Watson, *Sources of Chinese Tradition*, 768–71.
39. As Yan Xuetong notes, rejuvenation (*zhenxing*) implies a restoration of "China's lost international status rather than gaining something new." See Yan, "Rise of China in Chinese Eyes," 34.
40. Ong, *China Condensed*, 87; Mitter, *Bitter Revolution*, 149.
41. Hunt, "Chinese National Identity and the Strong State," 68.
42. Kirby, "Internationalization of China," 444.
43. Michael Alan Brittingham, "China's Contested Rise: Sino-US Relations and the Social Construction of Great Power Status," in *New Dimensions of Chinese Foreign Policy*, ed. Guo Sujian and Hua Shiping (Lanham, MD: Lexington, 2007), 94; Michael Schaller, *The US Crusade in China, 1938–1945* (New York: Columbia University Press, 1979), 89–90.
44. Brittingham, "China's Contested Rise," 95.
45. Cordell Hull, *The Memoirs of Cordell Hull*, vol. 2 (New York: Macmillan, 1948), 1583.
46. Brittingham, "China's Contested Rise," 94–97; John Garver, *Chinese-Soviet Relations, 1937–1945: The Diplomacy of Chinese Nationalism* (New York: Oxford University Press, 1988), 193–94.

47. Thus Garver argues that "what is remarkable is not that Chiang did not achieve more, but that, given the weakness of the Republic of China, he achieved so much." Wang Gungwu also notes that the nationalists had devoted "more than twenty years of effort to regain international respect." See Garver, *Chinese-Soviet Relations, 1937–1945*, 192–96, 229; and Wang, *China and the World since 1949*, 28.
48. Akira Iriye, "The United States as an Asian-Pacific Power," in *Sino-American Détente and Its Policy Implications*, ed. Gene Hsiao (New York: Praeger, 1974), 12; Brittingham, "China's Contested Rise," 96.
49. As Winston Churchill crudely put it, China's inclusion amounted to "a faggot vote on the side of the US." See Warren Cohen, *America's Response to China: An Interpretive History of Sino-American Relations* (New York: John Wiley & Sons, 1971), 162.
50. Ibid., 153.
51. The nationalist government might have had in mind domestic considerations when it tried to emphasize China's great-power status; that is, the Chinese nation had become "great" again under its leadership. See Wang, *China and the World since 1949*, 27.
52. Indeed, Gerald Segal argues that "one of the first steps in the PRC's emergence as a third great power upsetting the bipolar equation can be found prior to the declaration of the People's Republic." See Gerald Segal, "China and the Great Power Triangle," *China Quarterly* 83 (1980): 491. See also John Garver, *Foreign Relations of the People's Republic of China* (Englewood Cliffs, NJ: Prentice-Hall, 1993), 39–43.
53. Mao Zedong, "The Chinese People Have Stood Up," in *Selected Works of Mao Zedong*, vol. 5 (Beijing: Foreign Languages Press, 1977), 15–18.
54. Ibid.
55. Mao Zedong, "Long Live the Great Unity of the Chinese People," in *Selected Works of Mao Zedong*, vol. 5 (Beijing: Foreign Languages Press, 1977), 19.
56. Rosemary Foot, *The Practice of Power: US Relations with China since 1949* (Oxford, UK: Oxford University Press, 1995), 140–42.
57. The Soviets provided mainly military supplies, though there was also some limited combat activity. The most important Soviet contribution, however, was indirect: its deterrent value and the prospect that it might be drawn into the war. See Hao Yufan and Zhai Zhihai, "China's Decision to Enter the Korean War: History Revisited," *China Quarterly* 121 (1990): 94–115.
58. Mao Zedong, "Our Great Victory in the War to Resist US Aggression and Aid Korea and Our Future Tasks," in *Selected Works of Mao Zedong*, vol. 5 (Beijing: Foreign Languages Press, 1977), 115.
59. Chen Jian argues that one of the prime reasons underlying the Chinese decision to enter the Korean War related to Mao's desire to pursue "a glorious victory" over the Americans, so as to advance the PRC's "international prestige and influence." See Chen Jian, *Mao's China and the Cold War* (Chapel Hill: University of North Carolina Press, 2001), 116.
60. See Michael Yahuda, *China's Role in World Affairs* (London: Croom Helm, 1978), 60; Michael Yahuda, "China's Foreign Relations: The Long March, Future Uncertain," *China Quarterly* 159 (1999): 650.

61. Foot, *Practice of Power*, 146; Yuen Foong Khong, *Analogies at War: Korea, Munich, Dien Bien Phu, and the Vietnam Decisions of 1965* (Princeton, NJ: Princeton University Press, 1992), 143.
62. See *People's Daily* editorial cited in Zhai Qiang, "China and the Geneva Conference of 1954," *China Quarterly* 129 (1992): 121. According to Yongjin Zhang the Geneva Conference marked the first time that the PRC enjoyed international recognition as a great power. In his view the US and its allies had probably "unwittingly" granted great-power status to the PRC. See Yongjin Zhang, *China in International Society since 1949: Alienation and Beyond* (Basingstoke, UK: Macmillan, 1998), 37.
63. Cohen, "China's Rise in Historical Perspective," 695.
64. Mao Zedong, "Patriotism and Internationalism," in *Quotations from Chairman Mao Zedong* (Beijing: Foreign Languages Press, 1966), 180.
65. Foot, *Practice of Power*, 200–201.
66. John Gittings, "New Light on Mao: His View of the World," *China Quarterly* 60 (1974): 757–58.
67. Mao Zedong, "The Relationship between China and Other Countries," in *Selected Works of Mao Zedong*, vol. 5 (Beijing: Foreign Languages Press, 1977), 306.
68. Gittings, "New Light on Mao," 757.
69. Mitter, *Bitter Revolution*, 197.
70. Foot, *Practice of Power*, 212–13.
71. See Yahuda, *China's Role in World Affairs*, 121–26; Garver, *Foreign Relations of the People's Republic of China*, 133–63; and John Gittings, *Survey of the Sino-Soviet Dispute* (Oxford, UK: Oxford University Press, 1968). See also Chen Zhimin, "Nationalism, Internationalism, and Chinese Foreign Policy," *Journal of Contemporary China* 14, no. 42 (2005): 44. As Chen Zhimin notes, "China was able to obtain a sense of greater international status through its 'thought center' role in world revolutionary movements."
72. Peter Van Ness, "China as a Third World State: Foreign Policy and Official National Identity," in *China's Quest for National Identity*, ed. Lowell Dittmer and Samuel Kim (Ithaca, NY: Cornell University Press, 1993), 203–7.
73. Ibid., 206.
74. See Jonathan Pollack, "China and the Global Strategic Balance," in *China's Foreign Relations in the 1980s*, ed. Harry Harding (New Haven, CT: Yale University Press, 1984), 172; Jonathan Pollack, "Chinese Attitudes toward Nuclear Weapons, 1964–1969," *China Quarterly* 50 (1972): 244–71; and Alice Langley Hsieh, *Communist China's Strategy in the Nuclear Era* (Englewood Cliffs, NJ: Prentice Hall, 1962).
75. Foot, *Practice of Power*, 171.
76. Mao, "Relationship between China and Other Countries," 288.
77. Two months after China's successful atomic test, Zhou Enlai said, "Have we not exploded an atom bomb? Has not the label, 'sick man of the east,' fastened on us by Westerners, been flung off?" See Chong-Pin Lin, "From Panda to Dragon: China's Nuclear Strategy," *The National Interest* 15 (Spring 1989): 56. See also Chen Yi's statement about China degenerating into a "second-class or third-class nation" if it did not obtain nuclear weapons. Alice Langley Hsieh, "The Sino-Soviet Nuclear

Dialogue: 1963," in *Sino-Soviet Military Relations*, ed. Raymond Garthoff (New York: Praeger, 1966), 164.

78. Jonathan Pollack argues that there was "virtually no evidence to support the argument that decision makers in Peking began to view China's strategic position as qualitatively improved by the mere possession of limited nuclear capability." See Pollack, "Chinese Attitudes toward Nuclear Weapons," 249. On the notion of a nuclear order, see William Walker, "Nuclear Enlightenment and Counter-Enlightenment," *International Affairs* 83, no. 3 (2007): 431–53.
79. Yahuda, *China's Role in World Affairs*, 190.
80. Ibid., chap. 7.
81. Evelyn Goh, *Constructing the US Rapprochement with China, 1961–1974: From "Red Menace" to "Tacit Ally"* (Cambridge, UK: Cambridge University Press, 2005).
82. Gilbert Rozman, "China's Quest for Great Power Identity," *Orbis* 43, no. 3 (1999): 388.
83. Foot, *Practice of Power*, 46–51.
84. Ibid., 218–22.
85. Alexander Eckstein, *China's Economic Revolution* (Cambridge, UK: Cambridge University Press, 1977), 240–41.
86. Doak Barnett, *China and the Major Powers in East Asia* (Washington, DC: Brookings Institution, 1977), 193–200; Chen, *Mao's China and the Cold War*, chap. 7.
87. Wang Gungwu, "Power, Rights, and Duties in Chinese History," *Australian Journal of Chinese Affairs* 3 (1980): 1–26.
88. Kung-Chuan Hsiao, *A History of Chinese Political Thought*, vol. 1 (Princeton, NJ: Princeton University Press, 1979), 185.
89. Wang, "Power, Rights, and Duties in Chinese History," 5–11; Gerald Chan, *China's Compliance in Global Affairs* (Singapore: World Scientific, 2006), 15–16; John Fairbank, "The People's Middle Kingdom," *Foreign Affairs* 44, no. 4 (1966): 574–77.
90. Li, "Traditional Chinese World Order," 32–35.
91. Foreign peoples were assigned the inferior position of "barbarian" or "vassal," while the Chinese remained on the civilizational and social high ground.
92. To the extent that the Chinese emperor demonstrated "virtuosity" toward outsiders, it was a privilege extended, in Qianlong's words, "a kindly indulgence" rather than an obligation of the throne. See E. Backhouse and J. O. P. Bland, *Annals and Memoirs of the Court of Peking* (Boston: Houghton Mifflin, 1914), 330–31.
93. Ibid., 331.
94. Mao, incidentally, in his younger days (from 1912 to 1920) had writings that briefly explored a metaphysical interpretation of responsibility—one loosely based on the adage of "saving all under heaven as duty" (*jiu tianxia wei jiren*). See Fan Li, "Mao Zedong Zaoqi Wengao Zhong De Zeren Shiyi" (The explication of responsibility in Mao Zedong's early manuscripts), *Dali Xueyuan Xuebao (Journal of Dali College)* 2 (2003): 8–11.
95. See Sun Yatsen, *Sanmin Zhuyi (Three Principles of the People, 1924)* (Hunan: Yuelu Shushe, 2000), 68; "Sun Zhongshan De Xueshuo Shi Weixin Lun? Sun Zhongshan

Zou De Shi Ziben Zhuyi Daolu Ma?" (Are Sun Yatsen's words idealism? Is Sun Yatsen walking the path of capitalism?), Mingge Zhongyang (Revolutionary Committee of the Chinese Kuomintang Network), 2008, http://old.minge.gov.cn/minge/txt/2008-10/07/content_2505177_2.htm.

96. Li Benyi, "Sun Zhongshan Dui Huanghuo Lun De Pipan Jiqi Shijie Zeren Guan" (Sun Yatsen's criticism of the yellow peril theory and his world responsibility outlook), *Hubei Daxue Xuebao Zhexue Shehui Kexue Ban (Journal of Hubei University: Philosophy and Social Sciences)* 32 (2005): 599–600; "Sun Zhongshan De Xueshuo Shi Weixin Lun?"
97. Sun, *Sanmin Zhuyi.*
98. Li, "Sun Zhongshan Dui Huanghuo Lun De Pipan Jiqi Shijie Zeren Guan." Sun Yatsen also claimed that once the Chinese civilization fulfilled its destiny (*shiming*) of assuming greater world responsibility, it would become the "guiding lamp of mankind." See Li Xiufang and Yu Haixia, "Sun Zhongshan De Zhongxi Wenhua Guan" (Sun Yatsen's outlook on Chinese and western culture), *Xian Jiaotong Daxue Xuebao Shehui Kexue Ban (Journal of Xian Jiaotong University: Social Sciences)* 26 (2006): 86.
99. To be sure, there was some uncertainty as to how much of the ideas in *China's Destiny* were from Chiang Kai-shek himself, since there were claims that Tao Xisheng was Chiang's ghost writer. See Chiang Kai-shek, *China's Destiny*, trans. Philip Jaffe (London: Dennis Dobson, 1947), 103–4, 155, 214, 237.
100. Ibid., 107, 148–50, 157, 202–38.
101. Interestingly, the notion of responsibility is given considerable coverage in *China's Destiny* and is evoked on no less than thirty occasions.
102. A similar terminology used was "fundamental duty" (*genben renwu*). See Zhang Huimin, "Mao Zedong Tongzhi Dui Woguo Shehui Zhuyi: Jianshe De Daolu, Buzhou He Renwu De Tansuo" (Mao Zedong comrade and our national socialism: Probing its construction path, step, and duty), *Gansu Lilun Xuekan (Gansu Theory Research)* 5 (1993): 35–37.
103. See Wang Zhiyu, "Mao Zedong 'Yi Jingji Jianshe Wei Yiqie Renwu De Zhongxin' Lunduan Yanqiu" (Researching Mao Zedong's thoughts on "economic construction as the center of all duties"), *Shandong Nongye Daxue Xuebao Shehui Kexue Ban (Journal of Shandong Agriculture University: Social Sciences)* 34 (2007): 81–86.
104. Ibid.
105. Yang Zenghe, "Xin Zhongguo De Jiben Renwu He Shehui Zhuyi De Biaozhi" (New China's basic duty and the mark of socialism), *Xuexi Yu Yanjiu (Study and Research)* 3 (1988): 5–7. The journal is later retitled as *Qianxian (Frontline).*
106. Lin Huanfen, "Jianguo Tou Qinian Mao Zedong Guanyu Zhongxin Renwu: Zhuanyi De Lilun Guandian He Keguan Shijian" (Mao Zedong on the central duty during the first seven years of nation-building: Shifting theoretical viewpoints and objective practices), *Fujian Shifan Daxue Xuebao Zhexue Shehui Kezue Ban (Journal of Fujian Teacher Training College: Philosophy and Social Sciences)* 3 (1993): 1–5; Wang, "Mao Zedong 'Yi Jingji Jianshe Wei Yiqie Renwu De Zhongxin' Lunduan Yanqiu," 86.

107. Zhang, "Mao Zedong Tongzhi Dui Woguo Shehui Zhuyi," 37.
108. Zhang, *China in International Society since 1949*, 37.
109. Mao, "Patriotism and Internationalism," 179–80.
110. John Copper, *China's Foreign Aid: An Instrument of Peking's Foreign Policy* (Lanham, MD: Lexington, 1976), chap. 6.
111. Michael Yahuda, *Towards the End of Isolationism: China's Foreign Policy after Mao* (London: Macmillan, 1983), 100.
112. See Mao, "Patriotism and Internationalism," 178. The 1963 *CCP Proposal Concerning the General Line of the International Communist Movement* also noted that China's special role in revolutionary socialism meant "a heavier responsibility for the unity of the entire socialist camp and international communist movement." See William Griffith, *The Sino-Soviet Rift* (Cambridge, MA: MIT Press, 1964), 259.
113. Lin Biao, "Long Live the Victory of People's War," *Peking Review* 36 (1965): 24.
114. Shogo Suzuki, "China's Quest for Great Power Status: The Social Mechanisms of Delinquent Gang Formation," *University of Manchester Center of International Politics Working Paper Series* 29 (2007): 12–21.
115. Chen, *Mao's China and the Cold War*, 221–29.
116. Ibid., 237. Chen Jian goes as far as to argue that Beijing was seeking to "create a modern version of the relationship between the Central Kingdom and its subordinate neighbors."

2

INCIPIENT IDENTIFICATION AS A RESPONSIBLE GREAT POWER, 1978 TO 1996

Chapter 1 discussed the historical backdrop to China's responsible great-power identity. It showed that, historically, there were only ad hoc or indirect associations of the responsibility concept with Chinese great-power perceptions. Chapter 2 undertakes a more contemporary examination, focusing on the period from 1978 to 1996. In charting the topography of the RGP identity during this period, this chapter also aims to provide greater clarity on the genesis of this identity. Some scholars regard the period after 2005, in particular after the emergence of the "responsible stakeholder" discourse, to be the juncture at which China's RGP identity began to emerge. I offer a different interpretation: that a nascent Chinese RGP identity was already discernable in the early to mid-1990s, although, as previously noted, the preceding period, from the late 1970s to the 1980s, is important for understanding the context in which the RGP identity developed.

Continuing the previous chapter's approach, this chapter begins by genealogically tracking the two core narratives of the RGP identity—the notion of a great power and the idea of responsibility—as separate phenomena. This helps trace the point when these two narratives converged to express an aggregate RGP identity and tease out the intervening conditions and factors that led to its emergence. This chapter is organized as follows: first it explores the course of China's great-power identity in the 1980s; it then examines Chinese perceptions of responsibility during this period; next, in three segments it shows how China's great-power identity converged with the idea of responsibility during the early to mid-1990s; and finally it assesses the basis for China's desire to proclaim itself as a responsible great power.

Great Power Identity in the 1980s

The 1970s could be considered, on balance, to be a period of increased substantiation to Chinese perceptions of their country's great-power status. American statements, such as Richard Nixon's 1971 public assertion that the PRC would become "one of the five great economic superpowers," had provided some validation of China's great-power identity.[1] This validation was also supported by positive events, such as the US-China rapprochement and the ascension to UN Security Council permanent membership in 1971. Nevertheless, by the late 1970s it was discernable that a more moderated perspective was preferred. Deng and his colleagues clearly had a more realistic appraisal of Chinese power. Acknowledging China's considerable technological and economic gaps vis-à-vis the developed world, Deng openly admitted that China had been "stagnant and slow-developing for a long time" and it was "time for [China] to learn from other advanced countries in the world."[2] This declaration in effect called on the PRC to assume the role of a "student" vis-à-vis developed nations, cognizant of its shortcomings and keen to catch up. This student self-perception reflected Deng's pragmatic outlook on international politics, a departure from the more ideologically rooted Maoist era.

A greater recognition of China's limitations persisted for much of the 1980s. Chinese leaders frequently emphasized China's economic backwardness and underdeveloped status. In many ways this was a tacit admission of the failings of thirty years of Maoist rule.[3] It contributed to a revival of anti-traditionalist sentiments among the Chinese intelligentsia. For many Chinese intellectuals anti-traditionalism became associated with the idea of Westernization; Zhao Suisheng has described this as a "Western-learning fever" (*xixue re*). The controversial 1988 nationwide television series *Heshang* (River elegy), which contrasted a backward China with images of a progressive West, was one vivid expression of the "look West" attitude.[4]

In conjunction with the underdevelopment theme, the CCP leadership also made efforts to articulate a third-world identity for China.[5] Yet, unlike during the Maoist period, in the 1980s this seemed less about traditional Third World solidarity in the mold of anti-hegemony and economic self-reliance and more an acknowledgment of the PRC's impoverished position.[6] The reversal in Chinese foreign aid policy demonstrated this: the 1980s saw a sharp reduction in Chinese assistance to Third World countries, as China itself became a major recipient of international aid. By 1989 China had become the world's largest aid recipient, with incoming annual aid of almost US$2.2 billion.[7] The consequence was a reduction of China's ideological power within the Third World. For all its flaws, the former Maoist model of self-reliance represented a developmental alternative with considerable appeal among those Third World nations suspicious of foreign capitalists and aid. Deng's policies, however, moved away from the self-reliance logic and seemed to endorse economic dependency on or a strong economic relationship with the developed world.[8]

Alongside China's own reassessment of its relative power, American perceptions of China's national power became more measured and less prone to hyperbole. Initially, when President Ronald Reagan took office in early 1981, there appeared to be a continuation of the view that China was central to American geopolitical interests. Then-secretary of state, Alexander Haig, for example, had considered the PRC to be "the most important country in the world" for Washington.[9] However, by 1982 such an assessment came to be seen as untenable and the Reagan administration began to see China's role as "less than vital." In the US view China was basically "too technologically backward to do more than tie down Soviet forces that would otherwise be available for employment on other fronts."[10] In fact, China's perceived vulnerability vis-à-vis the Soviet Union was such that Washington saw little need to accommodate to various key Chinese interests (e.g., the Taiwan issue). The US felt it "could take China for granted," as China was ostensibly the more dependent party relative to the US.[11]

There was some evidence that this revised American judgment influenced Chinese leaders' own estimations of the PRC's strategic importance. In a study of US-China bargaining relations from the early to mid-1980s, Robert Ross argues that Beijing had been aware of Washington's assessment of China's limited role and that it eventually reconciled itself to this view, adopting a more conciliatory stance in the process.[12] In some ways Chinese leaders thus had "learned" about their country's diminished strategic role from interactions with American leaders. That said, the Sino-American relationship was not the only source of socialization and identity learning for China. Implementation of the opening-up policy in the 1980s meant that the PRC was essentially allowing the wider world to play a larger part in shaping its identity. China participated more in multilateral organizations; it permitted the import of foreign goods; it encouraged the entry of foreign capital, technology, and expertise; and it allowed its citizens to travel abroad for education, academic exchange, and tourism. These increased external exchanges helped the Chinese gain more knowledge of the outside world, but they also reinforced existing perceptions of national inadequacies by showing how less advanced the PRC still was in comparison to the developed world.[13]

Nevertheless, this trend of a more circumscribed great-power identity should not be overstated at the expense of other events that had encouraged, or were indicative of, a certain degree of consistency in the Chinese big-power mind-set. By 1980 China had successfully tested intercontinental nuclear weapons with a range theoretically capable of reaching US and Soviet targets. This was followed by the development of sea-based nuclear capabilities in 1982.[14] These were nontrivial technological breakthroughs and added credibility to China's nuclear power status. The year 1982 also saw the formal announcement of China's "independent" foreign policy, by which it would "never attach itself to any superpower, or enter into alliance or strategic relations with either of them."[15] From the perspective of US-China relations, Beijing was effectively signaling that it would not accept being relegated to a "subordinate role" vis-à-vis the US, even as ties between the two nations deepened. There were, of course, other reasons for adopting this strategic position, but Beijing evidently had misgivings of being perceived as a junior partner to the US.[16] This in some ways mirrored the PRC's previous pursuit of an autonomous path from the USSR and reflected a certain continuity in the big-power mind-set.[17] In 1984 the Chinese government successfully negotiated the transfer of Hong Kong's sovereignty from the United Kingdom to China. Effective from 1997, the handover agreement was generally considered to have been a major diplomatic victory, and it boosted Chinese national pride, addressing a long-standing issue symbolic of former humiliations at the hands of foreign aggressors.[18]

By the latter half of the 1980s China's economy was powering ahead with encouraging results. China's relations with the Soviet Union improved, as did relations with several other countries, including Japan. US-China relations also broadened with a reduction in frictions, and this helped facilitate increased sales of US military equipment to China. On the international front, therefore, a greater sense of security and stability emerged, which aided the advancement of Deng's domestic reform program. By 1986 Huan Xiang, a prominent scholar-diplomat who served as Deng's national security advisor, argued that "after revision of its domestic and international policy," China's "position in the three poles [US, USSR, and China] is definite."[19] A year later Huan, along with Gen. Yang Dezhi, went on to assert that "the mentality of being a world power" was imperative for China and that it "should not be satisfied with being a second-class power or regional power."[20] Also that year analyst Chen Feng, writing in the influential Chinese journal *Shijie Jingji Yu Zhengzhi (World Economics and Politics)*, noted that "China is a big power turning toward the world," one that would "inevitably produce a central impact on both the world system and itself."[21] Such analyses indicated a level of perceptual self-consistency regarding the PRC's great-power identity.

On the whole, Chinese leaders and intellectuals were realistic about China's capabilities in the 1980s. They frequently described a national self that was still relatively poor and backward. Up to a point this self-perception had been "learned" during China's interactions with the US and other developed nations. This did not imply that China eschewed its great-power perspective: on several occasions it continued to perceive international affairs through the lens of a big power. Rather, such thinking became more measured and less presumptuous. Deng's remarks at the time probably sum up the identity dichotomy best: "China is both a major power and a minor one. When we say it is a major power, we mean it has a huge population and a vast territory, although it has more mountains than arable land. But at the same time, China is a minor power, an underdeveloped or developing country. If we talk about China's ability to safeguard peace and deter war, it is certainly a minor one."[22]

Perceptions of Responsibility in the 1980s

Chinese statements alluding to the notion of responsibility were limited during the 1980s. Even so, Deng was one principal exponent of the concept, though he did not necessarily reference the idea of responsibility directly. As Deng stated: "China's contribution to the world is not small" and "if its material foundation and strength grow stronger, this contribution will inevitably become bigger."[23] On another occasion he emphasized that China's "primary foreign policy duty was to strive for peace," and it was critical for China to assume the role of a "peaceful, not-warlike" power.[24] In 1985 Chinese premier Zhao Ziyang added to this discourse with an implicit reference to the idea of big-power responsibility. Taking the unusual step of publishing in a foreign journal, *International Affairs*, Zhao expressed the view that as "a large country with a population of one thousand million, China is aware of its responsibility and its weight in international affairs."[25] While the significance of these remarks should not be exaggerated, they did hint at some awareness of China's international obligations and a belief that power begets additional responsibilities.

In 1988 Deng employed the Chinese term for responsible, *fuzeren*, to characterize China. In comments made to the visiting US secretary of defense, Frank Carlucci, Deng called China "a trustworthy nation, a responsible nation."[26] To be sure, Deng had given this characterization in response to American concerns about the alleged sales of the Silkworm missile to Iran; hence, it was a contingent remark and did not refer to a broader sense of global responsibility as such.[27] It was against this backdrop that the Ministry of Foreign Affairs proceeded to describe China in similar terms in its announcement of the "three principles of arms sales" the same year:

> China is a responsible country. Concerning the question of military products export, we always assume a serious, prudent, and responsible attitude. In this regard, we strictly adhere to three principles: first, our military products export should help strengthen the legitimate self-defense capability of the countries concerned; second, it should help safeguard and promote peace, security, and stability in the regions concerned; and third, we do not use the military sale to interfere in the internal affairs of other nations.[28]

Beyond the rhetoric, Chinese international behavior in the 1980s did seem more "responsible" than at any other time in the PRC's history.[29] From 1977 to 1988 China signed 125 multilateral treaties, an increase of more than fifteen times compared with the period of 1949 to 1970. Its membership in nongovernmental organizations increased from 71 to 574 during the same period.[30] By 1989 it had joined 37 major intergovernmental forums, which included, among others, the International Monetary Fund (IMF) and the World Bank.[31] China also became discernibly more supportive of and participatory within the United Nations, an institution it once derided as a "dirty international political stock exchange in the grip of a few big powers."[32]

China's support of the UN was most evident in the shift of Chinese policy regarding UN peacekeeping operations. In the 1950s and 1960s China viewed such activities negatively, considering them illegitimate, a form of neocolonialism, and a tool of big-power politics. In the 1970s its attitude toward UN peacekeeping had become less antagonistic but still indifferent overall. The critical watershed moment came on December 18, 1981. On that occasion the PRC voted for the extension of the UN contingent in Cyprus (UNFICYP), marking its first "positive approach" toward a mandate of UN peacekeeping forces.[33]

The following year it also started to assume its share of expenses relating to the UNIFIL (the UN Interim Force in Lebanon) and operations of the UNDOF (UN Disengagement Observer Force). By 1988 the PRC had become a full member of the UN Special Committee on Peacekeeping Operations. This facilitated a more active Chinese role in UN peacekeeping, and China subsequently voted in favor of the establishment of three new groups: the UN Iran-Iraq Military Observer Group (UNIIMOG), the UN Good Offices Mission to Afghanistan and Pakistan (UNGOMAP), and the UN Observer Group in Central America (UNOGICA).[34] In 1989 China sent twenty civilians to join the UN Transition Assistance Group in Namibia (UNTAG) and five military observers to serve in the UNDOF—its first ground involvement with UN peacekeeping forces.[35]

In the area of arms control and nonproliferation, notwithstanding its assistance to Pakistan's nuclear program and the sale of arms to Iran and Iraq during the 1980–1988 Gulf War, there were also nascent contributions from China.[36] Whereas in the Maoist period China mostly shunned or criticized such regimes, the 1980s marked the start of growing Chinese participation in them. Notable developments included joining the Conference of Disarmament (CD) in 1981, ratification of the Inhumane Weapons Convention in 1982, creation of the diplomatic post of special ambassador for disarmament in 1983, accession to the Biological Weapons Convention (BWC) and membership in the International Atomic Energy Agency (IAEA) in 1984, and ratification of the South Pacific Nuclear Weapons-Free Zone Treaty and the Convention on the Physical Protection of Nuclear Material in 1987 and 1989, respectively.[37] Chinese leaders and officials also made a number of notable announcements that indicated China would move in the direction of greater nonproliferation commitments. As early as 1985 Beijing declared that it "would be willing to reconsider its position" in regard to the formation of a nuclear test-ban body.[38] Another noteworthy announcement came in 1986, when Beijing formally confirmed that it "had not conducted atmospheric nuclear tests for many years and would thereafter not conduct [such] tests in the future."[39]

There was thus considerable evidence that 1980s China was a substantially different international actor from the earlier Maoist version. No longer seeking to be a disruptive influence on the extant global order, the PRC now endeavored to "link up with the international track" (*yu guoji jiegui*).[40] And, while it had yet to meet a number of the membership requirements of a Western-oriented international society, the general trend suggested a country leaning in that direction. It would be problematic, nevertheless, to link the overall more cooperative behavior to Chinese views of responsibility. Such rhetoric had been too limited and contingent in the 1980s to have formed a substantive role for China. At that time there were also few attempts by relevant "others," such as the US or the international society, to engage China from the normative perspective of responsibility.[41] China's behavior could be better and more simply understood as a consequence of its reform and opening-up policy: a more participatory international approach was seen as essential for gaining access to Western technology, expertise, and capital. At the same time, it was crucial for China to forestall a hostile external environment that could potentially thwart this access and derail its development. It was hence important that Chinese behaviors tried to align with, or at least not actively challenge, the prevailing global system.[42]

The Transitional Period of 1989 to 1991

The end of the 1980s came as a severe testing time for Beijing, as forces unleashed by the June 4, 1989, Tiananmen massacre threatened to destabilize the country. Internally the CCP was weakened by factional strife, a development that meant the temporary slowing down of economic reforms. Domestically the CCP faced serious questions over the legitimacy of its rule, a problem further exacerbated by the subsequent fall of several Eastern European communist regimes. On the external front the PRC met intense excoriation from Western governments, especially the US, resulting in diplomatic and material sanctions being imposed against it.[43]

The Tiananmen bloodshed had palpable implications for China's identity. As a result of the CCP's actions, the US and its allies effectively regarded the PRC as a pariah state in international society.[44] This negative identity perception was not lost on the CCP leadership, but in Beijing the message was interpreted differently. The PRC saw itself as the target of unjust American imperialism, whose ultimate goal was to subvert the Chinese political system. Sanctions by the Group of Seven and attempts to isolate China were likened to a gross interference in Chinese internal affairs and sovereignty. The upshot was that a historically informed victim identity increasingly came to the fore in Beijing. Deng's words were telling:

> I am a Chinese, and I know about the history of foreign aggression against China. When I heard that the seven Western countries had

> decided to impose sanctions on China, my immediate association was to 1900, when the allied forces of the eight powers (*baguo lianjun*) invaded China.[45]

Deng also concluded that the Tiananmen crisis reflected a failure in "ideological and political education," and his response was to initiate a patriotic education program that deliberately sought to remind the country about China's former humiliations at the hands of foreign powers.[46] This policy further perpetuated the Chinese self-perception as a victim of international realpolitik.

In addition, the ending of the Cold War, starting from around late 1989, compelled Beijing to reassess its international position. From a geopolitical perspective this situation did not seem propitious for China. Not only would Beijing lose the strategic leverage that it might once have enjoyed as a result of US-Soviet competition, it also meant that the strategic rationale that had underpinned the US-Sino relationship—the common Soviet threat—was basically gone. Of course, by the late 1980s tripolarity dynamics had been less of a factor, as both the United States and China pursued détente with the Soviet Union.[47] Still, because foreign policy had been conceived in largely globalist terms for most parts of the PRC's history, the end of the Cold War seemed to imply an inevitable reduction of China's global significance and influence. Its political position was also not helped by the fact that communism in the Soviet bloc countries was unraveling quickly.[48] Thus, the general conclusion among many analysts was that "China's global position and leverage have been weakened."[49]

Around this time Deng issued a twenty-eight-character axiom as a strategic compass for China's foreign policy direction: *Lengjing Guancha, Wenzhu Zhenjiao, Chenzhuo Yingfu, Taoguang Yanghui, Shanyu Shouzhou, Juebu Dangtou, Yousuo Zuowei*, which roughly translates to: "Calmly observe, secure our footing, handle the situation soberly, hide our capacities and bide our time, excel in keeping a low profile, avoid being the leader, but get some things done."[50] Although this dictum was prescribed in the context of a perceived precarious environment, it had implications for Chinese great-power identity. The words "hide our capacities and bide our time, excel in keeping a low profile, avoid being the leader" could be construed as advice for China to conceal or downplay the great-power aspects of its identity (albeit for the time being). However, the final part of the axiom, "get some things done," did suggest that China should undertake some limited activities. Deng later furnished additional insights into his strategic thoughts. In reference to some developing countries' hopes for China to assume a bigger global role, he replied, "China must not try to be the leader [*bu dangtou*]. This is one of our basic national strategies." In Deng's view, "China is not strong enough and cannot afford to be in this position" and that "to be in this role will not benefit China, but make China lose many initiatives."[51] One can see that there was thus a strategic dimension to Chinese identity construction: a bigger global role was seen as potentially detrimental, given China's extant level of development.

China's heightened sense of vulnerability was reinforced during and immediately after the 1990 Gulf War. The war vividly demonstrated the unmatched technological superiority of the American war machine and, conversely, highlighted the vast disparities between the US and Chinese militaries.[52] By comparison, the People's Liberation Army (PLA) seemed antiquated. The dominant view among the Chinese military was that "the American troops are very strong and powerful and we are not a match for them."[53] Furthermore, the ease with which the US had been able to orchestrate affairs within the UN to accommodate its military agenda was disconcerting to the Chinese.[54]

Yet, because the Gulf War was prosecuted under the aegis of the UN, it was also a timely reminder that China could not be ignored in world affairs; as one of the Permanent Five, Beijing retained the right to veto American initiatives through the Security Council.[55] More important, the conflict represented an opportunity for post-Tiananmen China to repair its relations with international society as well as improve its image. Consequently, China voted for all ten UN resolutions that imposed sanctions on Baghdad, abstaining only on Resolution 678, which authorized the use of force against Iraq. During the Gulf crisis, Chinese foreign minister Qian Qichen also made a special trip to Iraq to meet Saddam Hussein, after which the contents of the private meeting were shared with "relevant countries." This gesture, Qian later wrote in his memoirs, was greatly appreciated by the countries concerned and was considered by them to be an "indication of the serious, responsible spirit of China as a large country."[56] On one level Qian's account appears to suggest that other foreign nations were starting to engage China through the lens of international responsibility.

Interestingly, around this time China's support for UN measures had been on occasions expressed in the language of responsibility. For example, in response to media allegations that the PRC had violated the UN trade embargo against Iraq, Beijing declared: "China is a responsible country. We have been holding a very serious attitude toward the implementation of resolution 661."[57] That China would defend itself as a responsible state was perhaps not surprising. It had earlier asserted itself as such (in 1988), and that was also in an area connected to a Middle East security issue. As one Western diplomat who was cited in the *Washington Post* saw it, China's generally supportive gulf stance was linked to the importance of being perceived as "a friendly, responsible power."[58]

In 1991 the Soviet Union finally collapsed and Beijing was forced to confront an uncomfortable reality that had been looming for a while: it was now the last major socialist power. Recognizing the fundamentally contradictory nature of the Chinese and American political systems, residual CCP fears about a putative US ploy of peaceful evolution were stoked.[59] Nevertheless, many Chinese scholars still remained hopeful and argued that the overall trend portended a shift toward greater multipolarization (*duojihua*), reviving an argument that first took shape in 1986. Indeed, official rhetoric from 1991 to 1992 also indicated such an assessment, noting that "this is the initial stage of the evolution toward multipolarization." According to the multipolarization view, the coming global order would resemble a five-pole configuration comprising mainly the US, China, Japan, Russia, and Europe/Germany.[60] This greater leveling of power, it was claimed, would come primarily as an upshot of the US's strategic overextension, as evidenced by its increasing economic woes, domestic problems, and growing tensions with allies.[61] In effect, *duojihua* foretold a situation of growing power equivalence between the United States and China.

Comprehensive National Power and First References

By 1992, the post-Tiananmen diplomatic isolation was nearing an end. China's economic direction was also given greater clarity and impetus with Deng's high-profile trip to the south. Overall, the impression that Beijing conveyed was that it was committed to integrating China further with the world (human rights and democratic issues notwithstanding). Around this time Beijing began to give greater attention to the question of China's power status—what it is and how to measure it. The notion of comprehensive national power (CNP) (*zonghe guoli*) was proposed. While the idea originated in the 1980s at the behest of Deng, it was only at the 1992 Fourteenth Party Congress that it was included in official documents for the first time. Noting the inevitability of a "comprehensive national power competition," Jiang Zemin, the CCP general secretary, stated that "the core of [the] current international contest is comprehensive national power based on economic and political power."[62]

Huang Shuofeng, one of the principal proponents of the CNP idea, went on to give further conceptual flesh to the term in the monograph *Zonghe Guoli Lun* (*Discussing Comprehensive National Power*). In Huang's view a key objective of CNP was to "assess the comprehensive strength of enemies, friends, and one's own country in order to scientifically plan national strategic decision-making."[63] To this end, Huang defined CNP as comprising four main power "indexes": material, spirit, coordination, and environment. He explained: "The material power and spirit power indexes reflect a country's required [hard and soft] strength for survival and development; the coordination power index reflects the organization, command, management, and decision-making standards of the leadership system; and the environment power index reflects the limiting conditions of comprehensive national power." Based on Huang's CNP formulation, the PRC ranked sixth in the global power hierarchy in 1989.[64]

The official introduction of the CNP concept was a nontrivial juncture in the trajectory of China's great-power identity. In a sense it represented for the first time a Chinese attempt to formalize and systematize an assessment of great powerhood. Although CNP did not measure the notion of "greatness" per se, the concept sought to establish a country's relative power position within the international system, which was one indicator of whether that country was in or out of the great-power club. Furthermore, the notion of CNP took into account both tangible and intangible factors as well as exogenous and endogenous conditions. This suggested a degree of holism that more conventional power measures (i.e., military strength, gross national product, population, land size) lack. Compared to these one-dimensional indicators, CNP seemed more reliable in quantifying the rise (or fall) of China. The importance of CNP measurement on China's self-image was not lost on Zheng Yongnian; as he put it, CNP was "the new face" of Chinese identity.[65] Significantly, it aimed to estimate and verify the degree to which China would be able to categorize itself as a major power.

The year 1992 also marked another notable development. At a speech given at the luncheon of the US Foreign Policy Association, Qian Qichen declared China a "responsible great power" (*fuzeren daguo*). This was the first occasion that a senior Chinese leader combined both terms—"responsible" and "great power"—to express an aggregate PRC identity. Qian's elaboration of the RGP self-image went as follows:

> As one of the world's responsible great powers, China will strive for world peace and development in its foreign policy of independence and peace. As such, it will continue to observe the principles of mutual respect, equality, and noninterference in its relations with the world and neighboring countries. China will continue to participate in regional peace-making efforts. It will strengthen UN coordination and international cooperation in the maintenance of world peace and security as well as other major international issues. China will also unwaveringly work toward the establishment of a new international economic order that is just, reasonable and equal.[66]

Qian's words paint a China that seemed eager to work closer together with other powers in the pursuit of common international goods. Yet, the comment "establishment of a new international economic order" appears to imply some disenchantment with the status quo in the global economy. This might be due to the fact that at that point China was still subjected to the yearly American scrutiny of its most favored nation (MFN) status. Following Qian's proclamation, Jiang also began to incorporate the idea of responsibility into his speeches. At the 1993 Seattle Asia-Pacific Economic Cooperation conference, Jiang told his audience:

> But if the world continues to be chaotic, insecure, and plagued by economic troubles at the turn of the century, how are we going to account for this to the world's people? As we assumed leadership at a time of transition from the old to the new century, we were predestined to carry such a responsibility.[67]

It was likely that Qian and Jiang made these initial references to responsibility mainly out of an instrumental concern for China's external image. China had just broken out, or was on the verge of breaking out, of the post-Tiananmen isolation that had been foisted on it. Thus it was important that the country and its leaders be portrayed in a way that denoted a positive international orientation, one seemingly more aligned with global norms and more willing to make contributions. That both leaders chose to articulate the role of a responsible China in a foreign setting was indicative: it suggested that the target audience of this communication was external "others."

RGP Perceptions from Beijing and Washington

By the mid-1990s there was less Chinese reticence about categorizing the PRC as a great power even as Beijing continued to perpetuate a twin identity narrative of historical victim and underdeveloped country. Concerning the victim discourse, it was helped by the patriotic education program that had been steadily developing inside Chinese society since 1990. Emphasizing a version of the past that underscored China's "national humiliations," the program oversaw the production of textbooks and materials—for example, *Guochi Fen (The Indignation of National Humiliation)* (1990); *Guochi Shidian (Dictionary of National Humiliation)* (1992); and *Jianming Guochi Cidian (Simple Dictionary of National Humiliation)* (1993)—that highlighted the negative role perception of China as a victim of history. It also helped fuel a nationalistic domestic climate that inspired calls in 1995 to establish a "national humiliation day" as well as the publication of popular books such as Song Qiang's "China Can Say No" (1996).[68]

Yet, alongside the victim self-perception, Chinese confidence in assuming a big-power role was evidently growing. As noted in the introductory chapter, Chinese victim and great-power identities are not necessarily mutually exclusive; indeed, William Callahan has described this mixture of insecurity and self-confidence as "pessoptimism."[69] Thus, even as some intellectuals continued to promulgate the narrative of Chinese victimization, from around 1992 others were increasingly advocating that China should adopt a big-power mind-set. Many Chinese scholars held the view that while the US remained (and looked likely to continue as) the sole superpower, the PRC was nonetheless among the major powers of the world. This was encapsulated by the Chinese phrase *yichao duoqiang* (one superpower, many great powers).[70]

One prominent contributor to the great-power discourse in China at that time was Wang Yizhou, a scholar at the Institute of World Economics and Politics (IWEP) of the Chinese Academy of Social Sciences (CASS). Noting in 1994 that the nation had achieved annual economic growth rates of more than 10 percent for the three previous years, Wang wrote that the PRC's growing impact on the global balance of power was "indubitable." Wang's conclusion was that there had been increased "movement toward great-power affairs" (*daguohua*) in China's foreign policy.[71] Ye Zicheng, a scholar of international relations at Peking University, offered a more nuanced appraisal. In a detailed 1994 study of Chinese great-power identity, Ye called China "a great power that is not really a great power," an insight essentially predicated on Deng's earlier characterization of the country as both a major and minor power.[72] Nevertheless, Ye proceeded to identify what he defined as the core principles of Chinese "great-power consciousness" (*daguo yishi*). The first was a sense of "internal consciousness" that prioritized domestic development and needs. The second principle was to oppose great-power chauvinism and hegemony and superpower dominance. These were the "warped, perverted, and harmful" forms of great powerhood. The third principle was a "consciousness of peace," which Ye attributed to China's putative tradition of pacifism throughout its history. "On both paths before and after China becomes a 'global' great power," Ye further argued, "peace is necessary."[73]

In 1995 the IWEP produced what was the second major assessment (after Huang's 1992 study) of China's comprehensive national strength. Using an alternative methodology, the IWEP estimated that the PRC ranked tenth in the global CNP order. This placed China one place ahead of South Korea (eleventh) and suggested that the PRC was at best a second-tier power.[74] Nevertheless, in 1996 the idea of China as a great power received direct endorsement from the government. Chinese great-power identity, Jiang announced, would lead Beijing to embark on "great-power diplomacy" (*daguo waijiao*). This implied an emphasis on relations with other big powers, such as Russia, France, and the US, and it would be aimed at establishing "strategic partnerships" with these countries.[75] One example of such collaboration was the 1996 Sino-Russian "strategic cooperative partnership," which some Chinese analysts hailed as an "active model" of post–Cold War international relations.[76]

An important reason why Beijing was now more confident about articulating a big-power role related to its self-awareness that China was becoming a more significant actor in the global economy. Between 1978 and 1995 the PRC's total national output increased by around 400 percent, making it the fastest-growing economy in the world. Considering the size of China's economy on the basis of purchasing power parity (PPP), the World Bank estimated that China's 1994 gross domestic product (GDP) was already equivalent to the world's second-largest economy, behind only the US.[77] Economic factors aside, the increased centrality of UN institutions in world affairs in which Chinese involvement was crucial, China's relatively quick extrication from the post-Tiananmen isolation, and the continuing resilience of the Chinese political model were additional conditions prompting the development of the great-power self-categorization.

Important also to this identity formation was the role of the United States. In late 1992 Barber B. Conable Jr. and David Lampton, the chairman and president of the National Committee on US-China relations, respectively, argued that "China's strategic value is inaccurately perceived as having greatly diminished following the collapse of the Soviet Union," with the implication being that China remained an indispensable global power.[78] This perception was shared by the new Clinton administration. Assistant Secretary of State for East Asian and Pacific Affairs Winston Lord, for one, contended that China was "salient in new challenges that require global action."[79] Later, in 1994, the administration unexpectedly dropped its earlier policy of linking China's MFN status to the issue of human rights, which seemed to many to be a tacit admission of the PRC's rising economic clout. By the mid-1990s the US consensus was that China's strategic significance and power had been augmented overall since the end of the Cold War.[80]

Washington thus saw the PRC as a big power and, indeed, had communicated this role perception to Beijing. But its role prescription was more than that: it hoped that the PRC would assume the responsibilities that corresponded with its rising status. Clinton told Jiang in 1995:

> A stable, open and prosperous China—in other words, a strong China—is in our interest. We welcome China to the great power table. But great powers also have great responsibilities.[81]

The RGP rhetoric was repeated the following year by both Secretary of State Warren Christopher and Defense Secretary William Perry. In an important statement on US-China relations, Christopher stated that while the United States "strongly supports" China's emergence as a nation "that is taking its place as a world leader," the US would also try to "ensure" that China developed as "a strong and responsible member of the international community."[82] The defense secretary was more explicit still, directly exhorting China to behave as a "responsible world power." To Perry this meant that Beijing would be expected to eschew irresponsible behaviors, such as the exportation of nuclear technology, intimidation of Taiwan, and abuse of human rights.[83]

In many respects the American RGP call was a conditional affirmation of China's great-power identity: while the US considered China to be a great power, the latter had to behave "responsibly" for the US truly to recognize it as one. At the same time, it was also a reflection of the Clinton administration's policy of "constructive engagement" with China. Although the administration had initially appeared to be unsure of its China policy direction, it soon concluded that isolating or containing the PRC was not in the interest of the US. This view was further sharpened in 1995 with the publication of the US National Security Strategy, which argued that engagement would help coax Beijing to "define its interests in ways that would be compatible with the [US]."[84] In this respect the role prescription of a responsible great power was apposite. Joseph Nye, a former US assistant secretary of defense and principal author of the 1995 security strategy, thus publicly stated, "Nothing is more important than integrating the rising power of China as a responsible member of the international system."[85]

Interestingly, Chinese self-depiction as a responsible great power—not just a great power—was more evident during the mid-1990s, and it seems that Beijing was trying to align more closely with the American "role script" of China. In 1995, speaking at a luncheon hosted by American think tanks, President Jiang noted that China and the US are "two great countries," "major powers with global influence," and "permanent members of the UN security council." That was why, he added, both "share major responsibilities for world peace and development."[86] Jiang later made a similar RGP pitch at the 1996 Manila APEC conference, stating that both China and the US have "common responsibilities" as big powers.[87] Similarly, when Foreign Minister Qian visited Chicago in 1996, he insisted that China, as a member of the Permanent Five, "is fully aware of [its] responsibility for advancing world peace and stability and has always been working toward this end."[88]

It would be facile, nevertheless, to attribute Chinese RGP identification during this period solely to the influence of Washington. Certainly, Beijing wanted US validation (*rentong*) of its great-power identity, and in that sense would be more inclined to promote the narrative of China as a responsible great power. But, as a further reading of Qian's Chicago speech suggests, the Chinese foreign minister made the RGP references partly to refute the "China threat theory," an argument that was starting to gain currency in the US and elsewhere. Qian indicated that even though China had always worked toward fulfilling its great-power responsibilities as a member of the UN Security Council, there were still prejudiced "talks about the so-called China threat, a fallacy fabricated and disseminated with no regard to facts by some people around the world."[89]

At the same time, external role ideas do not automatically find their way into Chinese identity perspectives; how these ideas are interpreted and appraised by the Chinese is important. Indeed, evidence suggests that the American RGP exhortations were being viewed differently by some in China at that time.[90] For example, Song Yimin, a senior researcher at the China Institute of International Studies (CIIS) and a former Ministry of Foreign Affairs bureaucrat, suggested that such calls mainly reflected the limits of American power and influence and that Washington had "little choice" but to ask other leading states (such as China) to assume greater global responsibilities.[91] Yang Jiemian, a prominent scholar of US foreign policy, was similarly critical in his appraisal, writing in 1996 that such calls were nothing more than an attempt to use international rules to "constrain" (*yueshu*) China and to turn it into a responsible great power that was "only beneficial to the US."[92] Others critiqued the American RGP call by arguing that Chinese great-power responsibility should first be directed to the Asia-Pacific region. In this view the US-Japan security arrangement needed to be dismantled and replaced by a "just and rational" four-power order of China, US, Japan, and Russia; only then could the PRC assume the role of "core, balancer, and stabilizer" and partake in the big-power responsibilities of providing security for the region.[93]

Numerous scholarly contributions and ideas that arose between 1993 and 1996 might also have facilitated or supported the official RGP identity. Broadly grouped into two interrelated strands, the first connected with the theme of China's role in the world. One example was Ye Zicheng's 1994 study of Chinese great-power identity in the Peking University journal *Guoji Zhengzhi Yanjiu (International Politics Quarterly)*, in which he acknowledged the dialectical nature of this identity. Ye argued that, on the one hand, because China was a great power, it was necessarily different from other "normal" developing countries and should assume its "rightful, concomitant" responsibilities. On the other hand, because China was objectively still a developing nation, it should also recognize the limits of its influence and obligations.[94] Another scholar, Sheng Hong, advocated a change from a narrowly defined national "self" to a cosmopolitan Chinese identity based on the traditional concept of *tianxia* ("all under heaven"). He reminded his audience that, historically, China's development was underpinned by a "world" view rather than a "national" view.[95] This worldview, as epitomized by the concept of *tianxia*, meant that China was responsible not only to its people but also to the world, a moral imperative that would ultimately benefit China. Evoking a language reminiscent of early modern Chinese political discourse, Sheng wrote:

> Nationalism can save China but it cannot save the world. But if it cannot save the world, then it cannot ultimately save China because China has the largest share of the world's population.[96]

Ergo, "tianxia-ism," with its emphasis on a universal perspective, was preferable.

The second strand of thinking related to the subject of the PRC's strategic options vis-à-vis international society. Li Shenzhen, a former vice-president of CASS, believed that increasing Chinese integration in international society was inevitable. Thus, "if China would like to play a bigger role in the future . . . the only option is to learn and accept the established rules of the game."[97] Scholars such as Yan Xuetong and Wang Huning agreed but believed that a more active approach toward international society was needed. Yan, a leading exponent of realist IR thought in China, argued in 1995 that while participation in international society was essential, China should not "passively" (*xiaoji*) accept the extant Western-centric order. Rather, participation should be seen as a way for China to put forward its own "constructive ideas" to create an external environment conducive to its interests. Only then, Yan claimed, would China be able to "shoulder more of the responsibility of leading the world to a better future."[98] Wang, a well-known political scientist who was also an adviser to Jiang, advocated that China strengthen its "soft power" in international society, a factor that he saw as increasingly relevant to global political leadership.[99] Borrowing largely from Nye's original concept of soft power—the ability to influence other actors through attraction rather than coercion—Wang's discussion of soft power in 1993 marked the first time the idea entered into Chinese discourse. To the extent that responsibility in global affairs can be seen as a form of soft power, Wang's views promoted the idea of a more responsible China.[100]

Of course, actual Chinese behavior did not necessarily conform to the proclaimed RGP identity. For example, when the PRC unilaterally declared the South China Sea as part of its sovereign maritime area in 1992, it elicited consternation within the region and in Washington.[101] This was also the time when the idea that China's rise represented a threat began to foment.[102] China's perceived belligerence in the 1995–1996 Taiwan Straits crisis, its alleged sale of missile technology to Pakistan and chemical weapons to Iran, and its overall reluctance (as others saw it) to improve its human rights situation were damaging to its RGP rhetoric.[103] Not surprisingly, there was some skepticism in international society concerning the authenticity of the RGP self-image.

Yet, with regard to certain international norms, it is evident that Beijing was more willing to make efforts to conform.[104] As part of a policy trend that started in the 1980s, there was some expansion of Chinese involvement in UN peacekeeping. From 1992 to 1993 the PRC contributed a total of eight hundred military engineers and forty-nine observers to assist the United Nations Transitional Authority in Cambodia (UNTAC).[105] In 1993 and 1994 twenty Chinese military officers were sent to help UN forces monitor the cease-fire agreement in Mozambique (ONUMOZ). And, after 1993, China began sending personnel to the UN Mission in Liberia (UNOMIL).[106] Meanwhile, Chinese multilateral activities continued apace, especially at the regional level. By 1991 China was a member of APEC and in 1994 it took part in the inaugural ASEAN Regional Forum (ARF) meeting. In 1996 it joined the "Track-II" Council for Security Cooperation in the Asia-Pacific (CSCAP), and further consolidated its relations with the ASEAN (Association of Southeast Asian Nations), becoming a full dialogue partner.[107] Of particular significance that year was the formation of the Shanghai Five, a China-led security initiative that included Kazakhstan, Kyrgyzstan, Russia, and Tajikistan. Thus the PRC became not only a participant in multilateral organizations, it was also in some sense a regime entrepreneur. The Shanghai Five reflected China's "new security concept," which emphasized mutual "win-win" security instead of a Cold War–esque, zero-sum idea of security.[108]

Arguably, during this period the one area in which China made the most progress vis-à-vis its stated RGP identity was arms control/nonproliferation. In 1992 it agreed to observe the Missile Technology Control Regime (MTCR) and formally joined the Nuclear Non-Proliferation Treaty (NPT). When the NPT was up for review in 1995, China committed its support for an indefinite extension.[109] On that occasion Qian took the opportunity to declare that "China has never shied away from its due obligations for nuclear disarmament."[110] Earlier, at the UN Conference on Disarmament and Security Issues in the Asia-Pacific Region, Qian also stated that the largest nuclear powers should "bear special responsibilities" and "corresponding obligations in disarmament."[111] It would seem that China was keen to use its greater involvement in the arms control/nonproliferation regime to promote an RGP self-image. In 1996 China signed the Comprehensive Test Ban Treaty (CTBT), reportedly against the wishes of some within the military who had wanted additional testing. According to Bates Gill and Evan Medeiros, Beijing acceded to that treaty in large part due to concerns over its responsible great-power "stature."[112]

Conclusion

This chapter has examined the trajectory of China's RGP identity from 1978 to 1996, arguing that the incipient phase of this identity could be traced to the period between the early and mid-1990s. During this period Chinese leaders began to publicly identify China as a responsible great power and sought to draw linkages between China's responsibility and its great-power role. Rhetorically, this squared with American exhortations for China to play a bigger role in the international system and assume greater responsibilities, although some in China viewed such calls with skepticism. Chinese discussions on the related themes of the PRC's role and strategic course vis-à-vis the international society were also conducive to the official RGP narrative.

The broad thrusts of why the PRC began to pursue the identity of a responsible power relate predominantly to functionality (as in, it was a useful identity for achieving certain purposes) and social enhancement (as in, it promised social rewards). In the 1980s the idea of China as a responsible great power was a vague concept at best. Chinese perspectives on responsibility had mainly come in a non-great-power context, and when the explicit characterization of a responsible nation was first evoked, it related specifically to the issue of China's arms sales. Furthermore, during this period Beijing had a more circumscribed sense of its big-power identity, preferring instead to stress its underdeveloped status. However, in the aftermath of the Tiananmen violence, Beijing was deemed a pariah by several Western countries, a status that Chinese leaders clearly resented. This, together with the ending of the Cold War and its attendant repercussions, was clearly a time of major threat to China's great-power identity. Against this backdrop, involvement in the UN proceedings and diplomacy vis-à-vis the 1990 Gulf War was an opportunity for China to repair its damaged reputation and lessen its social isolation, and it used the occasion to strategically portray itself as being a responsible member of international society. This later culminated in official proclamations of China as a responsible great power in 1992–1993. The fact that these proclamations were first used in front of foreign audiences suggests that they had been made with a view to improving China's external image.

From 1993 to 1996 there were again incentives for China to continue and promote an official RGP identity. Strategically, as Qian's 1996 Chicago speech indicates, it was a useful conceptual tool for refuting the "China threat theory" that had been gaining currency. It was in the interests of Beijing to be characterized as a benign power that was receptive to the established "rules of the game" and lessen the prospect that others would consider it as a threat to be opposed, a scenario that would have been problematic for China's goals of economic development. Indeed, the notion that an RGP identity could and should benefit China's interests had been evident in the writings of scholars who had (directly or indirectly) discussed the subject. Although there were those who felt that this identity might constrain China's rise, certainly some advocates saw it as a useful identity that embodied a viable strategic path for navigating international politics.

Socially, the identity category of a responsible great power was helpful for furthering China's membership in international society. But, more than that, it was helpful to gaining potentially greater American recognition of Chinese big-power identity, which had become more pronounced by the mid-1990s. As mentioned earlier, Washington's RGP exhortations represented a conditional affirmation of China's great-power identity—that China had to behave "responsibly" for the US to accept it as one. This might have encouraged Chinese political elites to define China's global role in terms of big-power responsibility, at least at the official rhetorical level.

In sum, while there were some indications that Beijing was aware of its international responsibilities in the 1980s, the period in the early to mid-1990s basically marked the time when the initial contours of China's RGP identity started to form. From 1997 onward, the body of this proclaimed identity became more distinct, as Chinese RGP narratives expanded in quantity and range. The next chapter will explore that critical post-1997 phase.

Notes

1. Rosemary Foot notes that Nixon's statement had "caused enormous excitement among the Beijing leadership." See Rosemary Foot, *The Practice of Power: US Relations with China since 1949* (Oxford,UK: Oxford University Press, 1995), 105.
2. Deng Xiaoping, "Shixing Kaifang Zhengce, Xuexi Shijie Xianjin Kexue Jishu" (Adopt open policy and learn from the world's advanced science and technology), in *Deng Xiaoping Wenxuan Dierjuan (Selected Works of Deng Xiaoping),* vol. 2 (Beijing: Renmin Chubanshe, 1993), 132–33. See also Deng Xiaoping, "Liyong Waiguo Zhili He Kuoda Duiwai Kaifang" (Use foreign intellectual resources and open wider to the outside world), in *Deng Xiaoping Wenxuan Disanjuan (Selected Works of Deng Xiaoping)*, vol. 3 (Beijing: Renmin Chubanshe, 1993), 32.
3. As Suisheng Zhao observes, "Many Chinese intellectuals could not help asking why China was still so backward after thirty years of socialist revolution." See Suisheng

Zhao, "Chinese Intellectuals' Quest for National Greatness and Nationalistic Writing in the 1990s," *China Quarterly* 152 (1997): 726.

4. Ibid., 727–30. See also Merle Goldman, Perry Link, and Su Wei, "China's Intellectuals in the Deng Era: Loss of Identity with the State," in *China's Quest for National Identity,* ed. Lowell Dittmer and Samuel S. Kim (Ithaca, NY: Cornell University Press, 1993), 143–46.
5. See, for example, Deng Xiaoping, "Weihu Shijie Heping, Gaohao Guonei Jianshe" (Safeguard world peace, ensure domestic development), in *Deng Xiaoping Wenxuan Disanjuan (Selected Works of Deng Xiaoping),* vol. 3 (Beijing: Renmin Chubanshe, 1993), 56–57.
6. Peter Van Ness argues that "China had in fact turned its back on the Third World." See Peter Van Ness, "China as a Third World State: Foreign Policy and Official National Identity," in *China's Quest for National Identity*, ed. Lowell Dittmer and Samuel S. Kim (Ithaca, NY: Cornell University Press, 1993), 206.
7. Samuel S. Kim, "International Organizations in Chinese Foreign Policy," *Annals of the American Academy of Political and Social Science* 519 (1992): 152.
8. Foot, *Practice of Power*, 241; Samuel S. Kim, "China as a Regional Power," *Current History* 91, no. 566 (1992): 251.
9. Harry Harding, *A Fragile Relationship: The United States and China since 1972* (Washington, DC: Brookings Institution, 1992), 119.
10. Jonathan D. Pollack, "China and the Global Strategic Balance," in *China's Foreign Relations in the 1980s*, ed. Harry Harding (New Haven, CT: Yale University Press, 1984), 162.
11. Ibid.
12. Robert Ross, "China Learns to Compromise: Change in US-China Relations, 1982–1984," *China Quarterly* 128 (1991): 742–73.
13. Zi Zhongyun, "The Impact and Clash of Ideologies: Sino-US Relations from a Historical Perspective," *Journal of Contemporary China* 6, no. 16 (1997): 548.
14. Pollack, "China and the Global Strategic Balance," 71–72.
15. Foot, *Practice of Power*, 234.
16. Vladimir Petrov, "China Goes It Alone," *Asian Survey* 23, no. 5 (1983): 580–97.
17. Petrov describes the Chinese assertion of strategic independence as "audacity." See ibid., 589.
18. Jonathan D. Spence, *The Search for Modern China* (New York: W. W. Norton, 1999), 675.
19. Huan Xiang, cited in Michael Pillsbury, *China Debates the Future Security Environment* (Washington, DC: National Defense University Press, 2000), 11.
20. For Huan Xiang and Yang Dezhi's remarks, see Weixing Wu, "China's Security Agenda after the Cold War," *Pacific Review* 8, no. 1 (1995): 131.
21. Chen Feng, "Luelun Guoji Yicun" (A brief discussion of international mutual dependence), *Shijie Jingji Yu Zhengzhi (World Economics and Politics)* 2 (1987): 37.
22. Deng Xiaoping, "Heping He Fazhan Shi Dangdai Shijie De Liangda Wenti" (Peace and development are the two main issues in the world today), in *Deng Xiaoping*

Wenxuan Disanjuan (Selected Works of Deng Xiaoping), vol. 3 (Beijing: Renmin Chubanshe, 1993), 105.

23. Xu Shengxi, "Deng Xiaoping Guanyu Zengqiang Woguo Guoji Diwei De Sixiang" (Regarding Deng Xiaoping's thought on strengthening the nation's international position), *Guoji Zhengzhi Yanjiu (International Politics Quarterly)* 3 (1995): 76.
24. Wang Zhongshen, "Lun Deng Xiaoping De Zhongguo Xingxiang Guan" (Discussing Deng Xiaoping's view on China's image), *Fujian Lutan (Fujian Forum)* 6 (1994): 3.
25. Zhao Ziyang, "The Objectives of China's Foreign Policy: For Lasting Peace, Increased Friendly Cooperation and Co-Prosperity," *International Affairs* 61, no. 4 (1985): 578.
26. Sun Yi, "Deng Xiaoping Huijian Carlucci" (Deng Xiaoping meets Carlucci), *Renmin Ribao (People's Daily)*, September 8, 1988.
27. To a lesser extent Washington was also concerned about Chinese arm sales to Saudi Arabia, which Beijing did not deny. See Eden Y. Woon, "Chinese Arms Sales and US-China Military Relations," *Asian Survey* 29, no. 6 (1989): 611–14.
28. "Waijiao Bu Fayanren Qiangdiao: Zhongguo Chukou Junpin Yanshou Sanyuanze" (Ministry of foreign affairs spokesman stresses: China adheres to the three principles of arm sales), *Renmin Ribao (People's Daily)*, September 9, 1988.
29. There are, of course, competing interpretations of what constitutes responsible behavior in international society.
30. Samuel S. Kim, "China's International Organizational Behaviour," in *Chinese Foreign Policy: Theory and Practice*, ed. Thomas W. Robinson and David Shambaugh (Oxford, UK: Oxford University Press, 1994), 406–7.
31. Samuel S. Kim, "Thinking Globally in Post-Mao China," *Journal of Peace Research* 27, no. 2 (1990): 193.
32. Ibid.
33. See Yongjin Zhang, "China and UN Peacekeeping: From Condemnation to Participation," *International Peacekeeping* 3, no. 3 (1996): 1–3; Yitzhak Shichor, "China and the Role of the United Nations in the Middle East," *Asian Survey* 31, no. 3 (1991): 261.
34. Shichor, "China and the Role of the United Nations," 261–66.
35. Zhang, "China and UN Peacekeeping," 9.
36. Woon, "Chinese Arms Sales," 603.
37. See Alastair Iain Johnston and Paul Evans, "China's Engagement with Multilateral Security Institutions," in *Engaging China: The Management of an Emerging Power*, ed. Alastair Iain Johnston and Robert Ross (Abingdon, UK: Routledge, 1999), 235–72; Ann Kent, *Beyond Compliance: China, International Organizations, and Global Security* (Stanford, CA: Stanford University Press, 2007), 65–77; Zhou Baogen, "Zhongguo Yu Guoji He Bu Kuosan Jizhi De Yizhong Jiangou Zhuyi Fenxi" (A constructivist analysis of China and the international nuclear nonproliferation regime), *Shijie Jingji Yu Zhengzhi (World Economics and Politics)* 2 (2003): 23–27.

38. Kent, *Beyond Compliance*, 75; See also Evan S. Medeiros, *Reluctant Restraint: The Evolution of China's Nonproliferation Policies and Practices, 1980–2004* (Stanford, CA: Stanford University Press, 2007), 30–96.
39. Xie Yixian, *Zhongguo Dangdai Waijiao Shi, 1949–2001 (Contemporary Chinese Diplomatic History, 1949–2001)* (Beijing: Zhongguo Qingnian Chuban She, 2002), 388.
40. Hongying Wang, "Linking Up with the International Track: What's in a Slogan?," *China Quarterly* 189 (2007): 1–23.
41. This is not to say that the US and international society did not try to promote China's integration into the existing global order. See Foot, *Practice of Power*, 223.
42. Rana Mitter, "An Uneasy Engagement: Chinese Ideas of Global Order and Justice in Historical Perspective," in *Order and Justice in International Relations*, ed. Rosemary Foot, John Lewis Gaddis, and Andrew Hurrell (Oxford, UK: Oxford University Press, 2004), 223.
43. Joseph Fewsmith, *China since Tiananmen* (Cambridge, UK: Cambridge University Press, 2008), 21–47.
44. Yongjin Zhang, *China in International Society since 1949: Alienation and Beyond* (Basingstoke, UK: Macmillan, 1998), 248.
45. Deng Xiaoping, "Zhenxing Zhonghua Mingzhu" (Rejuvenate the Chinese nation), in *Deng Xiaoping Wenxuan Disanjuan (Selected Works of Deng Xiaoping)*, vol. 3 (Beijing: Renmin Chubanshe, 1993), 357.
46. William A. Callahan, *China: The Pessoptimist Nation* (Oxford, UK: Oxford University Press, 2010), 31–59.
47. Xiaoxiong Yi, "China's US Policy Conundrum in the 1990s: Balancing Autonomy and Interdependence," *Asian Survey* 34, no. 8 (1994): 679.
48. Rosemary Foot, *Rights beyond Borders: The Global Community and the Struggle Over Human Rights in China* (Oxford, UK: Oxford University Press, 2000), 138–39.
49. Bonnie S. Glaser, "China's Security Perceptions: Interests and Ambitions," *Asian Survey* 33, no. 3 (1993): 253.
50. "Lengjing Guancha, Chenzhuo Yingfu, Taoguang Yanghui, Juebu Dangtou, Yousuo Zuowei" (Calmly observe, handle the situation soberly, hide our capacities and bide our time, avoid being a leader, get some things done), Zhongguo Gongchan Dang Xinwen Wang (Chinese Communist Party News Network), http://theory.people.com.cn/n/2012/1028/c350803-19412863.html.
51. Deng Xiaoping, "Shanyu Liyong Shiji Jiejue Fazhan Wenti" (Be adept at using opportunities to solve our development question), in *Deng Xiaoping Wenxuan Disanjuan (Selected Works of Deng Xiaoping)*, vol. 3 (Beijing: Renmin Chubanshe, 1993), 363.
52. Jianhai Bi, "The Role of the Military in the PRC Taiwan Policymaking: A Case Study of the Taiwan Strait Crisis of 1995–1996," *Journal of Contemporary China* 11, no. 32 (2002): 551.
53. Harding, *Fragile Relationship*, 296.

54. Foot, *Practice of Power*, 248.
55. Deng was apparently pleased about this "reminder," as he reportedly said when he saw Qian Qichen's vote of abstention on UN resolution 678 on television: "By holding up his hand, he again showed the world that China has a decisive say in solving major disputes in the world." Incidentally, in 1990 Deng also declared China a "political big power." See Michael Yahuda, "Deng Xiaoping: The Statesman," *China Quarterly* 135 (1993): 565–66; Deng, "Zhenxing Zhonghua Mingzhu," 357.
56. Qian Qichen, *Waijiao Shiji (Ten Episodes in China's Diplomacy)* (Beijing: Shijie Zhishi Chubanshe, 2003), 96.
57. "Waijiao Fayanren Shuo: Zhongguo Zhixing Anlihui 661 Hao Jueyi Shi Renzhen De" (Foreign affairs spokesman: China's implementation of resolution 661 is serious), *Renmin Ribao (People's Daily)*, October 1, 1990.
58. Lena H. Sun, "China to Halt Arms Sales to Iraqis," *Washington Post*, August 6, 1990.
59. Qimao Chen, "New Approaches in China's Foreign Policy: The Post–Cold War Era," *Asian Survey* 33, no. 3 (1993): 238.
60. Rosemary Foot, "Chinese Strategies in a US-Hegemonic Global Order: Accommodating and Hedging," *International Affairs* 82, no. 1 (2006): 81.
61. Yong Deng, "Hegemon on the Offensive: Chinese Perspectives on US Global Strategy," *Political Science Quarterly* 116, no. 3 (2001): 345–46.
62. Zheng Yongnian, *Discovering Chinese Nationalism in China: Modernization, Identity, and International Relations* (Cambridge, UK: Cambridge University Press, 1999), 115.
63. Huang Shuofeng, *Zonghe Guoli Lun (Discussing Comprehensive National Power)* (Beijing: Zhongguo Shehui Kexue Chubanshe, 1992), 159.
64. Ibid., 162. In Huang's words, these indexes are *wuzhili* (material power), *jingshenli* (spirit power), *xietongli* (coordination power), and *huanjing* (environment). See 163–66 for a breakdown of the components in the indexes. For Huang's estimate of China's CNP in 1989, see table 3.3, 220–21.
65. Zheng, *Discovering Chinese Nationalism in China*, 119.
66. He Hongze, "Zai Meiguo Waijiao Zhengce Xiehui Shang Qian Qichen Waizhang Tan Zhongmei Guanxi Zhichu: Shuangfang Yingben Zhe Huxiang Zunzhong, Pingdeng Xiangdai, Xinshou Nuoyan, Zunshou Xieyi De Jingshen Chuli Liangguo Guanxi" (Foreign minister Qian Qichen discusses Sino-American relations at the US foreign policy association meeting: Both sides should adopt the spirit of mutual respect, mutual equality, keeping promises, and respecting agreements to handle bilateral relations), *Renmin Ribao (People's Daily)*, September 24, 1992.
67. Speech by President Jiang Zemin at the Informal APEC Leadership Conference, November 20, 1993, available at http://www.fmprc.gov.cn/mfa_eng/wjdt_665385/zyjh_665391/t24903.shtml.
68. Callahan, *China*, 31–59; Song Qiang, Zhang Zangzang, Qiao Bian, and Gu Qingsheng, et al., *Zhongguo Keyi Shuobu (China Can Say No)* (Beijing: Zhonghua Gongshang Lianhe Chubanshe, 1996).
69. Callahan, *China*.

70. Some scholars, like Wang Jisi, then-director of the Institute of American Studies at CASS, believed that "the superpower (US) is more super, and the many great powers are less great." See Wang Jisi, "Building a Constructive Relationship," in *China-Japan-US: Managing the Trilateral Relationship*, ed. Morton Abramowitz, Funabashi Yochi, and Wang Jisi (Tokyo: Japan Center for International Exchange, 1998), 22.
71. Wang Yizhou, "Gengjia 'Daguohua' De Yinian" (Another year of increasing "movement toward great power affairs"), *Shijie Zhishi (World Affairs)* 24 (1994): 2–3.
72. Ye Zicheng, "'Daguo Fei Daguo' Yu Zhongguo De Guoji Diwei" ("A great power that is not really a great power" and China's international position), *Guoji Zhengzhi Yanjiu (International Politics Quarterly)* 4 (1994): 1–2.
73. Ibid., 4–5.
74. The Committee for Research on Comprehensive National Power Comparison, Institute of World Economics and Politics, "Zhongguo Guoji Diwei De Bianhua Fenxi" (An analysis of changes in China's international position), *Taiping Yang Xuebao (Pacific Journal)* 1 (1995): 135–44.
75. H. Lyman Miller and Liu Xiaohong, "The Foreign Policy Outlook of China's 'Third Generation' Elite," in *The Making of Chinese Foreign and Security Policy in the Era of Reform, 1978–2000*, ed. David M. Lampton (Stanford, CA: Stanford University Press, 2001), 144.
76. Zhao Junjie, Wang Pingzhen, and Huo Yanping, "Jiang Zemin Yu Zhongguo Waijiao Xingeju" (Jiang Zemin and China's new diplomatic situation), Zhonghua Renmin Gongheguo Lishi Wang (The History of the People's Republic of China Network), http://www.hprc.org.cn/gsyj/wjs/gjzz/200909/t20090914_31183.html.
77. Samuel S. Kim, "China as a Great Power," in *The China Reader*, ed. Orville Schell and David Shambaugh (New York: Vintage, 1999), 450–51.
78. Barber B. Conable Jr. and David M. Lampton, "China: The Coming Power," *Foreign Affairs* 71, no. 5 (Winter 1992–93): 134.
79. Foot, *Practice of Power*, 255.
80. David M. Lampton, "China and Clinton's America: Have They Learned Anything?," *Asian Survey* 37, no. 12 (1997): 1099–1118.
81. Joseph S. Nye, "The 'Nye Report': Six Years Later," *International Relations of the Asia-Pacific* 1, no. 1 (2001): 98.
82. Warren Christopher, "American Interests and the US-China Relationship," Address to the Asia Society, the Council on Foreign Relations, and the National Committee on US-China Relations, May 17, 1996, available at http://dosfan.lib.uic.edu/ERC/briefing/dossec/1996/9605/960517dossec1.html.
83. Bill Gertz, "Perry Calls on China to Earn US Trust: Airs Complaints on Rights, Nukes," *Washington Times*, February 14, 1996. Another senior US official who had communicated a similar message was National Security Adviser Anthony Lake. Although Lake did not evoke the specific language of responsibility, he apparently told Chinese leaders (during his 1996 visit to China) that Washington wanted Beijing to be a co-manager of the twenty-first-century international order. See

Deborah Welch Larson and Alexei Shevchenko, "Status Seekers: Chinese and Russian Responses to US Primacy," *International Security* 34, no. 4 (Spring 2010): 84.

84. Nye, "Nye Report," 95–103.
85. Joseph S. Nye, "We Can't Afford to Lose China Again," *Los Angeles Times*, December 29, 1996.
86. Chinese President Jiang Zemin's Speech at a Luncheon Hosted in His Honor by Several US Organizations in New York, including the America-China Society, the National Committee on US-China Relations, the US-China Business Council, the Foreign Policy Association, the Council on Foreign Relations, and the Asia Society, October 23, 1995.
87. "Jiang Zemin Siwu Kelindun" (Jiang Zemin meets Clinton the fourth time), Zhongguo Wang (China Network), March 1, 2002. The Zhongguo Wang portal is under the auspices of the State Council Information Office. See http://www.china.com.cn/zhuanti2005/txt/2002-03/01/content_5112989.htm.
88. Speech by Vice-Premier and Foreign Minister Qian Qichen at Luncheon Hosted by Chicago Council on Foreign Relations, September 20, 1996.
89. Ibid.
90. The focus here is on those appraisals in the mid-1990s, in response to the initial RGP calls.
91. Song Yimin, "Meiguo Waijiao Zhengce De Xin Tiaozheng" (New readjustments in US foreign policy), *Guoji Wenti Yanjiu (International Studies)* 3 (1995): 33–36.
92. Yang Jiemian, "Meiguo Daxuan He Kelindun Zhengfu Tiaozheng Duihua Zhengce" (The American election and the shift in the Clinton administration's China policy), *Meiguo Yanjiu (American Studies)* 4 (1996): 132. For a similar view, see Jin Xiaochuan, "Lun Xinjiu Guoji Zhixu Zhuanhuan Zhong De Zhongguo Guoji Jiaose" (Discussing China's international role in the change from the old to new international order), *Xueshu Luntan (Academic Forum)* 6 (1996): 76.
93. Fei-Ling Wang, "Preservation, Prosperity and Power: What Motivates China's Foreign Policy?," *Journal of Contemporary China* 14, no. 45 (2005): 690.
94. Ye, "'Daguo Fei Daguo' Yu Zhongguo De Guoji Diwei," 2.
95. Sheng Hong, "Cong Minzhu Zhuyi Dao Tianxia Zhuyi" (From nationalism to Tianxia-ism), *Zhanlue Yu Guanli (Strategy and Management)* 1 (1996): 16.
96. Ibid., 18.
97. Zhao, "Chinese Intellectuals' Quest," 744.
98. Yan Xuetong, "Zhongguo Jueqi De Keneng Xuanze" (Possible options for China's rise), *Zhanlue Yu Guanli (Strategy and Management)* 6 (1995): 14. For a similar perspective, see Jin, "Lun Xinjiu Guoji Zhixu Zhuanhuan Zhong De Zhongguo Guoji Jiaose," 78.
99. Wang Huning, "Zuowei Guojia Shili De Wenhua: Ruan Quanli" (Culture as national strength: Soft power), *Fudan Xuebao: Shehui Kexue Ban (Fudan Journal: Social Sciences)* 3 (1993): 91–96.
100. Interview with Chinese scholar, Beijing, May 2011.

101. Allen Carlson, *Unifying China, Integrating with the World: Securing Chinese Sovereignty in the Reform Era* (Stanford, CA: Stanford University Press, 2005), 83.
102. Yong Deng, *China's Struggle for Status: The Realignment of International Relations* (Cambridge, UK: Cambridge University Press, 2008), 104–7.
103. Gertz, "Perry Calls on China."
104. Alastair Iain Johnston, "Is China a Status Quo Power?," *International Security* 27, no. 4 (2003): 5–56.
105. Bates Gill and Chin-Hao Huang, "China's Expanding Peacekeeping Role: Its Significance and the Policy Implications," *SIPRI Policy Brief* (February 2009): 2; Bonny Ling, "China's Peacekeeping Diplomacy," *China Rights Forum* 1 (2007): 47.
106. Allen Carlson, "Helping to Keep the Peace (Albeit Reluctantly): China's Recent Stance on Sovereignty and Multilateral Intervention," *Pacific Affairs* 77, no. 1 (2004): 17.
107. Jianwei Wang, "China's Multilateral Diplomacy in the New Millennium," in *China Rising: Power and Motivation in Chinese Foreign Policy*, ed. Yong Deng and Fei-Ling Wang (Lanham, MD: Rowman & Littlefield, 2005), 166–77.
108. Larson and Shevchenko, "Status Seekers," 82; Susan Shirk, *China: Fragile Superpower* (Oxford, UK: Oxford University Press, 2008), 128–29.
109. Foot, *The Practice of Power*, 253.
110. Statement by HE Mr. Qian Qichen, Vice Premier and Foreign Minister and Head of Delegation of the People's Republic of China, at the 1995 Review and Extension Conference of the Parties to the Treaty on the Non-Proliferation of Nuclear Weapons, April 18, 1995.
111. Speech by Mr. Qian Qichen, State Councillor and Foreign Minister, at the United Nations Conference on Disarmament and Security Issues in the Asia-Pacific Region, August 17, 1992.
112. Larson and Shevchenko, "Status Seekers," 83; Bates Gill and Evan S. Medeiros, "Foreign and Domestic Influences on China's Arms Control and Nonproliferation Policies," *China Quarterly* 161 (2000): 90.

3

EXPANSION OF THE RGP NARRATIVE AND US INFLUENCE, 1997 TO 2004

In chapter 2 I showed that, contrary to most perceptions, an embryonic Chinese RGP identity was already discernible in the early to mid-1990s. I now continue to investigate the development path of the RGP identity, focusing on the period from 1997 to 2004. It is argued that this period represents the second substantive phase of China's self-identification as a responsible great power, during which RGP identity narratives expanded considerably. The chapter begins by highlighting the major events connected to the development of the RGP discourse. It then explores ideas of international responsibility that had emerged in China and is followed by a discussion of related strategic concepts. China's general conduct during this period is briefly examined before the chapter concludes.

The Jiang-Clinton Summits

As previously noted, a more pronounced effort by Beijing to expand its ties with other major powers emerged around 1996. After the upgrade of Sino-Russian ties to a "strategic cooperative partnership" in 1996, China declared in 1997 that it would build a "long-term, comprehensive partnership" with France.[1] The following year China announced the start of "comprehensive partnerships" with the United Kingdom and the European Union.[2]

The top priority for China's big-power diplomacy, nevertheless, remained its relations with the US, and in this area there was discernible progress. At the invitation of President Clinton, in October 1997 Jiang Zemin became the first Chinese president to visit the United States in twelve years. Jiang's visit led to agreements between the two nations to increase cooperation in the fields of bilateral dialogue, nuclear energy, environmental protection, nuclear nonproliferation, trade, and law. More significantly, it culminated in the landmark joint statement that China and the US would work "toward a constructive strategic partnership"—the first time that the term "partnership" had been used formally to describe relations between the countries. Clinton elaborated on American expectations of this partnership at the joint press conference with Jiang: China ought to "join its strength and influence" with the US to "advance peace and prosperity, freedom and security."[3] For its part, rhetorically at least, the Chinese government appeared to share a parallel outlook, as Jiang acknowledged that China and the US, as nations of significant global influence, shouldered "common responsibilities" for the questions of human survival and development.[4] A similar point was also reiterated by Jiang during his speech at Harvard University, where he noted that both countries shared "common interests and responsibilities." According to Jiang, these encompassed areas such as international security, nonproliferation, environmental protection, and transnational crime.[5]

The call for China to work alongside the US in some form of a great-power concert was again made during Clinton's 1998 visit to China. In Beijing, Clinton stressed that it was in America's interest to see a "prosperous" China that assumed its global responsibilities. And, as if to draw attention to the kind of responsible actions that China should be doing more of, Clinton welcomed Chinese decisions or commitments on, inter alia, the International Covenant on Civil and Political Rights (ICCPR), the release of a number of high-profile political detainees, a restart to bilateral dialogue on human rights, a consideration of participation in the missile technology control regime, helping reinforce the Biological Weapons Convention, refraining from assisting missile programs in Iran and some South Asian countries, and further tightening its controls on nuclear exports.[6] The joint denunciation of India's 1998 nuclear tests was particularly appreciated by the Clinton administration and portrayed China as a co-guardian of the international nuclear order.[7] Later, in a speech at Peking University, Clinton commended the Chinese government for not devaluing the renminbi during the Asian financial crisis (AFC), saying that China had "steadfastly shouldered its responsibilities to the region and the world."[8] This marked the first time that an American president openly credited China for acting "responsibly."

The Jiang-Clinton visits presented further opportunities for the US to influence China vis-à-vis the RGP role. As noted earlier, from around 1995 there had been attempts by Washington to prod Beijing in a direction that corresponded to the American understanding of great-power responsibility. American rhetoric about China's expected role and conduct during the 1997–1998 summits reflected a continuation of that policy. For China, its leaders had begun to portray their nation as a responsible global power beginning in 1992, so it was no surprise to find continued Chinese positioning in this role. The Chinese certainly wanted American acceptance as a great power and were aware of the linkage of the responsibility issue to this goal.[9] Moreover, the RGP role had important strategic value and could help moderate concerns about China's growing power. Nevertheless, it would be difficult to link this more cooperative stance toward the US as solely a matter of RGP posturing. Aside from issue-specific considerations, pressure had been mounting on Beijing to take steps to improve Sino-American relations, which had been strained by events such as Lee Teng Hui's US visit in 1995 and the 1995–1996 Chinese missile tests in the Taiwan Strait.[10]

The Asian Financial Crisis

The 1997–1998 Asian financial crisis marked a turning point in the evolution of China's self-identification as a responsible power. During the crisis Beijing contributed a total of around US$4 billion to the IMF rescue fund, including aid packages of US$1 billion each to Thailand and Indonesia. Additionally, though it could have done so, Beijing did not opt for competitive devaluation of its currency, which surprised many observers. Economically this benefited those regional economies whose currencies had depreciated by 30 to 75 percent, enhancing their export competitiveness as well as attractiveness as foreign investment destinations relative to China. It also reduced pressure on those economies to further devalue their already weakened currencies.[11]

China's response to the AFC was widely welcomed in international society. Other than praise from Clinton, British prime minister Tony Blair and French president Jacques Chirac also applauded Beijing's actions, with the latter claiming that China had "shown the example of a great power that shouldered its responsibilities."[12] Regionally, China's AFC decisions were well received in ASEAN capitals, especially in contrast to what was perceived as harsh and conditional crisis prescriptions imposed by the IMF. It was thought that China's currency policy had been instrumental in stabilizing the crisis in Southeast Asia, leading one Thai leader to opine that "only China" had really assisted Thailand, and ASEAN secretary-general Rodolfo Severino to say that Beijing had emerged from the crisis with huge credibility.[13]

The positive reaction from the international community substantiated Beijing's sense of itself as a responsible big power and spoke to the impact of other external actors, besides the US, to lubricate the RGP conversation in China. Chinese analysts were quick to suggest that China's international "position" had risen.[14] They pointed to the fact that many countries had recognized China's "inescapable influence" in Asia's economic affairs, that China had maintained an impressive growth rate of above 8 percent in spite of the crisis, and that the relative decline of neighboring economies had accentuated the ascendancy of China's regional economic status.[15] Further, Chinese analysts (writing in various publication media, including Chinese textbooks) cited China's actions during the AFC as further evidence of an emerging identity as a responsible power. In this view China had demonstrated the "self-sacrificial" character of a responsible power when it chose to maintain the renminbi's value at the expense of its export competitiveness and investment inflow and had directly contributed to the stability of the international economic order.[16] It was also a matter of "trust and promise to the region and the world," according to Wang Yizhou. By keeping to its pledge of not devaluing the renminbi, Wang added, the Chinese government had laid down an important "marker" of an "open and responsible" attitude.[17]

Discussion of China's responsibility vis-à-vis the AFC led some scholars to ask questions about the corresponding roles of Japan and the United States. Japan, for example, was regarded as failing to do its part as Asia's strongest economy when it took the easy way out of joining the regional trend of currency devaluation.[18] In the case of the United States, some Chinese analysts argued that it should bear responsibility for the crisis's extension. It was suggested that, unlike its decisive response in the 1994 Mexican peso crisis, Washington's initial attitude of "watching from the sidelines" of the AFC led to the escalation of the contagion. Washington was also alleged to have compounded the problems of affected ASEAN economies—"adding frost to the snow" (*xueshang jialin*)—when it imposed conditions for aid.[19] In appraising the actions of Japan and the US during the crisis, these critiques essentially served to underline how, compared to China, the two other major Asia-Pacific powers had been less responsible and more concerned about their own narrow interests.

Yet, to say that Beijing had not considered its own interests during the AFC would be inaccurate. While China's decision to reject currency devaluation was made in part out of a concern for its declared RGP identity, there were also other important considerations at work. First and foremost, China could have become embroiled in the AFC had it not taken concrete measures to help limit the spread of the contagion.[20] Second, devaluation would have made imports more expensive and raised the price of many Chinese exports that depended on the processing of imported materials; this might ironically have resulted in reduced export competitiveness. It could also have potentially led to lose-lose cycles of competitive currency depreciations across the region. Third, devaluation could have further destabilized the Hong Kong dollar and put additional strain on the Hong Kong economy. At a time when the PRC had just regained sovereignty over Hong Kong, this would have been particularly damaging to Beijing's political credibility in the territory. Fourth, it would not have benefited China's bid to join the World Trade Organization (WTO) if it had been seen to be adopting policies (e.g., devaluation) that were counterproductive to the stabilization of the crisis.[21] Finally, China had been in a relatively comfortable monetary and fiscal position to uphold the renminbi's value, given its not-fully-convertible currency, currency restrictions, and sizable buffer of foreign exchange reserves.[22]

It should be pointed out that the RGP identity was not the only role narrative evoked during the financial conflagration. Two other identities—China as the developing nation and China as the victim—were also discernible in Chinese discourse during the crisis. On the former, some Chinese scholars noted that China had identified with developing nations on a number of occasions (e.g., the 1998 APEC summit in Kuala Lumpur).[23] In their view, while the crisis had proved that China can "uphold the interests of developing countries," it had also irrefutably demonstrated that the prevailing international financial and economic order marginalized the interests of developing countries. Ergo, they argued, China should strive and work together with these countries to "reform the order."[24] This perception of victimization was not limited only to the issue of economic development. There was also the sense that the AFC had presented an opportunity for some to cast unfair aspersions on Chinese intentions. "Hegemonic forces," it was argued, had tried to link the cause of the crisis to China's 1994 renminbi devaluation as well as portray China as a "Trojan horse" seeking regional domination via the crisis.[25]

The Failed WTO Bid and the Belgrade Embassy Bombing

By 1999 the earlier American optimism about China and its overall direction had dimmed considerably, and Chinese Premier Zhu Rongji openly commented that the political climate in Washington had become "anti-China."[26] It was in this mood that Zhu embarked on his visit to the US in April 1999, with the view to concluding bilateral negotiations on China's entry to the WTO. Despite the negative atmosphere, the Chinese government had high hopes that Zhu's trip would be successful and finally clear the foremost hurdle to China's WTO entry.[27] For the Clinton administration, the WTO issue was another opportunity to exert pressure on Beijing regarding its international obligations, even as the US recognized that China's WTO membership would, on balance, bring more benefits than costs to the US. Thus, on the eve of Zhu's visit Clinton publicly stated that American support for the WTO bid depended fundamentally on China's willingness to "accept the responsibilities that come with WTO membership" and "to play by the global rules of trade."[28]

Certainly, the Chinese government was keen to secure an agreement with the US on the issue of WTO admission. Although there were elements within Beijing that were apprehensive about the bid for WTO membership, overall there was broad consensus among the Chinese leadership that China had to join the WTO sooner rather than later.[29] Several reasons underpinned the pursuit of WTO membership, not least the belief that WTO accession would boost China's big-power standing. "When China joins the WTO," one article in the journal *Shijie Zhishi (World Affairs)* asserted, it would have another stage to "express its big-power influence and activism."[30] Yet this desire to project itself as a big power seems at odds with the insistence by Chinese negotiators that the PRC join the WTO as a developing state. It was argued that China's GDP per capita was still very modest as compared to many nations, making it "unfair and unacceptable" that China should bear "international obligations that did not match its development status."[31]

China's emphasis of its status as a developing state had been a point of contention during its WTO negotiations with Washington, but it was concerns about potential congressional opposition (on a WTO deal) that dissuaded Clinton from sealing an agreement during Zhu's visit. Naturally, Clinton's decision disappointed Zhu and the visiting Chinese delegation—it was "a slap in Zhu's face," as one scholar put it. Chinese unhappiness was further exacerbated when details of a draft agreement, documenting concessions offered by China, were unilaterally released online by the American side.[32]

Zhu's failure to secure a WTO deal as well as the leakage of details on the concessions provoked domestic reactions that referenced China's past victimization at the hands of foreign aggressors. China's WTO compromises were likened to the "new twenty-one demands selling out the country," an allusion to the harsh conditions imposed on China by Japan in 1915. Some even claimed that the government's embrace of globalization, as evidenced by its committed pursuit of WTO membership, was not too dissimilar from Wang Jingwei's traitorous collusion with the Japanese during World War II.[33] Such analogies are overblown, of course. But they are a reflection of "longer-standing historical memories of unfair trade" that inevitably cast a shadow on China's bid to join the WTO.[34]

Chinese sense of victimization was further heightened when the PRC embassy in Belgrade, Yugoslavia, was hit by American bombs in May that year. The Chinese government was already wary of the US-led NATO campaign to unilaterally bomb Yugoslavia using the justification that "human rights transcend sovereignty."[35] So, when the PRC embassy was also bombed, killing three Chinese reporters and injuring twenty others, Chinese outrage was neuralgic. Mass demonstrations erupted outside of American embassies and consulates in Beijing, Chengdu, and Guangzhou, as the Chinese government condemned the incident as "a crude violation of China's sovereignty."[36] The American explanation, that the bombing had been accidental, was dismissed as "lies" or "excuses" by Chinese commentators.[37] Meanwhile, rhetoric alluding to the Chinese victim identity quickly surfaced. In a speech welcoming returning diplomats from Belgrade, Jiang declared that China would never be "bullied."[38] Foreign minister Tang Jiaxuan responded similarly, asserting that China's reaction showed it would not be easily "bullied or humiliated."[39] A number of commentaries in Chinese publications saw the vestiges of history in the embassy bombing. One article in the journal *Guoji Zhanwang (Global Review)* claimed that the bombing was reminiscent of "late nineteenth to early twentieth century, old-style imperialism," while a *Renmin Ribao* opinion-editorial reminded its readers that "this is not the age when the Western powers plundered the Imperial Palace at will, destroyed the old Summer Palace, and seized Hong Kong and Macao."[40] The grim conclusion of several commentaries was that if a nation "lagged behind others" it faced the prospect of being "beaten up"; therefore, China had to unremittingly strengthen its comprehensive national power to avoid being bullied.[41]

The embassy incident crystallized the fears and concerns of Chinese intellectuals over the Kosovo War. To many of them it had demonstrated that "hegemonism and power politics" continued to thrive in the post–Cold War era, that the prevailing trends of "peace and development" were being challenged, and that Western powers could wantonly intervene in the affairs of other countries (the so-called new interventionism).[42] At a broader level, the Kosovo War led some scholars to moderate their estimations of China's relative position in the international order. The war had shown that the US could easily bypass the UN Security Council and act unilaterally, thus circumscribing China's veto power.[43] At the same time, it highlighted the continuing gulf in technological capabilities between the US and the PRC militaries (similar to an assessment derived in the wake of the 1990 Iraq War). Therefore, reasoned Chu Shulong and Wang Zaibang, scholars at the China Institutes of Contemporary International Relations, it is important that one "clearly and realistically" assess China's national strength and recognize that it remained backward in several areas.[44] For others, such as Yan Xuetong, it is evident that the world was not becoming more multipolar; rather, the "one superpower, many great powers" scenario had become more pronounced.[45]

Undoubtedly, the period from early to mid-1999 was a testing time for China's relations with the United States. Chinese policymakers and analysts were clearly concerned by what they perceived as increasing American proclivity toward hegemonic behavior. Indeed, some voices called for a more confrontational foreign policy toward the US, wherein China would align with Russia or the developing bloc to resist American hegemony. Nevertheless, a consensus quickly emerged in Beijing that, despite the diplomatic travails, "peace and development" were still the dominant currents in international society and there was neither the need nor the capacity to challenge the United States. Beijing recognized there was no real alternative to maintaining stable Sino-US relations, even if this relationship seemed to be moving further away from the stated ideal of a "constructive strategic partnership."[46] It was with these in mind that, shortly after the embassy incident, Jiang stressed that China had to build relations with the US even as it opposed hegemonism. High-level bilateral dialogues quickly resumed, and by September 1999 Jiang met Clinton on the sidelines of the seventh APEC leaders' meeting.[47]

"Bin Laden Saved China"

The last quarter of the Clinton administration's second term unfolded in a less turbulent direction for US-China relations. Rising Chinese nationalism and growing American anti-China sentiments were still troubling undercurrents, but in late 1999 Beijing finally reached a deal with the United States on its WTO accession. Clinton also publicly reaffirmed Washington's commitment to the "one China" status quo when Taiwan president Lee Teng-hui controversially characterized the cross-strait relationship as a "special state-to-state" relationship. Before the end of his second term Clinton signed legislation (after hard-won congressional approval) to grant permanent normal trading relations status to China.

But while Clinton got praise from Jiang by the end of his tenure, the election of George W. Bush to the American presidency in early 2001 caused initial consternation within Chinese policy circles.[48] As the Republican presidential candidate Bush had stated it would be a "mistake" to label China a strategic partner of the US, calling the country a "strategic competitor."[49] Condoleezza Rice, a key foreign policy consultant to Bush and later the US national security adviser, also argued earlier in the journal *Foreign Affairs* that China was not a "status quo power."[50] Such statements had not been lost on Chinese officials and analysts.[51] That being said, the first US visit by a Chinese leader after Bush assumed power went well. Meeting with Vice-Premier Qian Qichen in Washington, Bush stated his belief that Sino-American relations should be "constructive." Qian, on his part, tried to present China as a responsible power during the visit (as he had in earlier visits). At a luncheon attended by American policy elites, Qian pointed out that the "fundamental duty" of Chinese foreign policy was to "work toward a peaceful international environment" and that peace and stability of the Asia-Pacific region constituted the "mutual responsibilities" of China and the US.[52]

Qian's visit had barely passed when, in April 2001, Beijing and Washington found themselves embroiled in another major diplomatic crisis. An American EP-3 military surveillance plane had collided with a trailing PLA fighter jet in midair, killing the Chinese pilot and forcing the American plane to make an emergency landing on Hainan. Beijing's immediate reaction was to blame the collision on the American plane, accusing it of transgressing China's airspace and sovereignty. Demands for an apology and the US to stop its reconnaissance flights near the Chinese coastlines followed, but tensions were raised further when the Bush administration appeared reluctant to show contrition over the incident.[53] Unsurprisingly, anti-American sentiments ran high in China—and writings of how the PRC was again the victim of American hegemonic behavior began to emerge. One claimed that the US "always attempted to find trouble with China."[54] Another wrote of how "even though the aggressor was the US, it still treated a victimized China with an unreasonable and tyrannical attitude."[55] On the whole, however, the reaction in China was more restrained compared to the 1999 embassy bombing incident. This was, in part, the corollary of steps taken by the government to better manage the domestic fallout. Beijing was careful to rein in the excesses of Chinese nationalism that, left unbridled, could have had damaging consequences for Sino-American relations (and, potentially, for the CCP regime). It was perceived that relations with the US were simply too important to allow circumstances to drive it into a tailspin.[56]

For many Americans, however, the reaction of the Chinese appeared neither restrained nor was indicative of a nation aspiring to be a benign, responsible power. The view in Washington had been that the EP-3 plane was forced to land in circumstances beyond its control—the Chinese pilot was primarily at fault for the collision—so the American government and public were incensed when the PRC detained the EP-3 crew for eleven days and dismantled the EP-3 aircraft.[57] One Congressional Research Service (CRS) report described Beijing as having acted in a "hard-line" and "uncooperative" manner, while some American observers believed that China's behavior had strengthened the case of those who argued for a tougher foreign policy approach.[58] Against this backdrop, the Bush administration announced that same month the sale of arms to Taiwan that included eight diesel submarines and four Kidd-class destroyers.[59]

By mid-2001, however, there were signs that bilateral relations were starting to mend, even though Jiang was said to have expressed his misgivings about Bush's foreign policy outlook (which he described as "logically unsound; confused and unprincipled; unwise to the extreme").[60] One discernible indication was Secretary of State Colin Powell's visit to Beijing in late July.[61] Meeting the PRC leadership and addressing Chinese concerns that the new US administration appeared to pursue a more adversarial China policy, Powell publicly stated that Washington saw China "as a friend." The United States, according to Powell, wanted a "friendly relationship," with the view of getting China to "play a more active role in the world."[62] This conveyed the sense that the Bush administration, like the Clinton government, wanted China to assume more of the global responsibilities that came with its rising power. Powell's remarks had in fact squared with Assistant Secretary of State James Kelly's earlier testimony to the Senate Subcommittee on East Asian and Pacific Affairs, though Kelly's words were certainly more assertive. In May 2001, Kelly stated:

> We will hold China to its bilateral and international commitments. If China chooses to disregard its international obligations in areas as diverse as security issues, human rights, non-proliferation or trade, we

> will use all available policy tools to persuade it to move in more constructive directions . . . China's own interests—and its responsibility for the promotion of global peace, security, and prosperity—should guide the leadership in Beijing to uphold international standards in policy areas ranging from human rights to non-proliferation. China must live up to its global obligations.[63]

Ostensibly, one area in which China might be said to be "living up to its obligations" was counterterrorism.[64] In the wake of the terrorist attacks in the United States on September 11, 2001, Beijing was quick to show its cooperative side. It speedily offered its commiserations to the American people. It supported and collaborated with US international antiterrorism efforts, which included setting up a counterterrorism dialogue mechanism with Washington, clamping down on terrorist financing via Chinese banks, contributing intelligence on Islamist networks in the region, and establishing an FBI liaison office in Beijing. It publicly backed the US military campaigns against Al-Qaeda and the Taliban regime in Afghanistan and exercised its political leverage with Islamabad to help sway it to cooperate with American efforts against those elements. It voted for antiterrorism UN Security Council resolutions 1368 and 1373, marking the first Chinese votes in support of UN decrees with the scope for the use of force. And, as host of the APEC Summit held in Shanghai in October 2001, it assented to the inclusion of an antiterrorist agenda in the official statement.[65] These actions and more culminated in Bush's direct affirmation of China's power status at the October APEC meet, calling it a "great power." Bush stopped short of describing China as a responsible power but nonetheless praised Beijing for "stand[ing] side by side with the American people" in the fight against terrorism.[66] Later, Kelly addressed the House Subcommittee on East Asia and the Pacific, acknowledging that China had rendered valuable cooperation and support after 9/11.[67]

Bush visited China again four months later, a historical precedent. Standing together with Jiang at the Great Hall of the People's Republic of China on February 21, 2002, the thirtieth anniversary of Nixon's historic trip to China, Bush described China as "a force of peace" in the region. Bush also recognized China's rising economic power and took the occasion to remind the host nation that it had the "right and responsibility to fashion and enforce the rules of open trade." This corroborated the view that the Bush administration saw China emerging as a co-shaper and co-manager of the global economic order. On the part of the

Chinese leadership, Jiang did not deviate from embellishing his statements with customary RGP narratives, adding that both nations had "more rather than less common responsibilities" to the world.[68]

Such was the extent of the improvement in bilateral ties that by the end of 2002 the US destroyer *Paul Foster* was allowed to make a port call at Qingdao and Bush held his second meeting with Jiang in a year.[69] In fact, in October 2002 Jiang became one of the few world leaders to be invited to Bush's personal ranch in Crawford, Texas—a strong gesture of American friendship. That meeting resulted in a striking statement from Bush, that he considered China an "ally" in America's War on Terror.[70] Bush would reiterate a similar sentiment around a year later, when new Chinese premier Wen Jiabao visited Washington, hailing China and the US as "partners" in meeting the security challenges of the twenty-first century. On that occasion Bush also emphatically validated China's position in the global order, calling it a "great civilisation, a great power, and a great nation."[71]

Thus, following 9/11 there had been a substantial warming of US-China relations. Between then and the end of 2004, formal dialogue between Bush and PRC leaders took place eight times, while Powell met his Chinese counterpart, Li Zhaoxing, at least eleven times.[72] There were, of course, still several areas of policy difference and interest divergence between the sides, but it was patently clear that in the aftermath of the 9/11 attacks, there was a renewed momentum to ties between Beijing and Washington. Indeed, given the bilateral difficulties that had accompanied the initial months of the Bush administration, it was wryly suggested in China that "Bin Laden saved [the PRC]."[73]

Chinese analysts generally acknowledged that 9/11 had an impact on China's power status and its relations with the US, although there were differing assessments on the nature of this impact. On the one hand it compelled Washington to focus on the more pressing threats of Al-Qaeda and Jihadist terrorism instead of the potential threat of a rising China, which made it easier for Beijing to respond positively to the US and vice versa. This led antiterrorism to become part of the rationales that undergirded stable US-China relations, increasing opportunities for: (i) Sino-American dialogue and collaboration; (ii) a bigger Chinese role in global security governance; and (iii) establishing linkages between China's support for US counterterrorism efforts and its proclaimed RGP identity, as Jiang had tried to do at the 2001 APEC Summit.[74] On the other hand, 9/11 and its corollary effects also produced concerns about China's strategic position vis-à-vis the US. As shown by the 2003 invasion of Iraq, the Bush administration's panoptic vision of "fighting terror" could be used to justify preemptory military actions and interventionist policies. While Beijing had not opposed America's position during UN Security Council deliberations on Iraq, such a principle was at odds with China's state-centric view of sovereignty, whose strategists feared that it could be applied to the case of North Korea.[75] In fact, many of these strategists expressed skepticism of American intentions regarding Iraq—which were further heightened when the US Army failed to find concrete evidence of weapons of mass destruction—and saw that war as proof of enduring American hegemonism and imperialistic inclinations.[76] Nor were they unconcerned about the US's increased military presence in Central Asia, its growing influence in South Asia, and the ease with which it had been able to displace the Taliban and Saddam Hussein regimes.[77] These factors contributed to a sense that the United States had extended its strategic superiority over China, which by late 2001 had prompted Jiang to promote the study and strengthening of "national strategic capability" (*zhanlue nengli*) at a major PLA conference.[78] This sense of relative vulnerability was also not helped by the belief among several Chinese scholars that antiterrorism was a short-term common objective and that over the longer term the US might revert to a more adversarial attitude toward China.[79]

Debating International Responsibility

Yet, combating terrorism was never the only area in which the Bush administration wanted greater Chinese cooperation. As mentioned, even in the early months of the Bush government it had been apparent that there would be a continuation of the policy of pushing China to act as a responsible power on a range of international issues, from nonproliferation and the North Korea nuclear problem to international trade and human rights. Perhaps the clearest indication of this policy came from the director of policy planning at the State Department, Richard Haass, when he addressed the National Committee on US-China Relations in December 2002. Speaking on the question of China's international role, Haass stated unequivocally that China's leaders "must confront the reality that greater power brings with it the burden of greater responsibility." Haass noted that while the PRC had made considerable strides in integrating into the international system and signed "protocols and treaties," that was not enough. Nor was it sufficient merely that both sides had regular dialogues or "shared interests." What was more important, in Washington's view, was that the US and China cultivated a sense of shared purpose and identity, "one built on the basis of what [both countries] are *for*." The kind of "solidarity," Haass remarked, that George Kennan had envisioned the US as having with "other like-minded nations."[80] Haass's words suggest that Washington saw the issue of China's responsibility not only as a function of the latter's growing power but also increasingly through the prism of a solidarist society of states that perceives a responsible state as one that shares or contributes to the values and norms of a liberalist global order.[81]

For the Chinese leadership, its rhetoric had not moved beyond the general language of asserting common global responsibilities or pronouncing China as a contributor to international peace and security. Nevertheless, at the semi-official intellectual level, there was greater flavor to the discourse. As explored in the previous chapter, from around the early to mid-1990s Chinese scholars had begun to ponder the questions of China's role and responsibilities in international society. There would be a perpetuation and deepening of this discussion between 1997 and 2004.

One notable contributor was Renmin University scholar Pang Zhongying. Writing in the leading Chinese journal *Shijie Jingji Yu Zhengzhi (World Economics and Politics,* or *WEP),* Pang suggests that the PRC, despite its accession to the WTO in 2001, has yet to become a wholly "normal" country within the international system. From the viewpoint of history it is not normal for China to not become a world power, but, as Pang expounds, the question of China's "normalization" depends ultimately on whether it is inducted into the "mainstream" of international society and whether it shares the "interests and views" of this mainstream. Pang is of the view that since China "could not leave international society," it should align more with the norms of international society, even to the point of rethinking its traditional foreign policy emphasis on independence and autonomy. This "self-correction," he argues, will lead to the normalization of China's status as a responsible great power.[82]

Peking University scholars Ye Zicheng and Li Ying appear to share Pang's sentiments but criticize the national psychology of victimhood in preventing a more "normal" big-power outlook in China. They write: "Whenever difficulties arose with Western powers, one was often tempted to think about the eight-nation allied invasion or the late Qing dynasty's humiliations at the hands of foreign aggressors, reflecting a particular interpretation of history to understand modern reality." If China wants to become a great power, such negativity has to be jettisoned; it is more important that it develops "normal" big-power traits of self-confidence, optimism, and responsibility. On the last quality, Ye and Li remind their audience that Deng's diplomatic guideline "*taoguang yanghui*" (hide brightness, nourish obscurity) is followed by the phrase "*yousuo zuowei*" (do something useful), which implies a Chinese "spirit of responsibility and contribution" toward the world. This sort of diplomatic activism calls for China to "direct and establish international rules" and to assert its "voice" in international affairs, inasmuch as Deng's concept of strategic obscurity was still salient.[83]

The writings of Pang, Ye, and Li all connect to the belief that it is crucial for China's identity development to encompass a sense of great-power responsibility. But what is great-power responsibility, as conceived in China? Men Honghua and Huang Haili provide one interpretation in the influential policy journal *Meiguo Yanjiu (American Studies)*. Reflecting a conceptualization of great-power responsibility that is not too dissimilar from the English school conception, Men and Huang argue that "responsibility cannot be divorced from power"—ergo "great powers have greater responsibilities than other states." This bespeaks the duty of safeguarding international peace and security, as it necessarily falls on the shoulders of the powerful "few" (i.e., great powers), who also have "special responsibilities to more actively provide international public goods." Men and Huang do not particularly elaborate on the type of public goods that China should provide, but they do suggest the recovery of failed states as one area in which Beijing could provide leadership as a responsible power, as well as in its collaboration with the United States.[84]

Qu Congwen engages history to arrive at a similar view of great-power responsibility. Qu agrees with the notion that great powers have added responsibilities and that these responsibilities include the obligation to act with restraint and to improve the international system. Nevertheless, different historical epochs entailed different morality "requirements" for the "ways" of a great power, most of which were usually predetermined by the "forerunning powers" of the day.[85] In Qu's observation, beginning in the 1980s and continuing to the 1990s, the concept of the responsible great power had become the new moral benchmark for extant and aspiring powers, representing the continuing process of the "enlightenment" of the international system. International society has yet to achieve a complete consensus on the meaning of great-power responsibility, he notes, but there is little doubt that this idea is emerging as the "choice of history" for great powers in the twenty-first century.[86]

A more structural understanding of China's great power responsibility can be found in Xiao Huanrong's widely cited paper in the *WEP* journal. Xiao attempts to systematize great-power responsibility in terms of levels—domestic, regional, and global—that correspond to a state's power status. This ordering of power and responsibility is conceived as follows:

Table 3.1: Xiao's Power-Responsibility Matrix

	Domestic responsibility	Regional responsibility	Global responsibility
Basic great power	Seek basic security and prosperity	Pursuit of a strategic periphery	Of lesser importance or basic in nature
Regional great power	Realize basic security and prosperity	Establishment of a security ring	Of greater importance; pursue some global obligations
Superpower	Realize abundant security and prosperity	Establishment of spheres of influence	To manage the global order

Xiao's taxonomy leads to a measured assessment of China's responsibility-power juncture (*zeren dingwei*): first, China's domestic obligations correspond to those of a "basic great power" (i.e., in seeking basic security and prosperity) because, among other things, China still faces several developmental challenges and has not achieved reunification with Taiwan. Second, based on most readings of Chinese national power, China is already a regional big power. However, it has yet to fully meet its regional responsibility of establishing a "strategic periphery" of friendly states, much less a regional "security ring." Third, although China cannot be considered a superpower, it has inextricable influence and roles in global governance. Xiao concludes that, even as "appropriate" global responsibilities should be pursued, the focus of China's great-power responsibility should necessarily be focused on its regional obligations. This means an emphasis on Asian regionalism and its processes, which in Xiao's estimation will have a positive impact on enhancing China's regional leadership role as well as its ability to fulfill its domestic and global responsibilities.[87]

As is clear, Xiao perceives great-power responsibility as squaring with the needs of China's development and security. The same could be said of Men and Huang, who state that the pursuit of big-power responsibilities does not preclude the consideration of national interests (as they put it, ideally there should be a "confluence of responsibility, power, and interest").[88] Wang Yizhou, an authoritative voice in Chinese academia, sees little dichotomy between interest and responsibility, arguing that responsibility is both "an interest and a requirement" (*liyi yu xuqiu*) in Chinese foreign policy. Wang concurs with Xiao's assessment that Beijing should address its regional obligations more than its global obligations, given that China is still a developing state and has unresolved sovereignty issues. That said, China can still have meaningful contributions to the extant international order. In this area Wang suggests Beijing's responsibilities are: (i) helping establish a "fairer and more stable" global order; (ii) the "reaffirmation and bolstering of the moral authority and influence of the United Nations"; and (iii) helping reform the IMF and the World Bank so that the global financial regime more accurately reflects the development needs and risk capacities of member states. Wang is overall optimistic that as China's comprehensive national power rises, transforming its diplomatic priorities, "its great-power temperament and responsible persona will become more manifest."[89]

Yet, societal attitudes that indicate ideological dogmatism and a "retaliatory" mind-set of a victimized nation do not help China's RGP cause. It is therefore important, CASS scholar Shen Jiru argues, that a "healthy citizenry consciousness of China as a responsible great power" be cultivated. Shen points out that China is an important member of the "world family." External problems can quickly become China's problems, while China's internal difficulties could similarly affect others. It stands to reason, therefore, that China should seek an "alignment of interests" between the Chinese nation and the world's societies, Shen writes.[90]

Shen's advocacy of a "globally responsible citizenry" is reflective of the sanguinity many in China felt about their country's growing international stature and role. Certainly, among Chinese intellectuals there was rising interest of and receptivity to the narrative of China as a responsible power. Compared to the early to mid-1990s period, from 1997 to 2004 Chinese scholars appeared to be less cynical of the RGP vision, though this is not to say their views necessarily converged with those propounded in Washington or that perceptions of China's victimhood and developing status had faded. As we have seen, external events had served as an impetus to Chinese discussions on international responsibility. The 1997–1998 Asian financial crisis notably led many Chinese scholars and policymakers to assert China's RGP identity. Similar assertions were made about China's post-9/11 antiterrorism contributions and its membership in the WTO (that is, China as the "responsible developing power").[91] Meanwhile, various strategic concepts that had gained currency in Beijing during this period were also conducive to the RGP discourse. The next section looks at these ideas.

New Security Concept, Soft Power, and Peaceful Rise

The new security concept (NSC) marked the evolution of China's security diplomacy in the post–Cold War era. Building on security policy rhetoric of the mid-1990s, as well as on conceptual antecedents like the Five Principles of Peaceful Coexistence, the NSC came to be an authoritative doctrine (*tifa*) when it was outlined in China's 1998 national defense white paper. Its status as a major policy guideline was further enshrined when it was included in major Jiang speeches, in official statements at the Sixteenth Chinese Communist Party Congress, and in subsequent white papers on defense (in 2000, 2002, and 2004).[92]

The thrust of the NSC was that security should be underpinned by "mutual benefit, mutual trust, equality, and cooperation" between states instead of arms buildup and alliances. Such nomenclature had not been uncommon in Chinese diplomatic language, but in the area of security policy its use represented a new development. Important to their formulation in the NSC was the perspective that in an increasingly interdependent world, "no states can unilaterally achieve its security aims" and that the security of all states is inextricably linked. It is hence vital, the NSC argued, that states build trust with each other and pursue security cooperation. This cooperation was envisaged to extend to nontraditional threats such as terrorism, pandemics, and international crime, speaking to the notion of "comprehensive security" that had gained increased prominence following 9/11. The broad definition of security also dovetailed with the Chinese idea of comprehensive national power, conceiving security as coming with power, in multiple dimensions.[93]

The advocacy of the new security concept led to parallel Chinese RGP claims. It is noteworthy that the 1998 white paper that outlined the NSC also pronounced China as "a responsible great power, a firm force for upholding world peace and stability."[94] In academia, China Foreign Affairs University vice president Qin Yaqing was an influential voice who argued that the shift in security thinking demonstrates China's "willingness to be a responsible power of the international society."[95]

In some respects the positioning of China as a promoter of progressive security norms can be seen as Beijing's attempt to boost its soft power in the security arena. This should not be surprising. Since the late 1990s the idea of soft power had become increasingly prominent in Beijing, and many Chinese scholars and policymakers saw it as an integral aspect of China's comprehensive national power. In 2002 it received top-level endorsement when Jiang's report to the Sixteenth CCP Congress affirmed the strategic relevance of the concept. At the thirteenth collective study session of the Politburo of the CCP Central Committee in 2004, themes related to China's soft power were also raised.[96]

Generally concurring with the idea that soft power is about influencing others through attraction rather than coercion, Chinese discussions in this area centered on aspects such as a nation's culture, ideologies, image, and developmental model. At the heart of this discourse is the question of how these elements can ameliorate China's power position. It was perceived that soft power "competition" had become a core aspect of the international competition between states, and that for China's rise to be sustainable the strengthening of this dimension was crucial.[97] This was especially so, given China's aspiration to be a responsible big power, argued one scholar from the compilation and translation bureau of the central committee; it had to "possess the capacity to relate to other states."[98] A similar view was espoused by strategist Fu Xin. Writing in the influential policy journal *Guoji Wenti Yanjiu (International Studies)*, Fu suggests that China could not afford to ignore its responsibilities to international society if it wanted to augment its soft power and international image.[99]

A fundamental argument connecting the motifs of soft power and the new security concept was that China's rise would be peaceful. This message had been promulgated by Beijing for some time, but it was only in November 2003 at the Boao Forum that the *tifa* of China's "peaceful rise" was formally articulated by leading CCP political theorist Zheng Bijian. Zheng had earlier written and submitted a report on "the development path of China's peaceful rise" to Chinese president Hu Jintao, who publicly expressed his support for this concept by December 2003. There were subsequent statements of endorsement by key members of the CCP Politburo, but from around April 2004 Chinese leaders preferred to use the ostensibly more neutral terminology of "peaceful development" instead of "peaceful rise."[100]

Substantively, little changed and there remained considerable support in Beijing for the ideas advocated by Zheng. According to Zheng, China's rise would be a benign and nonhegemonic phenomenon. History had shown that the rise of new powers often destabilized the prevailing international order and caused wars, especially when these powers sought national aggrandizement through military means. This was why, Zheng claimed, China would never repeat the mistakes of these powers and go down the same "harmful" path; instead, it would pursue a "new" course of rising peacefully through internal reforms and participation in economic globalization. This obligated China to "strive" for a benign external environment, which meant avoiding confrontation with other big powers and cultivating good regional relations. Zheng was confident that China's emergence would have positive implications for the Asian region; as he put it, the peaceful rise of China constituted part of Asia's peaceful rise story.[101]

Official endorsement notwithstanding, the peaceful rise concept prompted an internal debate in China. Some emphasized the developing-state identity and thought it was premature to speak of China as a rising power. Others were concerned that the idea of peaceful rise weakened China's hand in employing force options against Taiwan, that it had no historical precedent and was thus not realistic, that it challenged Deng's earlier advice of adopting a low-profile international posture, that it diminished the rationale for China's military modernization, and that it potentially promoted nationalistic sentiments.[102] Supporters of the peaceful rise theory, on the other hand, saw linkages between this concept and China's RGP identity. Zheng himself made this connection at the 2003 Boao Forum, citing the elevation of Chinese living standards (i.e., of one-fifth of the world's population) as evidence that China had "shouldered its responsibilities toward mankind's development."[103] Similarly, at the 2004 Boao Forum it was asserted that China would emerge as a "nonhegemonic, peaceful, and responsible great power."[104] This outlook was evidently shared by several scholars writing in a special 2004 issue of the journal *Jiaoxue Yu Yanjiu (Teaching and Research)*, conceiving peaceful rise as entailing the fulfillment of China's obligations and role as a responsible power.[105] Qin Yaqing perceived a similar (if inverse) dynamic: China's RGP "political thought and practice" were proof that its rise would be peaceful.[106]

China's Conduct

Beyond the rhetoric, how did China's general behavior relate to its stated RGP identity during this period? As we have seen, in fighting the Asian financial crisis and international terrorism, China had generally evinced a more cooperative face. That side was again perceptible on the North Korea (DPRK) nuclear issue. China publicly voiced its opposition to the nuclearization of the Korean peninsula, took part in four-party talks with both Koreas and the US between 1997 and 1999, and supported the referral of the IAEA's report on the DPRK's violations to the UN Security Council. More significantly, it played a leading role in mediating the 2002–2003 nuclear standoff between Washington and Pyongyang, brokering first the US-China-DPRK trilateral talks in July 2003 and then persuading Pyongyang to accept a six-party talk format on negotiations (which China also hosted).[107] These actions and more were appreciated by Washington and led Colin Powell to hail China's assistance as a "vivid example" of the great-power concert that the US had come to expect with China.[108] Not surprisingly, many Chinese commentaries argued that Beijing had acted responsibly on the North Korea nuclear issue—although it was unclear from these writings the extent to which the RGP identity had been a factor in Beijing's response.[109] What was evident, though, was that China had substantial interests in getting North Korea to abandon its nuclear program. Pyongyang's pursuit of nuclear weapons was clearly destabilizing to China's regional security environment. There was also the risk of American military intervention, a scenario that could lead to a North Korean refugee crisis at Chinese borders and the loss of the DPRK as China's strategic buffer.[110]

In terms of broader nonproliferation / arms control efforts, China took a number of new steps to demonstrate its support. These included joining the Zangger Committee and ratifying the Chemical Weapons Convention (CWC) in 1997, issuing a control list of nuclear exports that accorded with those of the Nuclear Suppliers Group and eventually joining the group in 2004, assenting to an additional IAEA protocol in 1999 that permitted more stringent checks on China's civilian nuclear program, pledging in 2000 that it would withhold international assistance on the development of nuclear-capable missile-delivery systems, strengthening its control regulations on missile-related exports in 2002, and publishing its first white paper on nonproliferation in 2003.[111] These measures, however, were not enough to prevent a critical review of China's nonproliferation record in July 2003 by the Bush administration. The administration was particularly concerned with what it considered to be a lack of enforcement by Beijing to control the alleged sales of missile-related technologies to Iran and Pakistan by errant Chinese firms. It also stated its belief that China retained a clandestine chemical and biological weapons program.[112]

China's role in another area of maintaining international security—UN peacekeeping operations—was less contentious. Between 1997 and 2004 it participated in a total of eleven peacekeeping operations, increasing its number of sent peacekeepers by almost tenfold from 2001 to 2004. Examples of some of these operations with Chinese participation included: the UN missions in Sierra Leone (UNASMIL), Liberia (UNMIL), Ethiopia and Eritrea (UNMEE); the UN operations in Côte d'Ivoire (UNOCI) and Burundi (UNOB); and the UN Transitional Administration in East Timor (UNTAET).[113] The PRC's participation was still limited to noncombat activities, but to China's National Defense University scholar Tang Yongsheng, this involvement denoted not only the "practical" use of Chinese power but also China's "condition and image" as a "responsible and cooperative" power.[114]

This period also saw greater Chinese participation, enmeshment, and leadership in regional security mechanisms. For example, in 2001 China helped establish the Shanghai Cooperation Organization (SCO), which, among other things, promoted nontraditional security cooperation among its members (comprising also Russia, Kazakhstan, Kyrgyzstan, Uzbekistan, and Tajikistan). Its origin as the "Shanghai Five collective" was reflective of Beijing's central role within the group.[115] Additionally, China deepened its involvement in the ASEAN Regional Forum. Although Beijing had been initially skeptical about the ARF and its aims, it gradually came to the assessment that active engagement in this organization was not necessarily incompatible with Chinese interests. Thus, by 1997 Beijing was co-chairing a session on confidence-building initiatives with Manila. In 2003 Beijing broke new ground in its ARF approach with a proposal of an annual defense dialogue. This culminated in the unprecedented 2004 ARF Conference on Security Policy, which was attended by senior military and defense officials of all twenty-four member states. Given that one of the ARF's goals had apparently been to "socialize" the PRC to become a "responsible regional power," it could be argued that China had gone some way toward meeting this expectation (at least within the confines of the ARF).[116] Indeed, during this period China also signed a number of significant security-related documents with ASEAN, most notably the Declaration on the Conduct of Parties in the South China Sea and the association's Treaty of Amity and Cooperation. The former committed China to seeking peaceful solutions in regard to sovereignty disputes in the South China Sea, while the latter (in which the PRC had been the first non-ASEAN signatory) equally obligated China to renounce the threat or use of force in the settlement of conflicts. The last example related to regional governmental security dialogues and military exchanges. In both areas China upgraded its participation level. By 2004 Beijing had established security dialogue arrangements with the governments of Pakistan, Thailand, Japan, Mongolia, Kazakhstan, Kyrgyzstan, Australia, India, and Russia. Earlier, in 2003, China for the first time invited foreign military observers (which included officers from Thailand, Pakistan, Russia, and Singapore) to watch a large-scale PLA exercise. That year it also held joint military exercises with the navies of India, Pakistan, and Kazakhstan, marking a notable change from its long-standing policy of eschewing such collaboration.[117]

China's regional activism was not limited to the security domain. In terms of regional economic organizations, inter alia, Beijing continued to be an active player in APEC, signed up to join the development-oriented forum ASEAN Plus Three (which also included Japan and South Korea), and created its own regional economic dialogue institution, the Boao Forum (modeled after the World Economic Forum). In 2002 it signed a framework agreement that aimed to establish a China-ASEAN free-trade zone by 2010, which helped temper fears among ASEAN states that their economies risked being sidelined by the Chinese economic juggernaut.[118]

At the global level, China's 2001 entry to the WTO had an important impact on the free-trade regime. As previously noted, WTO accession had produced claims in China that it would act as a responsible power in the global economic order. That appears to be the case when China adopted a posture of moderation in the trade dispute between a coalition of developing states and the developed economies of Europe and North America at the 2003 Cancun WTO meeting. Beijing was praised by the US and others for its "constructive proposals and a moderating speaking tone" as well as in trying to "bridge the gap between developing and developed nations."[119] Washington was less complimentary, however, on the issue of China's WTO compliance. While in some aspects China committed itself to policies that were over and above what was required by the WTO, China's commitment in areas such as agriculture and service-sector policies, intellectual property rights, transparency, and market access drew concerns. Washington also made known its dissatisfaction with China's fixed exchange-rate system, which it saw as irresponsibly contributing to "imbalances that threaten the global economy."[120]

Meanwhile, Beijing took some steps—mainly procedural and relating to treaty signature—that signaled its awareness that recognition as a responsible power (especially by the US) depends in part on its alignment with the international human rights regime. China signed the International Covenant on Economic, Social, and Cultural Rights (ICESCR) and the ICCPR in 1997 and 1998, respectively, ratifying the former in June 2001. It engaged in bilateral human rights dialogues with more countries (e.g., UK, Australia, Norway, and Canada), and from 1998 it participated in formal dialogue with the office of the United Nations High Commissioner for Human Rights. It continued to permit village-level elections, which by the late 1990s covered nearly 80 percent of China's villages. And by 2004 it had published nineteen rights-related governmental white papers.[121] That year also saw the inclusion of the idea of human rights in the Chinese constitution for the first time.[122] Nevertheless, human rights is one area that China was always going to find hard to fully meet the expectations of American and other Western states because, among other factors, the Chinese definition of human rights emphasizes collective and development rights over individual and political rights, and because many in Beijing still interpret human rights in culturally relative terms rather than from a universal or organic standpoint.[123] There has been greater pluralism in Chinese perspectives on human rights, to be sure.[124] But these perceptual changes are obviously not enough to effect substantial change, as evidenced by continuing reports of Chinese abuses in areas such as labor rights, land rights, religious freedom, minority rights, and political rights.[125]

On environmental protection, China's ratification of the Kyoto Protocol in 2002 was a significant move that won it praise as a responsible power from several global leaders.[126] Its decision was made even more striking by the fact that the Bush administration pulled out of the protocol in 2001. Yet, arguably, ratifying the protocol had not been a particularly difficult decision for Beijing. Although China was obliged to implement "mitigating" ecological policies that would have an impact on domestic industries (e.g., the shutting down of older, coal-based power plants), as a Non-Annex I Party with developing-country status it was effectively exempted from binding emission quotas. This made it relatively easier for Beijing to accept the terms of the protocol. This is not to say that China considered environmental protection a peripheral issue. Numerous statements from Chinese leaders affirming the importance of sustainable development, the enactment of several environment-related legislations, and the inclusion of environmental protection targets in China's Tenth Five-Year Plan (2001–2005) were indications that China took environmental concerns seriously. On the specific problem of environmental warming, Beijing also stated that it saw its management as a "common" global responsibility—albeit "differentiated" in proportion to those of developed countries (which it believed should bear an increased burden).[127] Overall, nevertheless, it would appear that China's environmental protection record could be improved. As Minxin Pei points out, China's environmental conditions are worsening rather than improving.[128] Its emission levels had surged to the point that by 2002 it had become the world's second-largest producer of greenhouse gases.[129] This essentially discounts the possibility of having any meaningful solution on global warming without deeper Chinese involvement, even if much of China's emissions increase could be attributed to legitimate development needs.

Conclusion

The cartography of China's self-conception as a responsible great power in the period 1997–2004 bespeaks continuities and changes. The Clinton and Bush governments essentially continued the policy of seeking China to act more "responsibly" in international society. There was some pushing of the rhetorical envelope by Bush administration officials, as evidenced by the call for US-China relations to move beyond shared interests to include a sense of shared values. But, generally, the message to Beijing remained a consistent and simple one: the US welcomed China's rise, but its ascendancy should be matched by a willingness to shoulder the attendant global responsibilities. Washington never explicitly specified what it thought these responsibilities are, but it was apparent from American statements that they related to China's contributions toward regional and international security and its conformity to the major norms of the extant global order. In some of these aspects, as reviewed in the preceding section, it could be argued that China evinced a more cooperative side and had taken steps to improve its record. It is hard to tell the extent in which the proclaimed RGP identity was a factor in Beijing's behavior, but what is evident is that in several areas, Chinese writings sought to establish linkages between China's actions and the RGP identity.

Indeed, RGP narratives had proliferated in Chinese writings during this period, reflecting continued Chinese positioning in that role. At the official level Chinese leaders continued to embellish their statements with RGP references, but qualitatively these did not go beyond general assertions or claims. In effect there had been little variation in the rhetorical substance of official RGP discourse between this period and the earlier 1992–1996 phase. At the intellectual level, however, there was greater diversity and density to the discursive flow. As we have seen, Chinese scholars (some of whom are influential voices) engaged in a wide-ranging discussion on the questions of China's great-power role and its attendant responsibilities. Although there were perceptual differences in the emphasis and content of China's obligations, most concurred on the importance of Beijing's assuming greater global responsibilities. Interestingly, some of these views hewed toward a sense of noblesse oblige or a solidarist understanding of responsibility.

The expansion of the RGP discourse in China could be attributed in part to external events such as the Asian financial crisis and the 9/11 terrorist attacks, where Beijing's responses had prompted further claims and discussion of the RGP identity. The US's influence was still perceptible, as indicated by continuing Chinese acknowledgment of the importance of the responsibility issue to Washington. But, essentially, many of the Chinese arguments on international responsibility were endogenous conceptualizations that had not referenced American views of China's big-power conduct, reflecting what could be described as ideational "localization."[130] The rising domestic prominence of ideas such as the new security concept, soft power, and peaceful rise also squared with the development of the RGP discourse. This identity discussion would continue to evolve and deepen in the period after 2004. That phase will be examined next.

Notes

1. For a Chinese perspective on Sino-French relations, see Xue Longgen, "Zheng Zai Shenhua Fazhan De Zhongfa Quanmian Huoban Guanxi" (The deepening and development of the China-France comprehensive partnership), *Shijie Jingji Yu Zhengzhi Luntan (Forum of World Economics and Politics)* 5 (1999): 25–27, 64.
2. "Overview on China-UK Relations," The Embassy of the People's Republic of China in the United Kingdom of Great Britain and North Ireland, October 2010, available at http://www.chinese-embassy.org.uk/eng/zygx/introduction/; and ibid., 64.
3. Transcript of President Bill Clinton and President Jiang Zemin press conference, October 29, 1997, available at http://china.usc.edu/ShowArticle.aspx?articleID=750.
4. Jiang Zemin, "Zai Baigong Huanying Yishi Shang De Jianghua" (Speech at White House welcome ceremony), in *Jiang Zemin Wenxuan Dierjuan (Selected Works of Jiang Zemin)*, vol. 2 (Beijing: Renmin Chubanshe, 2006), 50. In another speech, given just before departing Los Angeles, he repeated his view that "China and the US are two great countries with significant responsibilities toward the world." See

"Zhongguo He Meiguo Yi Jianli Xianshi Zhuyi Xin Guanxi" (China and US have already established doctrine of realism, new relations), *Lianhe Zaobao (Zaobao Daily)*, November 5, 1997.

5. Jiang Zemin, "Zengjin Xianghu Liaojie, Jiaqiang Youhao Hezuo" (Enhance mutual understanding, strengthen friendly cooperation), in *Jiang Zemin Wenxuan Dierjuan (Selected Works of Jiang Zemin)*, vol. 2 (Beijing: Renmin Chubanshe, 2006), 64.
6. Transcript of President Bill Clinton and President Jiang Zemin's news conference in Beijing, June 27, 1998, available at http://china.usc.edu/ShowArticle.aspx?articleID=739.
7. Michael Yahuda, *The International Politics of the Asia-Pacific*, 3rd ed. (Abingdon, UK: Routledge, 2011), 281.
8. Transcript of President Bill Clinton's speech at Beijing University, June 29, 1998, available at http://china.usc.edu/ShowArticle.aspx?articleID=514.
9. Several Chinese scholars have noted and documented the importance of the responsibility issue to the Clinton administration. Jin Canrong, for example, identifies that a key part of Clinton's China strategy had been to use "engagement to induct China into the American-led international order, turning it into a responsible member of the international society." Similarly, Ding Kuisong and Niu Xinchun write that the US "sought to promote greater Chinese responsibility" as part of its China policy. See Jin Canrong, "Geng Duo De 'Jianshe Xing': Ping Jiang Zhuxi Fangmei Yilai De Zhongmei Guanxi" (More "constructiveness": Appraising Sino-American relations since chairman Jiang's visit to the US), *Dangdai Yatai (Contemporary Asia-Pacific)* 6 (1998): 6; Ding Kuisong and Niu Xinchun, "Zai Tansuo Hezuo Zhong Fazhan De Zhongmei Guanxi" (Probing developing Sino-American relations amid cooperation), *Xiandai Guoji Guanxi (Contemporary International Relations)* 12 (1999): 80.
10. Joseph Fewsmith, *China since Tiananmen* (Cambridge, UK: Cambridge University Press, 2008), 213.
11. See Zhang Xuebin, "Lun Zhongmei Liangguo Zhengfu Zai Yazhou Jinrong Weiji Zhong De Biaoxian" (Discussing the performance of the Chinese and American governments during the Asian financial crisis), *Guoji Zhengzhi Yanjiu (International Politics Quarterly)* 2 (1999): 40–42; Wang Hongying, "A Responsible Great Power? China's International Image Management in the 1990s," *East Asian Institute Working Paper* no. 44 (July 2000): 13–18.
12. Clinton also praised the Chinese government for showing "great statesmanship and strength." See Transcript of President Clinton and President Jiang Zemin's News Conference in Beijing. Indeed, various Chinese writings on the AFC stress the positive reaction of world leaders. See Yang Chengxu, "Zhongguo Guoji Diwei Jiju Tigao" (The rapid rise of China's international position), *Liaowang (Outlook)* 51 (1998): 20–21; Chen Fengjun, "Jinrong Weiji Hou Yatai Geju De Bianhua" (The changes in Asia-Pacific regional structure after the Asian financial crisis), *Guoji Zhengzhi Yanjiu (International Politics Quarterly)* 2 (1999): 27–28; Yu Changmiao, "Guanyu Renminbi Huilu Zouxiang De Sikao" (Reflecting on

the direction of the renminbi's exchange rate), *Zhonggong Zhongyang Dangxiao Xuebao (Journal of the Party School of the Central Committee of the CPC)* 7, no. 4 (2003): 108–12; Special Commentator, "Zai Kaoyan He Tiaozheng Zhong Fazhan De Guoji Xingshi" (International situation in tests and readjustment), *Xiandai Guoji Guanxi (Contemporary International Relations)* 12 (1999): 12.

13. Joshua Kurlantzick, *Charm Offensive: How China's Soft Power Is Transforming the World* (New Haven, CT: Yale University Press, 2007), 36. The Kuala Lumpur Declaration of the 1998 APEC summit also described China's currency policy as having acted as an "anchor" to the crisis's stabilization. See "APEC Economic Leaders Declaration: Strengthening the Foundations for Growth," Kuala Lumpur, November 18, 1998, 2.
14. See, for example, Zheng Bijian, "Zhuazhu Jiyu Yu Lilun Wuzhuang" (Grasping opportunity and theoretical augmentation), *Qiushi (Seeking Truth)* 7 (1999): 6; Wang Haihan, "Dui Dangqian Zhongmei Guanxi Jiqi Fazhan Qianjing De Jidian Kanfa" (Some perspectives on current Sino-American relations and their development prospects), *Guoji Wenti Yanjiu (International Studies)* 4 (1998): 9; Zhai Fengyu, "Yingjia, Shujia, Haishi Youying Youshu? Ping Zhongmeiri Sanguo Zai Dongya Jinrong Weiji Zhong De Deshi" (Winner, loser, or both win and lose? Reviewing the gains and losses of China, US, and Japan in the Asian financial crisis), *Shijie Jingji Yu Zhengzhi (World Economics and Politics)* 7 (1998): 38–39; Yang, "Zhongguo Guoji Diwei Jiju Tigao," 20–21; and Chen, "Jinrong Weiji Hou Yatai Geju De Bianhua," 27–29.
15. Zhou Zhongfei, "Mianxiang 21 Shiji De APEC Yu Zhongguo" (Toward the twenty-first century, APEC and China), *Guoji Zhanwang (Global Review)* 23 (1998): 5; Zhai, "Yingjia, Shujia, Haishi Youying Youshu?," 39; and Chen, "Jinrong Weiji Hou Yatai Geju De Bianhua," 28.
16. Some examples are Chen Hongbin, "Zhongguo Zhengzai Chengwei Fuzeren Daguo" (China is becoming a responsible great power), *Baike Zhishi (Encyclopaedic Knowledge)* 2 (1999): 29–30; Li Zhiye, "Daguo Guanxi Chubu Daowei, Liangxing Hudong Shijian Chengxiao" (Preliminary positioning of great-power relations, benign interactions start to show results), *Xiandai Guoji Guanxi (Contemporary International Relations)* 12 (1999): 86; "Jinrong Weiji Yinfa De Huati" (Topics raised by the financial crisis), *Shijie Zhishi (World Affairs)* 1 (1999): 33; Wang Mongkui, "Yazhou Jinrong Weiji Yu Zhongguo" (The Asian financial crisis and China), *Qiushi (Seeking Truth)* 21 (1998): 47; and Special Commentator, "Zai Kaoyan He Tiaozheng Zhong Fazhan De Guoji Xingshi," 12. See also the Chinese Academy for Social Sciences (CASS) postgraduate history textbook by Tao Wenzhao and He Xingqiang, *Zhongmei Guanxi Shi (A History of China-US Relations)* (Beijing: Zhongguo Shehui Kexue Chubanshe, 2009), 303.
17. Wang Yizhou, "Quanqiu Hua Guocheng Yu Zhongguo De Jiyu: Yazhou Jinrong Weiji Beijing Xia De Jidian Sikao" (Globalization and China's opportunities: Some thoughts against the backdrop of the Asian financial crisis), *Dangdai Shijie Yu Shehui Zhuyi (Contemporary World and Socialism)* 3 (1998): 19.

18. Zhai, "Yingjia, Shujia, Haishi Youying Youshu?," 39.
19. Zhang Xuebin, a Peking University scholar, criticized American support for ASEAN states as "shockingly little." Zhai Fengyu, an official at the former Ministry of Foreign Trade and Economic Cooperation (renamed the Ministry of Commerce in 2003), was also cynical of American intentions, asserting that the US had achieved its aim of using the crisis to "weaken Asia." See Zhang, "Lun Zhongmei Liangguo Zhengfu Zai Yazhou Jinrong Weiji Zhong De Biaoxian," 43–47; and Zhai, "Yingjia, Shujia, Haishi Youying Youshu?," 40–41.
20. Rong Dianxin, "Dongya Jinrong Weiji Yu Zhongguo De Kaifang Zhengce" (The Asian financial crisis and China's open up policy), *Shijie Jingji Yu Zhengzhi (World Economics and Politics)* 7 (1998): 31.
21. Samuel S. Kim, "China's Path to Great Power Status in the Globalization Era," *Asian Perspective* 27, no. 1 (2003): 64; Wang, "Quanqiu Hua Guocheng Yu Zhongguo De Jiyu," 18–19; Wang, "Yazhou Jinrong Weiji Yu Zhongguo," 20.
22. David Shambaugh, "China Engages Asia: Reshaping the Regional Order," *International Security* 29, no. 3 (Winter 2004–5): 68.
23. See, for example, Xu Mingqi, "Fengxian, Duice, Zeren: Zhongguo Yu Guoji Jinrong Tixi" (Risk, measures, responsibility: China and the international financial system), *Shijie Zhishi (World Affairs)* 7 (2000): 28; and Zhou, "Mianxiang 21 Shiji De APEC Yu Zhongguo," 6.
24. Ibid.; and Zhang, "Lun Zhongmei Liangguo Zhengfu Zai Yazhou Jinrong Weiji Zhong De Biaoxian," 42.
25. Zhang, "Lun Zhongmei Liangguo Zhengfu Zai Yazhou Jinrong Weiji Zhong De Biaoxian," 42–43; Wang, "Dui Dangqian Zhongmei Guanxi Jiqi Fazhan Qianjing De Jidian Kanfa," 9.
26. Avery Goldstein, "The Diplomatic Face of China's Grand Strategy: A Rising Power's Emerging Choice," *China Quarterly* 168 (2001): 852; "Guowuyuan Zongli Zhu Rongji Da Jizhe Wen" (Interview with premier Zhu Rongji), *Renda Gongzuo Tongxun (News Report of Work of the People's Congress of China)*, 1999, 39.
27. In Zhu's opinion, "99 percent of the road toward a WTO deal had been completed." See Pan Rui, "Xi Zhongmei Guanyu Zhongguo Jiaru Shimao Zuzhi Tanpan" (Analyzing Sino-American negotiations regarding China's WTO entry), *Guoji Zhanwang (Global Review)* 9 (1999): 10. See also Joseph Fewsmith, "China and the WTO: The Politics behind the Agreement," *NBR Analysis* 10, no. 5 (1999): 24.
28. William Clinton, "Remarks to the United States Institute of Peace," *Public Papers of the Presidents of the United States* (National Archives and Records Administration, Maryland, January 1–June 30, 1999), 509.
29. Wei Liang, "China's WTO Negotiation Process and Its Implications," *Journal of Contemporary China* 11, no. 33 (2002): 706–18.
30. Zhen Bingxi, "Toushi Zhongguo Jiaru WTO De Jincheng Ji Libi" (Comprehending the process as well as pros and cons of China's entry to WTO), *Shijie Zhishi (World Affairs)* 22 (1999): 26.

31. Ibid., 25. Zhang Jianqing writes that the "objective reality" of China's developing status had been ignored. See Zhang Jianqing, "Guanyu Zhongguo Jiaru Shijie Maoyi Zuzhi De Ruogan Sikao" (Several thoughts on China's entry to WTO), *Shijie Jingji Yu Zhengzhi (World Economics and Politics)* 10 (1999): 64–65.
32. Susan Shirk, *China: Fragile Superpower* (Oxford, UK: Oxford University Press, 2008), 228–31.
33. Fewsmith, "China and the WTO," 30–31.
34. Rana Mitter, "An Uneasy Engagement: Chinese Ideas of Global Order and Justice in Historical Perspective," in *Order and Justice in International Relations*, ed. Rosemary Foot, John Lewis Gaddis, and Andy Hurrell (Oxford, UK: Oxford University Press, 2004), 223.
35. Rosemary Foot, "Chinese Power and the Idea of a Responsible State," *China Journal* 45 (2001): 44.
36. "Jiu Beiyue Daodan Longji Wo Zhunan Dashi Guan Shijian, Tang Jiaxuan Waizhang Zaici Xiang Meifang Tichu Yanzheng Jiaoshe Bing Dijiao Zhengshi Zhaohui" (Concerning the incident on NATO's attack on the PRC Belgrade embassy, foreign minister Tang Jiaxuan again lodges solemn representations with the United States), *Zhonghua Renmin Gonghe Guo Guowu Yuan Gongbao (Gazette of the State Council of the People's Republic of China)* 19 (1999): 800.
37. "Nuhou De Zhongguo" (China roars), *Liaowang (Outlook)* 20 (1999): 12–16.
38. Jiang Zemin, "Zai Huanying Woguo Zhu Nansilafu Lianmeng Gongheguo Gongzuo Renyuan Dahui Shang De Jianghua" (Speech at ceremony to welcome staff of the Chinese embassy in Yugoslavia), *Zhonghua Renmin Gonghe Guo Guowu Yuan Gongbao (Gazette of the State Council of the People's Republic of China)* 19 (1999): 774.
39. Interestingly, in the same speech Tang also claimed that China's "constructive" actions during the Kosovo War—e.g., firm opposition toward foreign intervention—showed it was a responsible great power. Tang's speech at an internal MFA conference can be found at "Zhongguo Buke Qi, Zhongguo Renmin Buke Wu" (China cannot be bullied, Chinese people cannot be humiliated), *Shijie Zhishi (World Affairs)* 11 (1999): 7–8.
40. Gu Ji, "Renquan Weishi De Fan Renlei Baoxing" (The violent, anti-humanity actions of the human rights defender), *Guoji Zhanwang (Global Review)* 9 (1999): 2; Han Zhongkun, "Zhongguo, Bushi Yibajiujiu" (China, this is not 1899), *Renmin Ribao (People's Daily)*, May 12, 1999.
41. For a representative work on the so-called backwardness begets beatings argument, see Fang Ning, "Luohou Aida Suixian" (Backwardness begets beatings: Some thoughts), *Dangjian Yanjiu (Party Construction Research)* 9 (1999): 39–40. See also "Fazhan Jingji, Zengqiang Guoli" (Develop economy, strengthen national power), *Liaowang (Outlook)* 20 (1999): 56–62.
42. Wang Fuchun, "Kesuowo Zhanzheng Yu Zhongguo De Waijiao Zhanlue" (The Kosovo war and China's foreign policy strategy), *Guoji Zhengzhi Yanjiu (International Politics Quarterly)* 4 (1999): 24; Xu Xueyin and Zhu Xian, "Pin Xin Ganshe

Zhuyi" (Assessing new interventionism), *Xiandai Guoji Guanxi (Contemporary International Relations)* 8 (1999): 19–22.

43. Wang, "Kesuowo Zhanzheng Yu Zhongguo De Waijiao Zhanlue."
44. Chu Shulong and Wang Zaibang, "Guanyu Guoji Xingshi He Wo Duiwai Zhanlue Ruogan Zhongda Wenti De Sikao" (Reflections on the international situation and important questions of China's foreign strategy), *Xiandai Guoji Guanxi (Contemporary International Relations)* 8 (1999): 6.
45. Yan Xuetong, "Guoji Huanjing Ji Waijiao Sikao" (International environment and China's foreign relations), *Xiandai Guoji Guanxi (Contemporary International Relations)* 8 (1999): 7–8.
46. Goldstein, "The Diplomatic Face of China's Grand Strategy," 853–54.
47. Tao and He, *Zhongmei Guanxi Shi*, 327–31.
48. Guan Li, *Ruhe Yu Meiguo Gongchu: Lengzhan Hou Zhongguo Duimei Fangzhen Yu Zhongmei Guanxi (How to Coexist with America: China's US Diplomatic Guideline and Sino-American Relations after the Cold War)* (Beijing: Jiuzhou Press, 2010), 162–63.
49. Thomas Lippman, "Bush Makes Clinton's China Policy an Issue," *Washington Post*, August 20, 1999.
50. Condoleezza Rice, "Promoting the National Interest," *Foreign Affairs* 79, no. 1 (January–February 2000): 56.
51. Tao and He, *Zhongmei Guanxi Shi*, 336–37.
52. Guan, *Ruhe Yu Meiguo Gongchu*, 164–65.
53. Joseph Y. S. Cheng and King-lun Ngok, "The 2001 'Spy' Plane Incident Revisited: The Chinese Perspective," *Journal of Chinese Political Science* 9, no. 1 (2004): 63–83; Yu Zhang, "Chinese Nationalism and the 2001 US Spy Plane Incident," *International Studies* 42, no. 1 (2005): 77–85.
54. "Meiguo You Biyao Shenke Fansi" (America needs to have a profound self-review), *Shijie Zhishi (World Affairs)* 9 (2001): 11.
55. Wu Jianxin, "Weihu Guojia Zhuquan He Zunyan, Fandui Baquan, Badao He Baqi: Jianxi Zhongmei Zhuangji Shijian" (Defend national sovereignty and dignity, oppose hegemony, tyranny, and domineering attitude: Analyzing the US-China plane collision incident), *Sixiang Zhengzhi Ke Jiaoxue (The Teaching of Thought and Political Study)* 5 (2001): 56.
56. Shirk, *China*, 236.
57. Ibid.
58. Shirley Kan, "China-US Aircraft Collision Incident of April 2001: Assessments and Policy Implications," *Congressional Research Service Report*, October 10, 2001, 9–22.
59. Steven Mufson and Dana Milbank, "Taiwan to Get Variety of Arms," *Washington Post*, April 24, 2001.
60. Lanxin Xiang, "Washington's Misguided China Policy," *Survival* 43, no. 3 (2001): 8.
61. Other positive early indications include the Bush administration's decision to extend China's normal trading status in June 2001 and a phone conversation between Bush and Jiang on July 5, 2001, which concluded with both leaders affirming the importance of US-China relations. See Guan, *Ruhe Yu Meiguo Gongchu*, 167.

62. Transcript of Secretary of State Colin Powell's Interview on CCTV, July 28, 2001, available at https://2001-2009.state.gov/secretary/former/powell/remarks/2001/4330.htm.
63. James Kelly, "The Future of US-China Relations," *Testimony before the Senate Foreign Relations Committee, Subcommittee on East Asian and Pacific Affairs*, May 1, 2001, https://2001-2009.state.gov/p/eap/rls/rm/2001/2697.htm.
64. Deborah Welch Larson and Alexei Shevchenko describe China as having acted as a "responsible global citizen" in "addressing Washington's new concerns about terrorism." See Deborah Welch Larson and Alexei Shevchenko, "Status Seekers: Chinese and Russian Responses to US Primacy," *International Security* 34, no. 4 (Spring 2010): 85.
65. See Rosemary Foot, "Bush, China, and Human Rights," *Survival* 45, no. 2 (2003): 167–68; Jia Qingguo, "The Impact of 9/11 on Sino-US Relations: A Preliminary Assessment," *International Relations of the Asia-Pacific* 3, no. 2 (2003): 164–65; Tao and He, *Zhongmei Guanxi Shi*, 344.
66. Transcript of Remarks by President Bush and President Jiang Zemin during Press Availability, October 19, 2001, https://2001-2009.state.gov/s/ct/rls/rm/2001/5461.htm.
67. James Kelly, "US-East Asia-Pacific Relations," *Statement before the House International Relations Committee, Subcommittee on East Asia and Pacific*, February 14, 2002, https://2001-2009.state.gov/p/eap/rls/rm/2002/8024.htm.
68. Transcript of President Bush's Meeting with Chinese President Jiang Zemin, February 21, 2002, https://2001-2009.state.gov/p/eap/rls/rm/2002/8564.htm.
69. Francis Markus, "US Warship Docks in China," *BBC News*, November 24, 2002. In September 2003 Powell proclaimed that US-China relations "are the best they have been" since Nixon's 1972 visit. See Colin Powell, Remarks at the Elliot School of International Affairs, September 5, 2003, https://2001-2009.state.gov/secretary/former/powell/remarks/2003/23836.htm.
70. Bush-Jiang Crawford Summit—Transcript of Bush-Jiang Press Conference, October 25, 2002, http://www.presidency.ucsb.edu/ws/index.php?pid=18.
71. Transcript of Remarks at Arrival Ceremony: President Bush and Premier Wen Jiabao, December 9, 2003, https://2001-2009.state.gov/p/eap/rls/rm/2003/27184.htm.
72. In this period Bush met Jiang in October 2001, February 2002, and October 2002; Hu Jintao in May 2002, June 2003, October 2003, and November 2004; and Wen Jiabao in December 2003. On the frequency of Powell and Li's meetings, see Colin Powell, Remarks at Conference on China-US Relations, November 5, 2003, https://2001-2009.state.gov/secretary/former/powell/remarks/2003/25950.htm; and Transcript of Remarks with Chinese Foreign Minister Li Zhaoxing after Their Meeting, September 30, 2004, https://2001-2009.state.gov/secretary/former/powell/remarks/36641.htm. Indeed, the men had established such a strong personal rapport that they eventually stopped using prepared talking points. Li even called Powell at his home and joked that both men might get a "gold medal" for the most number of "phone calls between foreign ministers." See aforementioned citations.
73. Shirk, *China*, 241.

74. See Jia Qingguo, "One Administration, Two Voices: US China Policy during Bush's First Term," *International Relations of the Asia-Pacific* 6, no. 1 (2006): 23–36; Qin Yaqing, "Guannian Tiaozheng Yu Daguo Hezuo" (Adjusting perspective and big-power cooperation), *Xiandai Guoji Guanxi (Contemporary International Relations)* 3 (2002): 8; Jin Canrong, "Yingxiang Zhongguo Guoji Huanjing De Lianglei Xin Yinsu Pinggu" (Assessing the two new factors affecting China's international environment), *Xiandai Guoji Guanxi (Contemporary International Relations)* 11 (2002): 7–8. On Jiang's statement at the 2001 APEC conference, see Transcript of the Remarks by President Bush and President Jiang Zemin during Press Availability. One CCTV news editor, writing in the *International Politics Quarterly,* also claimed that China established the "image" of a responsible great power at the "post 9/11 APEC meeting." See Shen Jianing, "APEC Shanghai Huiyi Yu Zhongguo De Guoji Xingxiang" (Shanghai APEC conference and China's international image), *Guoji Zhengzhi Yanjiu (International Politics Quarterly)* 1 (2002): 115–18.
75. China had, in fact, voted for UNSC Resolution 1441, which stated that Iraq breached its disarmament obligations. Assistant Secretary Kelly also complimented Beijing for critcizing "Baghdad's attempts to play games with the UN Security Council." Nevertheless, it was clear that Chinese thinkers were disturbed by the American preemption doctrine and the ensuing Iraq War. See, for example, Xia Liping, "Yilake Zhanzheng Dui Guoji Zhanlue Geju Yanbian Ji Woguo Anquan Huanjing De Yingxiang" (The impact of the Iraq war on international strategic structural development and China's security environment), *Lilun Cankao (Theoretical Reference)* 1 (2004): 27–29; Zhang Shengjun, "Quanqiu Jiegou Chongtu Yu Meiguo Baquan De Hefa Xing Weiji" (Global structural conflict and the legitimacy crisis of American hegemony), *Meiguo Yanjiu (American Studies)* 3 (2003): 30–41. On American appreciation of China's response, see James Kelly, "US Policy on China and North Korea," Remarks to the World Affairs Council, January 30, 2003, https://2001-2009.state.gov/p/eap/rls/rm/2003/17164.htm.
76. See the section on American hegemony in *Zhongguo Xuezhe Kan Shijie—Guoji Zhixu Juan (Chinese Scholars View the World—Volume on International Order),* ed. Wang Jisi and Qin Yaqing (Beijing: Xin Shijie Chubanshe, 2007), 89–157. See also Liu Jinzhi, "Shiping Xiao Bushi De Diguo Waijiao" (Appraising junior Bush's diplomacy of imperialism), *Guoji Zhengzhi Yanjiu (International Studies Quarterly)* 4 (2004): 83–92.
77. Mohan Malik, *Dragon on Terrorism: Assessing China's Tactical Gains and Strategic Losses Post-September 11* (Carlisle, PA: Strategic Studies Institute, 2002), 28–31.
78. Jiang Zemin, "Yingzao Youli Zhanlue Taishi, Zengqiang Guojia Zhanlue Nengli" (Create a favorable strategic situation, enhance national strategic capability), in *Jiang Zemin Wenxuan Disanjuan (Selected Works of Jiang Zemin)*, vol. 3 (Beijing: Renmin Chubanshe, 2006), 352–65. Following the Iraq War one analyst described the American military as "unbeatable under the heavens." See Guo Xuetang, "Baquan Zhouqi Lun De Pinkun—Jianxi Meiguo Baquan Shifou Zouxiang Shuailuo" (Poverty of the theory of hegemonic cycle—An analysis of whether

American hegemony is going downhill), *Meiguo Yanjiu (American Studies)* 3 (2003): 42–51.

79. See, for example, Pan Zhongqi, "Zhongmei Guanxi De Zhanlue Jichu: Guoqu, Xianzai Yu Weilai" (The strategic foundations of US-China relations: Past, present, and future), *Guoji Guancha (International Review)* 3 (2002): 33–37; Ni Shixiong and Zhuang Jianzhong, "Bushi Zhengfu Dui Hua Xin Zhanlue Yu Zhongguo Duimei Xin Zhanlue Chutan" (Preliminary inquiry of the Bush government's new China strategy and China's new America policy), *Meiguo Wenti Yanjiu (Fudan American Review)* (2002): 19–32.
80. Richard Haass, "China and the Future of US-Sino Relations," Remarks to the National Committee on US-China Relations, December 5, 2002, https://2001-2009.state.gov/s/p/rem/15687.htm.
81. For more on the notion of a liberal solidarist society of states, see Andrew Hurrell, *On Global Order: Power, Values, and the Constitution of International Society* (Oxford, UK: Oxford University Press, 2007), chap. 1.
82. Pang Zhongying, "'Shijie Daguo' Yu 'Zhengchang Guojia': Lun 'Zhengchang Guojia' Fanshi Yu Guojia De Shijie Guan Zhongsu" ("Global great power" and "normal country": Discussing the model of the "normal country" and the remolding of the national worldview), *Shijie Jingji Yu Zhengzhi (World Economics and Politics)* 11 (2002): 12–16.
83. Ye Zicheng and Li Ying, "Goujian Daguo Waijiao Zhihun: Zhengchangxin, Zixinxin, Leguanxin" (Constructing the soul of a great power's diplomacy: Normalcy, self-confidence, optimism), *Shijie Jingji Pinglun (International Economic Review)* 3 (2001): 22–23.
84. Men Honghua and Huang Haili, "Yingdui Guojia Shibai De Bujiu Cuoshi: Jianlun Zhongmei Anquan Hezuo De Zhanlue Xing" (Remedial measures for failed states: A strategic dimension of Sino-American security cooperation), *Meiguo Yanjiu (American Studies)* 1 (2004): 26–27.
85. Yan comes to a comparable conclusion, stating: "The norm of international responsibility is defined by the strong." See Yan Xuetong, "The Rise of China in Chinese Eyes," *Journal of Contemporary China* 10, no. 26 (2001): 37.
86. Qu Congwen, "Fuzeren De Daguo Guan" (The concept of the responsible great power), *Shijie Jingji Yu Zhengzhi (World Economics and Politics)* 10 (2002): 72–77.
87. Xiao Huanrong, "Zhongguo De Daguo Zeren Yu Diqu Zhuyi Zhanlue" (China's great-power responsibility and the strategy of regionalism), *Shijie Jingji Yu Zhengzhi (World Economics and Politics)* 1 (2003): 48–51.
88. Men and Huang, "Yingdui Guojia Shibai De Bujiu Cuoshi," 27.
89. Wang Yizhou, "Sanda Xuqiu: Fazhan, Zhuquan Yu Zeren" (Three great requirements: Development, sovereignty, and responsibility), *Shijie Zhishi (World Affairs)* 5 (2000): 9–10. A longer version of this article can be found at Wang Yizhou, "Mianxiang 21 Shiji De Zhongguo Waijiao: Sanzhong Xuqiu De Xunqiu Jiqi Pingheng" (Toward China's twenty-first-century diplomacy: Seeking and balancing three kinds of requirements), *Zhanlue Yu Guanli (Strategy and Management)* 6 (1999): 18–26.

90. Shen Jiru, "Fuzeren Daguo De Gongmin Xintai" (The national mentality of a responsible great power), *Zhanwang (Outlook Weekly)* 2 (2004): 1.
91. See, for example, Wang Jian, "Zhongdong Fankong Xingshi Ji Zhongguo De Zuoyong" (The anti-terrorism situation in the Middle East and China's role), *Shijie Jingji Yanjiu (World Economy Research)* 12 (2004): 69–73; Song Hong, "Fuzeren De Fazhan Zhong Daguo: Woguo Zai Shijie Maoyi Zuzhi Zhong De Diwei He Zuoyong" (The responsible developing power: Our nation's position and role in the world trade organization), *Shijie Jingji Yu Zhengzhi (World Economics and Politics)* 12 (2002): 28–33.
92. Although the ideas associated with the new security concept first appeared around 1996, I agree with Bates Gill that the concept attained formal policy status with its inclusion in the 1998 white paper. See Bates Gill, *Rising Star: China's New Security Diplomacy* (Washington, DC: Brookings Institution Press, 2007), 4–7.
93. State Council Information Office, "Zhongguo De Guofang Baipi Shu" (White paper on China's national defense) (1998), 840–43; Jianwei Wang, "China's Multilateral Diplomacy in the New Millennium," in *China Rising: Power and Motivation in Chinese Foreign Policy,* ed. Yong Deng and Fei-ling Wang (Lanham, MD: Rowman & Littlefield, 2005), 161–62.
94. "Zhongguo De Guofang Baipi Shu," 839.
95. Qin Yaqing, "Guojia Shenfen, Zhanlue Wenhua He Anquan Liyi: Guanyu Zhongguo Yu Guoji Shehui Guanxi De Sange Jiashe" (National status, strategic culture, and security interests: Three hypotheses on China's relations with international society), *Shijie Jingji Yu Zhengzhi (World Economics and Politics)* 1 (2003): 10.
96. Young Nam Cho and Jong Ho Jeong, "China's Soft Power: Discussions, Resources, and Prospects," *Asian Survey* 48, no. 3 (2008): 453–72; Li Mingjiang, "China Debates Soft Power," *Chinese Journal of International Politics* 2, no. 2 (2008): 287–308.
97. For some notable examples of Chinese writings on soft power between 1997 and 2004, see Pang Zhongying, "Guoji Guanxi Zhong De Ruan Liliang Ji Qita" (Soft strength and others in international relations), *Zhanlue Yu Guanli (Strategy and Management)* 2 (1997): 49–51; Zhang Ji and Sang Hong, "Wenhua: Guoji Zhengzhi Zhong De 'Ruan Quanli'" (Culture: "Soft power" in international politics), *Shehui Zhuyi Yanjiu (Socialism Studies)* 3 (1999): 38–41; Zhu Majie, "Xin Shiji Guoji Guanxi Zhong De Ruan Guoli Jingzheng" (Competition for soft power in international relations in the new century), *Guoji Zhanwang (Global Review)* 2 (2001): 7–11.
98. Yuan Shan, "Guan Yu 'Beijing Gongshi' Yanjiu De Ruogan Wenti" (Concerning the several problems of research on the "Beijing consensus"), *Dangdai Shijie Yu Shehui Zhuyi (Contemporary World and Socialism)* 5 (2004): 20.
99. Fu Xin, "Quanqiuhua Shidai De Guojia Xingxiang: Jiandui Zhongguo Mouqiu Heping Fazhan De Sikao" (A nation's image in the age of globalization: Reflecting on China's pursuit of peaceful development), *Guoji Wenti Yanjiu (International Studies)* 4 (2004): 17.
100. Bonnie S. Glaser and Evan S. Medeiros, "The Changing Ecology of Foreign Policy-Making in China: The Ascension and Demise of the Theory of 'Peaceful Rise,'" *China Quarterly* 190 (2007): 291–310.

101. Zheng Bijian, "Zhongguo Heping Jueqi Xin Daolu He Yazhou De Weilai" (China's new path of peaceful rise and Asia's future), Xinhua, November 24, 2003; Study Times' Interview with Zheng Bijian, "Heping Jueqi: Zhongguo Tese Shehui Zhuyi De Yige Ji Zhongyao De 'Zhongguo Tese'" (Peaceful rise: The most important "Chinese characteristic" in Socialism with Chinese characteristics), *Xue Lilun (Theory Research)* 8 (2004): 4–6.
102. Glaser and Medeiros, "Changing Ecology of Foreign Policy-Making," 301–6.
103. Zheng, "Zhongguo Heping Jueqi Xin Daolu He Yazhou De Weilai."
104. This claim was made by Long Yongtu, a senior Chinese diplomat and secretary-general of the Boao Forum. See "Long Yongtu Shuo: Zhongguo Jiang Chengwei Buchengba, Heping, Fuzeren De Daguo" (Long Yongtu says: China will become a nonhegemonic, peaceful, and responsible great power), *Shenzhou (Divineland)* 6 (2004): 13.
105. In particular, see the articles by Song Xinning, Liu Xige, and Yang Yi in *Jiaoxue Yu Yanjiu (Teaching and Research)* 4 (2004).
106. Qin Yaqing, "Shijie Geju Yu Zhongguo De Heping Jueqi" (Global structure and China's peaceful rise), *Dangjian (Party Construction)* 5 (2004): 12.
107. Shirk, *China*, 123–27.
108. Powell, Remarks at Conference on China-US Relations.
109. See, for example, Guan, *Ruhe Yu Meiguo Gongchu*, 187.
110. Shirk, *China*, 126.
111. Gill, *Rising Star*, 74–99; Gerald Chan, *China's Compliance in Global Affairs: Trade, Arms Control, Environmental Protection, Human Rights* (Singapore: World Scientific, 2006), 111–40.
112. Paula DeSutter, "China's Record of Proliferation Activities," Testimony before the US-China Commission, July 24, 2003, https://2001-2009.state.gov/t/vci/rls/rm/24518.htm.
113. Jin Canrong, *Daguo De Zeren (Big Power's Responsibility)* (Beijing: Zhongguo Renmin Daxue Chubanshe, 2011), 38–46.
114. Tang Yongsheng, "Zhongguo Yu Lianheguo Weihe Xingdong" (China and United Nations peacekeeping operations), *Shijie Jingji Yu Zhengzhi (World Economics and Politics)* 9 (2002): 42.
115. Chien-peng Chung, "The Shanghai Cooperation Organization: China's Changing Influence in Central Asia," *China Quarterly* 180 (2004): 989–1009.
116. Gill, *Rising Star*, 29–34; Rosemary Foot, "China in the ASEAN Regional Forum: Organization Processes and Domestic Modes of Thought," *Asian Survey* 38, no. 5 (1998): 425–40.
117. Shambaugh, "China Engages Asia," 64–99.
118. Ibid.
119. Alan Larson, "China's Role in the World Economic System," Remarks to the Students and Faculty of the University of International Business and Economics at Beijing, November 5, 2003, https://2001-2009.state.gov/e/rm/2003/27026.htm; Rosemary Foot, "Chinese Strategies in a US-Hegemonic Global Order: Accommodating and Hedging," *International Affairs* 82, no. 1 (2006): 87.

120. Larson, "China's Role in the World Economic System"; Randall Schriver, "China and the WTO: Compliance and Monitoring," Testimony before the US-China Economic and Security Commission, February 5, 2004, https://2001-2009.state.gov/p/eap/rls/rm/2004/28957.htm.
121. Chan, *China's Compliance in Global Affairs*, 173–202; Merle Goldman, *From Comrade to Citizen: The Struggle for Political Rights in China* (Cambridge, MA: Harvard University Press, 2005), 1.
122. Dingding Chen, "Explaining China's Changing Discourse on Human Rights, 1978–2004," *Asian Perspective* 29, no. 3 (2005): 156.
123. I prefer not to use the phrase "international" expectations because, as Alastair Iain Johnston has pointed out, China has consistently been able to garner support at the United Nations to vote down motions critical of its human rights record. See Alastair Iain Johnston, "Is China a Status Quo Power?," *International Security* 27, no. 4 (2003): 20; Andrew Nathan, "Human Rights in Chinese Foreign Policy," *China Quarterly* 139 (1994): 622–43.
124. Chen, "Explaining China's Changing Discourse," 155–82.
125. See, for example, Lorne Craner, "Prospects on Human Rights and Democracy in China," *Statement before the East Asian and Pacific Affairs Subcommittee, Senate Foreign Relations Committee*, April 22, 2004, https://2001-2009.state.gov/g/drl/rls/rm/31721.htm.
126. Xiao Cong, "Zhongguo Shi Fuzeren De Daguo" (China is a responsible great power), *Shishi Baogao Zhongxue Shengban (Current Affairs High School Edition)* 2 (2002): 31.
127. Ann Kent, *Beyond Compliance: China, International Organizations and Global Security* (Stanford, CA: Stanford University Press, 2007), 167–72; Chan, *China's Compliance in Global Affairs*, 143–71.
128. Minxin Pei, "China's Governance Crisis," *Foreign Affairs* 81, no. 5 (September–October 2002): 104–5.
129. Kent, *Beyond Compliance*, 147.
130. Amitav Acharya, *Whose Ideas Matter? Agency and Power in Asian Regionalism* (Ithaca, NY: Cornell University Press, 2009).

4

AMERICA'S "RESPONSIBLE STAKEHOLDER" CALL AND THE SHARPENING OF DEBATE, 2005 TO 2012

Chapter 3 explored the trajectory of the Chinese RGP self-conception in the period 1997–2004. This chapter continues the empirical analysis, tracing the RGP identity's development from 2005 to 2012; the cutoff point of 2012 reflects the end of the Hu Jintao era in Chinese political history. The chapter unfolds with an assessment of the external and internal narratives that had an impact on Chinese deliberations of their country's big-power role and responsibilities. Next it examines how developments during the second term of the Bush administration contributed to a strengthening of Chinese great-power perceptions. The chapter moves on to discuss a major global event, the 2008–2009 financial crisis, and considers its implications for the RGP identity. It then assesses the trajectory of the RGP identity against the backdrop of growing Chinese diplomatic assertiveness and a more contentious Sino-American relationship from around 2010. In the penultimate section I analyze the key schools of thought in the Chinese RGP debate—the internationalist, developmental, and skeptics' positions—that had become more distinct over the 2005–2012 period. The last section closes with a discussion of the chapter's findings.

The Responsible Stakeholder

The introduction of the "responsible-stakeholder" concept by US deputy secretary of state Robert Zoellick in September 2005 marked a significant point in the evolving American rhetoric on China. Addressing the National Committee on US-China Relations, Zoellick spoke of the need for China to be "more than just a member" of the international system—it also needed to be a responsible stakeholder. His contention was that China had been a prime beneficiary of the extant international system and thus had an obligation to bolster and sustain the system that "enabled" its rise. This called for China to take greater ownership over global challenges such as nuclear proliferation, environmental protection, and international financial stability, and to work with the United States in the management of these issues. This sense of shared global responsibility should be based on more than just common interests between the two powers, Zoellick suggested. Reiterating an earlier American call, he urged both countries to define their relationship on the basis of "what both are for," building a sense of shared purpose and values.[1]

By the end of 2005 the concept of the responsible stakeholder had become even more prominent in US policy discourse, with Zoellick calling it "a strategic framework" to guide Washington's approach to Beijing.[2] The call for China to act as a responsible stakeholder was echoed by other senior officials of the Bush administration. In a speech in Beijing in 2006 Treasury Secretary Henry Paulson emphasized that the US would "welcome China's role as a responsible stakeholder in international organizations."[3] Similarly, Deputy Assistant Secretary for East Asian and Pacific Affairs Thomas Christensen, speaking to the US-China Economic and Security Review (ESR) Commission in 2006, stressed that the "crux" of American policy toward China was to "channel" the latter down the path of being a responsible global stakeholder.[4] This strategy also received support from the US military, with its 2006 Quadrennial Defense Review affirming the importance of getting China to act as a responsible stakeholder.[5] In 2007 Christensen provided an update to the ESR Commission, underlining that China had yet to become the "truly" responsible stakeholder envisioned by Zoellick and that the US would continue its policy of "encouraging" the PRC to evolve as one.[6]

The usage of the vocabulary of stakeholder did not change the fact that the core message from Washington remained the same: China's international responsibilities should match its burgeoning power. The concept, however, marked a different approach from earlier American rhetoric in that it sought to speak more directly to Chinese interests. In characterizing China's role as a stakeholder of the international system, the suggestion is that it is in Beijing's interests to maintain or improve this system. There were certainly indications that many in China interpreted this concept from the vantage point of interests.

For one, the dominant Chinese transliteration for the term "stakeholder" was *liyi xiangguan zhe*, which literally means "actors with related interests."[7] Yet this was a balance of interests skewed in favor of the United States, claimed some Chinese analysts. According to Lin Fengchun, the stakeholder concept implies the leveraging of China's strength to bolster the US's "hegemonic" position in international society.[8] China Institutes of Contemporary International Relations assistant president Yuan Peng expresses a similar outlook, opining that the "strategic" obligations expected of China have a "unilateral American flavor."[9] Nevertheless, most Chinese analysts did not seem too critical of the responsible-stakeholder concept. While some wondered if the US could really relinquish its "market share" in world politics and treat China as an equal partner, the primary sentiments were that the concept validated the PRC's growing international status and position, implied American acceptance of China's inevitable rise, was a more positive US engagement approach, and portended a shift from the "tough" China threat discourse toward the more "reasonable and moderate" China responsibility theory.[10]

The stakeholder concept had the effect of drawing further global attention to the question of China's international obligations, squaring with the increasing willingness of other actors outside Washington to assess their relationships with Beijing in similar terms. Notably, in 2006 the European Union published the policy paper "EU-China: Closer Partners, Growing Responsibilities," which called for China to assume a "more active and responsible international role" in its growing partnership with the union. The paper also argued that China is "a major beneficiary of the international trading system" and should therefore undertake "responsibility commensurate with those benefits."

But perhaps the more telling impact of the stakeholder idea came at the domestic level. The concept added new impetus to continuing Chinese identity discourses about China's great-power role and responsibilities, with many of the post-2005 discussions citing Zoellick's seminal speech as a reference point.[11] At a later point of this chapter those discussions will be explored in greater detail.

Harmonious World and the Chinese Development Model

Domestic conversations on the responsible-stakeholder framework during this period were paralleled by the emergence of two other related policy discourses. The first related to the "harmonious world" idea (*hexie shijie*), which was initially articulated by Hu Jintao at the Asian-African Summit in 2005 and further outlined during Hu's speech at the sixtieth anniversary of the UN that year.[12] Its status as a diplomatic guideline was further consolidated when it was referenced in the 2005 white paper "China's Peaceful Development Path," the 2006 *Government Work Report*, the 2006 Central Committee Foreign Affairs Work Conference, and *Hu's Report to the Seventeenth CCP Congress*.[13]

As the foreign policy counterpart to the policy framework of "harmonious society," the harmonious world idea represented both a rhetorical refurbishment of the Chinese diplomatic outlook and an extension of the peaceful-rise thesis.[14] Among other things, the concept called for amity and equality among nations, greater international cooperation and inclusiveness, the pursuit of common security and development, a more "democratic" international society, and the accommodation of the world's cultural and civilizational diversity.[15] Qualitatively these did not diverge too much from ideas advocated in the Five Principles of Peaceful Coexistence or the new security concept, while the advocacy for greater pluralism in international society was not new and had been previously espoused by Jiang Zemin.[16] What was relatively different, however, were: (i) its use of the Confucian philosophy of *he* (harmony) to express China's vision of international order; and (ii) the attempt to synchronize foreign policy with domestic policy at the strategic conceptual level.[17]

Chinese analysts were quick to laud the putative strengths of the harmonious world concept. It was suggested that the conception was the externalization of Chinese traditional virtues, marking a uniquely Chinese contribution to global normative development. Apparently, it correctly grasped "the pulse of the times" and was hence more effective than the West's "confrontational" approach in addressing the contradictions of a multicultural, multicivilizational world; constituted a more proactive international approach that met both internal and external needs; represented a road map toward a more "just and reasonable" global order; and conveyed China's big-power outlook and commitment to peaceful development.[18] It was claimed that Deng's 1993 "puzzle" on the kind of world that should be ushered in during the twenty-first century had finally been answered.[19] Unsurprisingly, connections were made between the harmonious world idea and the declared RGP identity. According to a number of Chinese scholars, the advocacy of a harmonious world signals China's "will and ambition" to shoulder international responsibilities, keeping with its "promise" to "uphold global peace and development as a responsible great power."[20] It is Beijing's "reply" to the burgeoning expectations of its RGP role in international society, notes Zhao Lei, an analyst at the Central Party School.[21] It is also one that demonstrates the "self-discipline" of a responsible power, Qin Yaqing suggests, alluding to the apparent restraint and moderation of the harmonious world idea.[22]

The second related policy discourse that emerged around this time centered on the Chinese politico-economic model. Like discussions on the responsible-stakeholder concept, Chinese debates in this area arose as a response to an external idea. This catalyst was Joshua Cooper Ramos's provocative 2004 writings on the Chinese development model. Labeling this paradigm the "Beijing Consensus," Ramos argues that China's approach presents a competitive and viable alternative to the more conventional American development model, the "Washington Consensus." As opposed to the Washington Consensus's prescription of free-market economics with democratic governance, the Beijing Consensus speaks of a seemingly efficacious development path that combines state capitalism with political autocracy. To be sure, Ramos did not explicitly express the Beijing Consensus in such a way, preferring instead to explicate what he notes as three defining features of the Chinese approach: the turn to innovation to complement reform; a more holistic sense of development that looks beyond the traditional GDP per-capita measure and toward aspects such as equality and sustainability; and an emphasis on developmental self-autonomy.[23]

Ramos's arguments stirred energetic reactions in China, where efforts were made to reinterpret the notion of the Beijing Consensus (*Beijing Gongshi*) or China model (*Zhongguo Moshi*).[24] Political scientist Yu Keping, for example, characterized the Beijing Consensus as essentially a "strategic choice" to effect modernization under globalization.[25] For others it was about the "coordination and balance between reform, development, and stability," "reform incrementalism," or the synthesis of "socialist democracy and socialist market economy." Regardless of the differing understandings, many Chinese commentators agreed that China's development strategies, taken together, can be regarded as a particular brand of political and economic model.[26]

That said, initial Chinese assessments about this model's implications or impact were mixed. One view was that while the China model had been an unqualified economic success, it seemed to generate or exacerbate problems such as environmental pollution, rising income gap, social inequities, market deficiencies, and corruption; hence, the ideal China model should be a "low-cost" development path. Some were also concerned that the narrative of a China model cast an unnecessary spotlight on the country's political, human rights, and environmental protection record and created the perception that the PRC represents an ideological challenge to the United States and the West, adding grist to the "China threat" mill. Questions were also raised about the fact that the China model encompassed only a relatively short history of success, had yet to achieve full recognition in international society, and was still arguably a "work in progression."[27]

Those more optimistic, on the other hand, believed that talk of the China model indicated the improvement of China's soft power. To the extent that the model had replicable elements, it was perceived that China's development experience appealed to and held valuable lessons for other developing countries and emerging powers. Optimists pointed out how in the wake of the Washington Consensus's "experimentation" failures in Latin America and elsewhere, leaders in Africa, India, and Russia had started to look toward Beijing for development insights and as a model to "emulate."[28] The China model, Tao Wenzhao argues, broke the "myth" that there was only one right way of modernization (i.e., the Washington Consensus).[29] But its greatest impact, in the view of several Chinese commentators, was its elevation of 70 percent of the world's poor (who reside in China) out of absolute destitution, contributing greatly to the improvement of the human condition. These assessments stopped short of making direct reference to the RGP identity but maintained that the China model was a positive force for humanity.[30] Finally, there was the belief among some that China's global status had been raised. That the PRC's development system was now looked on as a potential alternative to the more established American model implied the perspicacity of Chinese strategic choices and affirmed China's rising status as a political power and potential peer of the US. Thus, as one scholar puts it, the China model is also a "model of a great power's rise."[31]

Heightening Great Power Perceptions

Chinese scholars' attention to their nation's international status should not be surprising. As previous chapters have shown, elites in China have always been concerned about perceptions—both internal and external—of their nation's position and rank in international society. Indeed, moving beyond the traditional measurement of comprehensive national power, beginning in 2003 the government think tank Shanghai Academy of Social Sciences started publishing the *China's International Status Report* (*Guoji Diwei Baogao*), which qualitatively tracked the annual status gains and losses of the PRC.[32]

By the end of 2008 there seemed to be a stronger sense within China that its global status had risen. "The year 2008," *China's International Status Report* asserted, "was the year the PRC finally grew up [*cheng ren*] . . . it was transforming from a regional big power to an emerging world power."[33] Insofar as the developing state identity continued to be perpetuated, such perceptions could be attributed to a number of material developments: among others, the continuing robustness and performance of the Chinese economy; the expanding Chinese economic presence in Latin America and Africa; the successful conduct of China's first anti-satellite weapons test; the launch of the Shenzhou-7 mission, which executed China's first spacewalk; and, most notably, the triumphant hosting of the 2008 Olympic Games.[34] These factors and more helped boost national pride and strengthened China's great-power identity.

The role of the United States in reinforcing Chinese status perceptions was significant as well. The second half of the Bush administration saw greater institutionalization and levels of interaction between the Chinese and American governments, spanning more than fifty bilateral dialogues, meetings, and working groups. These included but were not limited to: (i) the Senior Dialogues, the leading regular US-China summit on political and security affairs and its economic counterpart, the Strategic Economic Dialogue; (ii) the regular subdialogues on regional issues between the US assistant secretaries of state and China's vice-foreign ministers; (iii) the Energy Policy Dialogues between, primarily, the US Department of Energy and China's National Development and Reform Commission; (iv) the Global Issues Forum, co-led by the US Department of State and the Chinese Ministry of Foreign Affairs and aimed at strengthening US-China cooperation on common transnational concerns; (v) the bilateral discussions on trade and commerce issues via the Joint Commission on Commerce and Trade; and (vi) the bilateral military dialogues that encompassed the Defense Policy Coordination Talks, the Defense Consultative Talks, and the Military Maritime Consultative Agreement Meetings.[35] In Washington's view such "real" dialogues extended beyond immediate bilateral concerns and increasingly focused on the coordination of responses between the US and China on a range of regional and global issues.[36] This unprecedented level of diplomatic engagement between the two powers probably fell short of Hedley Bull's idea of a great-power concert, but it nonetheless fostered the impression of a global order increasingly shaped or contested in the capitals of the US and China (typified by talk of the so-called Group of 2 or "Chimerica").[37] In Beijing many viewed these dialogues, especially the Senior Dialogue and the Strategic Economic Dialogue, as suggesting that the prevailing hegemon, the US, was willing to engage a rising China on an equal basis (*ping tai*), which helped reinforce Chinese estimations of their nation's big-power status.[38] Moreover, these meetings and exchanges frequently featured remarks by senior US officials that affirmed or implied China's great-power status. In his closing address to the second Senior Dialogue, for instance, Robert Zoellick referred to China as "a major global player."[39] Likewise, during a preparatory visit to China for the 2007 Strategic Economic Dialogue, Henry Paulson stated, "China is already a global economic leader and deserves to be recognized as a leader."[40]

As with earlier American rhetoric and the stakeholder language, such references were made with more than just recognition of China's growing global influence in mind; equally they related to expectations for Beijing to use its influence in a "responsible" way. Interestingly, Chinese behaviors on a number of global issues between 2005 and the end of 2008 suggest some willingness to address these expectations. Beijing continued to play a crucial role in hosting the Six-Party Talks by helping broker a 2005 statement that committed Pyongyang to renounce its nuclear program. When this commitment was contravened by North Korea's subsequent missile and nuclear tests, China supported international measures to sanction its traditional ally. In 2007 Pyongyang disabled its nuclear reactors at Yongbyon, a development that appeared to have stemmed from direct Chinese pressure. On the Iran nuclear issue there was some alignment between Beijing's actions and its stated aim of preventing Iranian nuclear weapons capability. While its economic and energy links with Tehran were perceived as undermining efforts to check Iranian nuclear ambitions, China voted in favor of a number of UN Security Council resolutions that sanctioned Iran for its alleged nuclear transgressions (in particular, resolutions 1737, 1747, and 1803). The less reluctant attitude toward the use of sanctions squared with Beijing's increasing willingness to bend its traditional position on noninterference in the internal affairs of other states. Thus, from an initial hands-off approach to the Darfur human rights crisis in Sudan, Beijing moved to endorsing the UN three-phase plan for stabilizing the region, eventually getting its officials (including the personal involvement of Hu) to persuade Khartoum to accept the establishment of a joint UN–African Union peacekeeping force. This more flexible approach toward the noninterference principle was also evident when, in a first for the Chinese military, the PLA sent warships to the Gulf of Aden to help combat piracy off the Somalian coast in 2008. Signally, this effort was met with UN Security Council approval—with China's support—for international policing forces to pursue pirates into Somalian maritime territory.[41]

Of course, Washington's expectations of Beijing's big-power conduct went well beyond these, and it would have liked China to do more. But US officials also recognized that some of Beijing's actions during this time were unprecedented and suggested a degree of progression toward meeting US hopes of a more "responsible" China. As Christensen later wrote in *Foreign Affairs*, Beijing had "responded impressively, although only partially" to the Bush administration's responsible-stakeholder call.[42] A similar assessment was put forward by Deputy Secretary of State John Negroponte. In an update to the Senate Foreign Relations Committee in 2008, Negroponte testified that China's traditional observance of the noninterference principle was "giving way to diplomatic interventions that highlight [its] stated ambition to be seen as a responsible major power."[43]

The Global Financial Crisis and Chinese Responses

That said, the main area in which Washington wanted greater cooperation from Beijing by late 2008 was support in addressing the global financial crisis (GFC). The financial tsunami that had originated in the US was now threatening to engulf the global economy and China. With its substantial US Treasury holdings and the world's largest foreign exchange reserves of around US$1.9 trillion, Beijing was seen as a potentially vital partner for dealing with the crisis. On September 21, 2008, President Bush personally called Hu to express his hope that both countries worked together to shore up international financial stability.[44] Similar sentiments were relayed by Paulson to Vice-Premier Wang Qishan, the Chinese leader in charge of Beijing's financial crisis committee.[45] When the Obama administration succeeded the Bush government in early 2009, it too lost no time in looking for Chinese cooperation. New secretary of state Hillary Clinton was sent to visit China (and three other Asian nations) on her first official trip abroad, marking a departure from diplomatic tradition. Such was the importance attached to Chinese support vis-à-vis the crisis that the Obama administration initially appeared willing to downplay the traditional US concern over human rights in China: while en route to Beijing, Clinton underlined that human rights issues should not "interfere" with efforts to address the GFC.[46]

The United States was not alone in looking to Beijing for support in the crisis. In Europe many saw China as a potential "white knight" that could help bail out stricken economies.[47] These international expectations prompted further assertion of the RGP identity in Beijing, as Chinese leaders conveyed assurances that the country would act "responsibly" over the GFC. "As a responsible country," Vice-Premier Wang told visiting former German chancellor Gerhard Schroeder, China would "always emphasize communication and cooperation with the world's nations to jointly uphold international financial and economic stability."[48] Premier Wen Jiabao made a similar pledge in October 2008, telling British prime minister Gordon Brown that "China would continue to adopt a responsible attitude in its active efforts" to deal with the crisis.[49]

Chinese pledges, nevertheless, came with a catch: to the extent that Beijing would work together with other nations in responding to the crisis, its priority and primary duty would be to ensure the continued stability of its domestic economy. As the Chinese leadership saw it, China's "greatest contribution" to the world would be to first manage its own economic affairs well.[50] A *China Daily* editorial captured this perspective trenchantly:

> It is only fair to say China, by saving itself, is contributing to the world at large. If this does not sound convincing, just imagine what would follow if the Chinese economic locomotive loses steam.[51]

Beijing certainly had reasons to fear an economic slowdown in China. Not only could this lead to attendant problems such as social unrest and popular discontent; an enduring downturn could well call into question the legitimacy of a CCP regime that had increasingly rested on ensuring high economic growth.[52] Beijing's answer was to implement a series of expansionary fiscal policies designed to boost domestic spending and stimulate the Chinese economy. These included two massive stimulus programs with a combined worth of ¥4.23 trillion to boost infrastructure spending and prop up key industrial sectors, an ¥850 billion spending plan to expand basic health care services and coverage, a housing appliance subsidy plan for all rural residents to encourage consumption spending, and employment measures worth ¥42 billion to help create new urban jobs.[53]

China's preference to prioritize its resources for domestic needs corresponded with its general reluctance to commit significantly more capital to buy US and European debt. Such a move would have helped bolster the US and European economies, and Beijing keenly understood that the health of these economies was inextricably linked to its own. However, Chinese leaders were hesitant to raise their country's holdings of US and European assets for a number of reasons. For one, the safety and prospects of these assets in a bearish economic climate were a major concern; already the depreciation of China's US holdings had sufficiently concerned Wen that he openly commented that he was "a little worried."[54] There were also perceived political and strategic risks. Within China such investments would have created the perception that Beijing was bailing out rich foreigners at the expense of its citizens, an impression not helped by the fact that a considerable number of Chinese people were still living in poverty and that many Chinese saw the financial crisis as a consequence of Western fiscal ill-discipline. Outside of China, investments could have accentuated anxieties that Beijing might one day use its accumulation of American and European financial assets as a means by which to coerce or pressure the US and its allies.[55]

For these reasons China's external response to the crisis was less a debt bailout of distressed economies and more a broad effort to stimulate global growth through monetary contributions to international bodies, multilateral economic diplomacy, and the reduction of trade barriers. It committed US$40 billion to the IMF to reinforce its crisis response capacity. It established a US$10 billion investment cooperation fund with ASEAN and pledged credit support of up to US$15 billion to the association's member states. It promised preferential credit of US$10 billion to the Shanghai Cooperation Organization and Africa, where, in the latter's case, the least-developed states were additionally granted debt waivers and tax relief for 95 percent of their imports to China.[56] But perhaps the most visible aspect of its external response was its involvement in the G20 Forum, the economic bloc now seen as the leading institution to coordinate a global response to the crisis. From late 2008 to 2009, the crisis's most severe period, China participated in all three G20 leaders' summits and, among other things, pledged to improve macroeconomic policy coordination with other G20 states, avowed to oppose domestic economic protectionism, and generally agreed to expand its domestic consumption to help rebalance the global economy. Yet this involvement also suggested a sense of dissatisfaction toward the extant global financial architecture. The view from Beijing was that the crisis had been caused in part by deficiencies in the international financial system. It argued, along with others in the G20, that the system should be reformed to encompass new "widely accepted [financial] standards and norms" and allow developing economies a bigger role and "say" (*huayu quan*) in international financial bodies such as the IMF and World Bank.[57] Influential voices in China were also heard calling for "fairer" alternatives to the US dollar as the international reserve currency.[58]

The call for a more representative, less US-centric international financial system was reflective of perceptions in China that the crisis had "adjusted" the international status quo and that a realignment of the global order was under way. Most Chinese analysts believed that the PRC's international position had clearly been raised relative to others, especially in relation to the United States. That the US and Europe were seemingly unable to come up with concrete measures to address their economic problems, while China's economy performed better than most during this period, were two reasons often cited for this positional improvement. "Others sank while we floated up," said Tsinghua University scholar Yan Xuetong.[59] Chinese analysts did not believe, however, that the fundamental structure of "one superpower, many great powers" had been changed: the US remained the sole global hegemon even if its power gap vis-à-vis China and other emerging powers had become smaller and less pronounced.[60] Still, many analysts agreed that the crisis had been a "*jiyu*" (accidental opportunity) for China in a number of ways. Along with the amelioration of its global position, it was perceived that the crisis had resulted in: (i) the extension of China's big-power influence; (ii) the affirmation of its development model and enhancement of its soft power; and (iii) further opportunities to realize its "role transformation" in international society as a responsible great power.[61]

Concerning the last point, there was certainly the belief among Chinese policymakers and analysts that the country had acted responsibly over the crisis, in line with its early assurances. Foreign minister Yang Jiechi publicly stated that the PRC's responses showed it was a responsible actor that had made "vital contributions" to promote global economic recovery.[62] Chinese commentators also lauded Beijing's leadership in the G20, calling it the "preparatory class" for China's emergence as a responsible power.[63] Outside of China, however, assessments about its contributions were mixed. While it was acknowledged by the World Bank, the IMF, and others that China's domestic stimulus package had prevented the global financial crisis from worsening, some felt that Beijing had not sufficiently pulled its weight in leading the global economic recovery. A 2009 European Council on Foreign Relations policy report, for example, argued:

> Efforts to get Beijing to live up to its responsibility as a key stakeholder in the global economy by agreeing to more international coordination have been largely unsuccessful. The G20 Summit in London in early April 2009 demonstrated Beijing's ability to avoid shouldering any real responsibility; its relatively modest contribution of $40 billion to the IMF was effectively payment of a "tax" to avoid being perceived as a global deal-broker.[64]

By the time of the 2010 Seoul G20 Summit, the sentiment that China had not done enough vis-à-vis efforts to revive the world economy had grown. There was in Washington, in particular, a growing perception and frustration that Beijing had persistently acted in an "irresponsible" or "unfair" manner to keep the yuan artificially low, which many Americans thought contributed to the US's ballooning trade deficit with China and undermined its recovery efforts. These arguments, predictably, were rejected by Beijing. Noting that the yuan had appreciated by almost 24 percent since 2005, its reply was that Chinese currency policy had been "coherent and responsible." It also pointed out that the US position was hypocritical because its policy of printing money to stimulate the economy (the so-called quantitative easing) was tantamount to a planned weakening of the American dollar.[65] Reactions from Chinese commentators, meanwhile, were generally defensive. One analyst argued that the US perspective basically sought to encumber China with more financial obligations than it could manage, revealing the "intertwining of Western jealousy, expectation, suspicion, and fear." Another thought that the currency calls failed to "distinguish between truth and falsehood" and were essentially an "irresponsible moral trap."[66]

Perceived Chinese Assertiveness and the Obama Administration's Approach

In addition to Beijing's perceived intransigence over the yuan's valuation, Chinese responses to a number of international issues from late 2009 also increasingly concerned Washington. Regarding North Korea, for example, China's reluctance to castigate Pyongyang over two major provocations in 2010—the attack on the South Korean naval ship *Cheonan* and the bombardment of South Korea's Yeonpyeong Island—seemed to Washington and others to be overly protective of its traditional ally.[67] Neither was Washington positively impressed with the continuing reports of sales of restricted arms and missile technologies by Chinese entities, the increasing restrictions on internet freedom in China, and what it saw as Beijing's more determined clampdown on human rights activism in the wake of democratic advances in the Middle East and North Africa.[68]

Particularly disquieting for the Obama administration were signs that Chinese diplomacy was taking on a more assertive tone. When the US announced the sale of a US$6.4 billion arms package to Taiwan in January 2010, China condemned the move as a violation of its "core interests" and warned of retaliatory "consequences," such as military dialogue suspension and possible sanctions on US defense equipment firms.[69] It reacted similarly strongly when Obama proceeded to meet the exiled Tibetan leader the Dalai Lama the following month, charging again that its core interests were being undermined.[70] But rising Chinese assertiveness appeared to be most perceptible on issues relating to the country's maritime sovereignty. Hillary Clinton's 2010 characterization of the South China Sea territorial dispute as a US "national interest" was met with not only strident objections from Beijing but also blunt warnings to ASEAN states against attempts to involve the US in the matter (which, according to one Chinese vice foreign minister, would be akin to "playing with fire").[71] As a result of perceived Chinese "bullying" over competing maritime claims, China's relations with some ASEAN states, in particular the Philippines and Vietnam, deteriorated sharply. A more muscular attitude was also palpable in Chinese diplomatic jousts with Japan over the contested Senkaku/Diaoyu Islands. In one notable example in 2010, when a Chinese captain was detained following his vessel's collision with Japanese patrol ships near the disputed islands, Beijing reacted by summoning the Japanese ambassador six times, halting high-level bilateral exchanges, allegedly curtailing its rare earth exports to Japan, and demanding an official apology and compensation.[72]

Against this backdrop of a seemingly more assertive China, around late 2010 the Obama administration signaled that it would reorient the US strategic focus away from the Middle East and Afghanistan and toward the Asia-Pacific region.[73] Termed as "forward-deployed diplomacy" by Hillary Clinton, this shift envisioned a rise in US economic, political, and military investments in the region. More specifically it aimed to: (i) shore up existing US regional alliances (i.e., with Japan, South Korea, the Philippines, Thailand, and Australia); (ii) forge more robust relationships with other major regional actors (such as India and Indonesia); (iii) expand US trade with Asia-Pacific nations; and (iv) establish a more active and visible American presence in regional multilateral forums (such as the ARF and the East Asia Summit). At the heart of this realignment was more than just acknowledgment of the Asia-Pacific's centrality to the twenty-first century; it also implied recognition of the significance of China's role in this centrality and how a more engaged American leadership in the region potentially could be productive in steering China toward a path that in US perceptions would be beneficial for regional stability and growth.[74] "To get China right, you have to get the region right" was how some in Washington put it.[75] Yet many in China did not see how this US strategic repositioning was "right." To many Chinese scholars the policy adjustment was yet another affirmation of the lingering suspicion that the US saw China as a threat and intended to keep it down to maintain the US regional hegemonic status. For others it typified the American realist approach in that Washington returned to its "old game of hedging against China" and was less "conciliatory" once it deemed that the PRC had become less critical to, or was less willing to assist in, its economic recovery.[76]

However, even as Washington looked to "shape" the regional environment of China's rise, it continued to apply rhetorical pressure on the question of China's international obligations.[77] Like the earlier two administrations, the idea and language of China's great-power responsibility had been a crucial feature of the Obama government's China policy. Through enhanced dialogue mechanisms, such as the US-China Strategic and Economic Dialogue (SED), as well as existing bilateral and multilateral forums, the Obama administration sought to impress on the Chinese leadership that the PRC's rising power must be matched by increasing global responsibilities. This message was calibrated and communicated to Beijing in a number of ways. For one, there was discernibly less usage of the stakeholder jargon, even as US officials strove to convince the Chinese that it was ultimately in their interests to act as a responsible global player.[78] Second, the Obama administration emphasized that it was important for China to act in ways that reassured the world about the nature and trajectory of its rise. In other words, it did not regard China's emergence in itself as naturally beneficial. "China's rise is potentially good for the world," Obama pointedly remarked in the presence of Hu during a joint White House press conference, "to the extent that [it] is functioning as a responsible actor on the world stage."[79] Third, from around 2011 the US rhetoric increasingly shifted to a discourse of how China needed to observe "the rules of the road," the implication being Beijing had been acting less responsibly than expected, especially in the economic sphere. This spoke to more than just US frustrations with Chinese currency policies, as mentioned earlier; it also related to America's overall misgivings over what it saw as the "unfair" and mercantilist practices of Chinese state capitalism. The Obama administration warned that if Beijing was seen to be trying to "game the system" to the detriment of others and avoid making its due contributions, the country risked an international reaction that could impact both global and Chinese development.[80]

To be sure, the tougher tenor of the US rhetoric on China did not mean that the Obama administration did not recognize Chinese efforts to cooperate in some areas. Washington acknowledged and welcomed, among other things, China's support for additional sanctions on North Korea after Pyongyang's 2009 nuclear and missile tests (e.g., UN resolutions 1716 and 1874), its declaration of opposition to Iran's alleged nuclear activities and its involvement with the P5+1 process to manage this issue, its financial contributions to Afghanistan's reconstruction efforts and reaffirmation of support for US counterterrorism efforts, and its pledge to lower national emissions levels and to report on such mitigation work (albeit on a nonbinding basis).[81] Both governments also worked at creating additional mechanisms of bilateral dialogue, which by 2012 led Hillary Clinton to claim that both powers "literally consult with each other almost on a daily basis about every consequential issue facing our nations and the world today."[82] Earlier, in 2010, Deputy Secretary James Steinberg told a Washington audience that the "balance sheet" on US-China collaboration could be considered a "pretty positive one."[83] On the whole, nevertheless, the Obama administration was realistic about the extent to which it could expect cooperation from China, especially by the latter half of its first term. While there had been pockets of progress, it was under little illusion that China was moving toward matching Washington's own expectations of what it took to be a responsible global actor.[84]

Debating China's Responsibility: Three Schools of Thought

Beijing certainly did not share the American perspective that alluded to its less-than-responsible ways in international society. It continued to rely on standard rhetorical responses that asserted how "China, as a major country, does not shirk its responsibilities" or how China and the US, as great powers, shouldered "important responsibilities on a host of major issues."[85] Such statements could be attributed in part to a degree of embeddedness of RGP narratives within the Chinese policy system (i.e., as an official pronounced identity) and in part to continuing Chinese awareness of the importance of the responsibility issue to US-China relations and American recognition of China's great-power status.[86] They could also be linked to growing Chinese concerns about the country's worsening image problem abroad. It was not lost on Beijing that perceptions of a more belligerent China had been gaining ground internationally (especially from around 2010), and that such perceptions bolstered the China threat discourse. This was apparent when Premier Wen took the unusual step of addressing these concerns at the 2010 National People's Congress. Noting that there had been talk of China becoming "more arrogant and tough" and that "some are putting forward a theory of Chinese triumphalism," Wen's response was to claim: "China is a responsible country" that "has called for and taken an active role in international cooperation on economic and political issues in [the] world."[87]

At the subofficial, intellectual level, domestic views on China's responsibility were considerably more colorful. Between 1997 and 2004, in conjunction with the domestic expansion of the RGP discourse, Chinese scholars had already started engaging in a wide-ranging discussion on questions of the PRC's big-power role and responsibilities. This trend continued into the period of 2005 to 2012, but it is noteworthy that during this time, the various key positions in the Chinese RGP debate became further sharpened. This is not to imply that these perspectives did not exist earlier; rather, the distinct stances in the RGP debate became more discernible in the 2005–2012 period. These could be broadly grouped into what I label the internationalist, the developmental, and the skeptics' positions.[88]

The internationalist perspective generally concurs with the notion that China should take on more global responsibilities. This argument is informed by a number of interrelated narratives. The first connects with the Bullian belief that great powers, by virtue of their stronger capacities, have greater responsibilities in international society. In this view Beijing needs to better comprehend the "responsibility of [its] power" (*quanli de zeren*) and redefine its obligations to the world to match its burgeoning strength.[89] Liu Jianfei of the Central Party School points out that due to power disparities in the international system, it is natural that there would be differences in responsibilities that states bear; ergo, for a swiftly rising China it is "reasonable" that international society has expectations that it "[shoulder] more international responsibilities and [serve] a bigger function in international affairs."[90] But great-power responsibility is more than just an issue of burden sharing in international relations, others note. There is also an element of noblesse oblige, in that a great power's exalted status behooves it to do more for international society. Conversely stated, if aspiring powers failed to "positively engage with international society and did not solve its problems," Renmin university scholar Jin Canrong notes, they would find it difficult to earn the great-power recognition they craved.[91] Hence, for China to "regain its historical status as a great world power, it must act like a great world power."[92] This calls for, among other things, the maintenance of international peace and stability, improved transparency in foreign policymaking, participation and leadership in international institutions, provision of global public goods, and greater activism in promoting regional cooperation and security.[93] Fundamentally it is about acting as a "humane authority" in global affairs, writes one prominent Chinese strategist.[94]

Another narrative in support of the internationalist position comes closer to a solidarist understanding of responsibility. Drawing on Chinese ideas such as "all under heaven" (*tianxia*) and "common responsibility," it is argued that China is morally and normatively accountable to the "shared" and "common" world of which it is a part. This narrative speaks of a less nationalistic worldview and emphasizes that China's future and interests are inextricably linked to the world's, while promoting a perception of international relations from the standpoint of human survival and progress and underlining that global challenges are the responsibility of all nations.[95] This more communal conception of international relations is also consistent with Hu's harmonious world idea, it is claimed.[96]

A strategic or pragmatic outlook toward international responsibility is also counseled by some Chinese scholars. One reason cited is that as the beneficiary of the current globalized international system, it is in China's interests to contribute to its continued sustainability and well-being: it would not benefit China if this system were to become unstable. These scholars also remind readers that China needs a relatively benign external environment for development, and in this respect it cannot afford to be "isolated" or treated like a "heretic" in international society. This requires that Beijing tries its best to address expectations of its conduct or at least give the appearance of doing so.[97] It will not help China's "grand strategy," notes Shi Yinhong, a prominent intellectual and advisor to the CCP government, if it is perceived to be an irresponsible "free-rider." In Shi's view China's pledge to rise peacefully has not been enough to assure others of its benign intentions and "prudence"; hence, it needs to commit itself to "responsible emergence with words as much as deeds."[98] Wu Xinbo, a Fudan University scholar, offers different advice. Presupposing a link between international duties and rights, he suggests that Beijing should leverage its responsible-power role to push for a larger and more proportionate share of rights in international society.[99]

However, even as several Chinese scholars argue that Beijing could and should shoulder more international responsibilities, it is equally stressed that these obligations should not be decided unilaterally by others and that, at a minimum, China should seek to "coordinate" with outside powers on what these obligations entail.[100] As one Chinese analyst puts it, "One can only be responsible for something that one accepts."[101] Liu Ming of the Shanghai Academy of Social Sciences agrees but goes further to caution that external interpretations of China's responsibilities should not be allowed to cast the country in a "morally defensive" position; Beijing needs to take greater initiative in defining its global obligations. For Liu, ideally, China should be a "distributor" (*fenpei zhe*) of responsibilities vis-à-vis the international order.[102] Such views, in a sense, reflect the limits of the internationalist perspective.

Yet this is still a less conservative position when compared with the developmental position, which argues against Beijing's taking on "excessive" global responsibilities—not because it is unwilling but because it lacks the "objective" capacity to do so (*meiyou nengli*). The developmental position does not deny that China should make an "appropriate" level of international contribution. Rather, it is wary that external obligations risk the prospect of national overextension. The core of the developmental narrative, therefore, is an estimation of China's power position that accentuates its developing status. This particular argument underscores that the PRC's national income per capita is still comparatively modest (around one-fifth of US levels), that the PRC still has more than 100 million people living below the poverty line, that its "socialist" development is still at a nascent stage and faces severe challenges from corruption and a rising income gap, that its export/investment-based economic model is potentially unsustainable in the long run, and that the country has yet to attain complete territorial sovereignty.[103] Under these conditions, Li Jie of the MFA's Policy Research Department contends, it would be "unrealistic" to expect China to "shoulder international responsibilities that are not commensurate with its capability and development stage, especially those that would entail sovereignty, security, and development costs."[104] It could also be politically difficult to justify, Jin Canrong suggests, noting that many Chinese questioned why a "poor China" should seek to behave "generously" to others when it should be (in their view) helping itself first.[105] For these reasons, proponents of the developmental position argue that Beijing should prioritize its internal responsibilities and focus on national "self-strengthening"; it has a "right" to develop. In so doing, it is claimed, China would not only fulfill a major responsibility to the world (i.e., by improving the living standards of one-fifth of the world's population, by creating positive economic externalities, etc.), it would also build a stronger "foundation" to better shoulder its international responsibilities.[106]

While the developmental perspective raises questions about Chinese great-power identity and advocates a more circumspect and inward-looking approach toward China's responsibilities, it accepts the overall idea that Beijing should act "responsibly" (albeit in accordance with its national conditions). The same could not be said about the skeptics' position, which is suspicious of the responsibility concept. The primary argument here is that the RGP discourse, in particular those emanating from the US and Europe, encompasses a hidden agenda to: (i) hamper China's rise by saddling it with "unreasonable" and disproportionate international burdens; (ii) pass the buck on most of the world's problems to China (i.e., "billing" Beijing), diverting attention away from the "fact" that others were primarily to blame and responsible for these problems; and (iii) exploit China's growing strength to perpetuate American hegemony.[107] Given these ostensible motives, it is alleged that the RGP discourse is fundamentally a "cousin to the China threat theory and China collapse theory," with the main difference being only that it is more "gentle" in expression. Ma Zhengang, a former senior diplomat and president of the China Institute of International Studies cautions: "We should not blindly think that the US looks up to us when it requests China to take on more global responsibilities, much less revel in self-importance."[108] A similar view is espoused by Huo Jianguo, a senior scholar-official at the Ministry of Commerce. In an interview entitled "Why Is China Supposed to Be Responsible for the World?," Huo asserts that the idea of China as a responsible power (as articulated by the US) is "dangerous" and amounts to a way of "killing China with flattery." In Huo's opinion, the US and others had grown increasingly "jealous" of China's success, especially in the aftermath of the 2008–2009 global financial crisis, and they were seeking to "invent more excuses" to burden China and check its development.[109]

It might be tempting at this juncture to ask, Which was the leading perspective in the Chinese RGP debate during this period? Short of a large-scale phased national survey of relevant Chinese opinion-makers and intellectuals, it would be difficult to say with some degree of confidence. Yan Xuetong has claimed that the skeptics' position represents the Chinese "mainstream" but cites no evidence at how he arrived at this assertion.[110] The results of my field interviews and discussions with Chinese interlocutors in 2011, on the other hand, suggest that Chinese analysts were inclined to understand the responsibility discourse from lenses that encompass elements of both the internationalist and developmental perspectives.[111] This is not to say that among those with whom I had spoken there had been no cynicism expressed about the RGP concept. But it appears that most lean toward some combination of the internationalist and developmental views. Admittedly, these interviews and discussions comprise only a small sample size and entail a certain degree of interpretative subjectivity. Thus they should not be understood as anything more than an estimate of perceptions in the RGP debate during a specific period. Nevertheless, caveats aside, they can be potentially indicative. Field data suggest that among Chinese analysts it is less a question of whether China should behave responsibly and more a question of how China should behave responsibly (that is, whether to tilt toward external or internal obligations).

Conclusion

Overall, the years 2005 to 2012 mark a period of further entrenchment of the RGP identity at both official and intellectual levels.[112] This period saw an unprecedented level of dialogue and policy engagement between the US and China, which reinforced perceptions of China's great-power identity but also created additional opportunities for Washington to focus attention on questions of Chinese behavior. When comparing the Bush and Obama administrations, the tenor of the latter's rhetoric on China appears to be more forceful (especially from around 2010). But by and large the message to Beijing remained the same: its global responsibilities should be commensurate with its rising power. There was evidence that some of this rhetoric had an impact on Chinese deliberations, as seen by the advocacy of the stakeholder concept that had spurred discussion of the responsible great-power role in China.

Of course, the continued proliferation of Chinese RGP narratives relates to more than just responses to American arguments. Domestic debates about the harmonious world concept and the Chinese development model facilitated this discourse, while events such as the 2008–2009 global financial crisis also played a role. As with the 1997–1998 crisis, Beijing saw the 2008–2009 GFC as a useful opportunity to assert identity claims as a responsible global actor, believing that it had responded "responsibly" over the crisis. But, unlike the 1997–1998 crisis, assessments of Chinese contributions the second time were more mixed, and many believed that it could have done more to help boost global economic recovery. Indeed, by 2010 Washington was more vocal in arguing that some of China's trade and economic practices, in particular its currency valuation policy, were "unfairly" undermining efforts to restore the global economy.

Those sentiments were part of a broader perception in Washington that the gap between Chinese behavior and American expectations was growing. Compared with the period between 2005 and 2008, when US commentators and officials argued that some of Beijing's actions indicated it had "responded impressively although only partially" to the responsible stakeholder call, by the second half of the Obama administration's first term, this view had changed. It had become apparent to US officials that Beijing was increasingly acting in ways that suggested not only a more abrasive China but also one that still had much ground to make up in terms of addressing US expectations of its conduct.

Unpacking the evolving Chinese arguments on the RGP identity might well shed some light on why US-China political divergence had grown during this period. As the chapter has shown, from 2005 to 2012 there was a sharpening of the RGP debate in China, with at least three distinct schools of thought emerging, among which only the internationalist position advocating that Beijing take on more global responsibilities. But even this more liberalist position is qualified by the insistence among Chinese analysts that these responsibilities should not be unilaterally determined by others. In fact, all three major positions in the debate (internationalist, developmental, and skeptics') involve narratives that speak implicitly or explicitly to Chinese interests. While not problematic in itself, this implies differences in responsibility "standards" between China and others when Chinese interests diverge from others' interests. Taken together these identity arguments suggest limits on how Beijing will behave as a responsible power.

Notes

1. Robert B. Zoellick, "Whither China: From Membership to Responsibility?," Remarks to the National Committee on US-China Relations, September 21, 2005, https://2001-2009.state.gov/s/d/former/zoellick/rem/53682.htm.
2. Robert B. Zoellick, Deputy Secretary Zoellick's Statement on the Conclusion of the Second US-China Senior Dialogue, December 8, 2005, https://2001-2009.state.gov/r/pa/prs/ps/2005/57822.htm.
3. Henry Paulson, Statement from Treasury Secretary Henry Paulson at the Closing of the US-China Strategic Economic Dialogue, December 15, 2006, https://www.treasury.gov/press-center/press-releases/Pages/hp200.aspx. For similar remarks by Paulson, see also Henry Paulson, "Growth and Future of China's Financial Markets," Prepared Remarks in Shanghai, March 7, 2007, https://2001-2009.state.gov/p/eap/rls/rm/2007/81671.htm.
4. Thomas Christensen, "China's Role in the World: Is China a Responsible Stakeholder?," Remarks before the US-China Economic and Security Review Commission, August 3, 2006, https://2001-2009.state.gov/p/eap/rls/rm/69899.htm.
5. US Department of Defense, "Quadrennial Defense Report" (2006), 29. See also Richard Lawless, "China: Recent Security Developments," *Prepared Statement before the House Armed Forces Committee*, June 13, 2007, available at http://ogc.osd.mil/olc/docs/testLawless070613.pdf.
6. Thomas Christensen, "The State of US-China Diplomacy," Remarks before the US-China Economic and Security Review Commission, February 2, 2007, https://2001-2009.state.gov/p/eap/rls/rm/2007/79866.htm.
7. Other less common terms were *can guren* (shareholder) and *gongtong jingying zhe* (coadministrator). Interviews with Chinese scholars in Beijing and Shanghai, April–June 2011.
8. Lin Fengchun, "Fuxi? Huoxi? 'Zhongguo Fuzeren Lun' Jiedu" (Fortune? Misfortune? Interpreting the "China responsibility theory"), *Shehui Guancha (Social Outlook)* 4 (2006): 42–43.
9. Quoted in ibid.
10. Indeed, several Chinese commentators viewed the stakeholder concept from the perspective of "the US's positioning of China." See Liu Wanyuan, "Meiguo Chongxin Dingwei Zhongguo: Liyi Xiangguan Zhe" (America repositions China: Stakeholder), *Zhongguo Xinwen Zhoukan (China Newsweek)*, November 2005, 40–41; Wu Xingtang, "Ruhe Kandai Meiguo Dui Zhongguo De Dingwei" (How to understand America's positioning of China), *Dangdai Shijie (Contemporary World)* 2 (2006): 14–15; Wang Lianhe, "Meiguo Dui Huazhengce Xin Siwei? Ping Zuolike De Jianghua (New thinking for America's China policy? Assessing Zoellick's speech), *Guoji Guancha (International Review)* 1 (2006): 33–37; "Zaikan Zuolike 9.21 Yanjiang" (A look again at Zoellick's September 21 speech), *Guoji Zhanwang (Global Review)* 2 (2006): 10; Li Peng, "Cong 'Zhanlue Jingzheng Zhe' Dao 'Liyi Xiangguan Zhe': Meiguo Dui Hua Zhanlue Dingwei Zhuanbian Yu Taiwan Wenti"

(From "strategic competitor" to "stakeholder": The change in the US's strategic positioning of China and the Taiwan problem), *Taiwan Yanjiu Jikan* (*Taiwan Research Quarterly*) 1 (2006): 1–13; Yu Zhengliang, "Shilun Meiguo Duihua De Duichong Zhanlue" (Discussing America's hedging strategy against China), *Guoji Guancha (International Review)* 1 (2006): 2–8.

11. It did not escape Zoellick's attention that the Chinese quickly picked up on the stakeholder concept. He said he was "very pleased that the stakeholder concept has generated some good discussion and debate in China." See Robert B. Zoellick, Press Conference in China, January 24, 2006, https://2001-2009.state.gov/s/d/former/zoellick/rem/2006/59659.htm. For Zoellick's September 21, 2005 speech (as reproduced in the Chinese language), see "Waikan Lun Zuolike Dui Meizhong Guanxi De Xin Dingwei: Liyi Xiangguan Zhe" (Foreign publications discuss Zoellick's new positioning of Sino-American relations: Stakeholder), *Guoji Zhanwang (Global Review)* 2 (2006): 8–9.
12. Qi Pengfei, *Zhongguo Gongchan Dang Yu Dangdai Zhongguo Waijiao, 1949–2009 (Chinese Communist Party and Contemporary Chinese Diplomacy, 1949–2009)* (Beijing: Gongchan Dangshi Chubanshe, 2010), 98.
13. State Council Information Office, "Zhongguo De Heping Fazhan Daolu" (China's peaceful development path) (2005), section 5; *Zhengfu Gongzuo Baogao (Government Work Report)* (2006), http://www.gov.cn/test/2009-03/16/content_1260216.htm; "Zhongyang Waishi Gongzuo Huiyi Zaijing Juxing: Hu Jintao Wen Jiabao Zuo Zhongyao Jianghua" (Central committee foreign affairs work conference held at capitol: Hu Jintao, Wen Jibao make important speech), *Renmin Ribao (People's Daily)*, August 24, 2006; *Hu Jintao Zaidang De Shiqida Shang De Baogao (Hu Jintao's Report to the Seventeenth CCP Congress)* (2007), http://cpc.people.com.cn/GB/64093/67507/6429855.html.
14. As one party-published historiography claims, "Harmonious coexistence transcends peaceful coexistence" among nations. See Qi, *Zhongguo Gongchan Dang Yu Dangdai Zhongguo Waijiao, 1949–2009*, 99. The party school scholar Liu Jianfei makes a similar point, claiming that a harmonious world is even "better" than a peaceful world. See Liu Jianfei, "Heping Jueqi Shi Zhongguo De Zhanlue Xuanze" (Peaceful rise is China's strategic choice), *Shijie Jingji Yu Zhengzhi (World Economics and Politics)* 2 (2006): 40.
15. Hu Jintao, "Nuli Jianshe Zhijiu Heping, Gongtong Fanrong De Hexie Shijie" (Build toward a harmonious world of lasting peace and common prosperity), *Renmin Ribao (People's Daily)*, September 16, 2005.
16. Jiang Zemin, "Rang Women Gongtong Dizao Yike Geng Meihao De Shijie" (Let us jointly create a better world), in *Jiang Zemin Wenxuan Diyijuan (Selected Works of Jiang Zemin)*, vol. 1 (Beijing: Renmin Chubanshe, 2006), 476–82; Jiang Zemin, "Gongtong Chuangzao Yige Heping Fanrong De Xin Shiji" (Jointly construct a peaceful and prosperous new century), in *Jiang Zemin Wenxuan Disanjuan (Selected Works of Jiang Zemin)*, vol. 3 (Beijing: Renmin Chubanshe, 2006), 472–78.

17. Yongnian Zheng and Sow Keat Tok, "'Harmonious Society' and 'Harmonious World': China's Policy Discourse under Hu Jintao," *China Policy Institute Briefing Series*, no. 26 (2007): 8.
18. See the report on the Harmonious World and China's Diplomacy Conference, with contributions from a number of leading Chinese IR scholars: Wu Jianmin, Yu Xintian, Liu Zhenmin, Wang Jisi, Rao Geping, Bai Yansong, Feng Shaolei, Cai Tuo, Qin Yaqing, Zhang Tuosheng, Zhang Yan, Jin Canrong, Ma Xin, and Li Zhaojie, "Hexie Shijie Yu Zhongguo Waijiao" (Harmonious world and China's diplomacy), *Waijiao Pinlun (Foreign Affairs Review)* 87 (2006): 15–20. See also Xu Jian, "Zonglun Guoji Xingshi Yu Zhongguo Waijiao" (On the international situation and China's diplomacy), *Guoji Wenti Yanjiu (International Studies)* 2 (2007): 18–19, 31; Yu Xintian, "'Hexie Shijie' Yu Zhongguo De Heping Fazhan Daolu" ("Harmonious world" and China's peaceful development path), *Guoji Wenti Yanjiu (International Studies)* 1 (2007): 7–12, 18; and Wang Yusheng and Yin Chengde, "Guanyu 'Goujian Hexie Shijie' De Sikao" (Thoughts on "constructing a harmonious world"), *Lilun Cankao (Theoretical Reference)* 5 (2007): 11–12.
19. Qi, *Zhongguo Gongchan Dang Yu Dangdai Zhongguo Waijiao, 1949–2009*, 99.
20. See, for example, Pu Ping, "Heping Fazhan Daolu Yu Hexie Shijie Linian" (Peaceful development path and the harmonious world concept), *Jiaoxue Yu Yanjiu (Teaching and Research)* 11 (2007): 53–54; Yue Xiaoyong, "Dui Tuidong Jianshe Hexie Shijie Lilun De Chubu Renshi" (Preliminary thoughts on promoting the construction of a harmonious world), *Guoji Wenti Yanjiu (International Studies)* 4 (2007): 5; Xu, "Zonglun Guoji Xingshi Yu Zhongguo Waijiao," 15. In a *China Daily* commentary, analyst Qin Xiaoying of the China Foundation for International and Strategic Studies writes that the harmonious world idea demonstrates "the CPC's handling of international relations is maturing and China is becoming a responsible global power." See Qin Xiaoying, "China's Path to World Peace and Prosperity," *China Daily*, October 30, 2007.
21. Zhao Lei, "Yi 'Hexie Shijie' Linian Tisheng 'Fuzeren Daguo' Xingxiang" (Promote the self-image of a "responsible great power" with "harmonious world" concept), *Zhongguo Dangzheng Ganbu Luntan (Chinese Cadres Tribune)* 12 (2007): 47–48.
22. See Wu et al., "Hexie Shijie Yu Zhongguo Waijiao," 18.
23. Joshua Cooper Ramos, *The Beijing Consensus* (London: Foreign Policy Centre, 2004).
24. Reactions to Ramos's views were confined not only to China, of course. Elsewhere there were vigorous debates on the notion of a Beijing consensus. See, for example, Suisheng Zhao, "The China Model: Can It Replace the Western Model of Modernization?," *Journal of Contemporary China* 19, no. 65 (2010): 419–36; Scott Kennedy, "The Myth of the Beijing Consensus," *Journal of Contemporary China* 19, no. 65 (2010): 461–77; and Stefan Halper, *The Beijing Consensus: How China's Authoritarian Model Will Dominate the Twenty-First Century* (New York: Basic, 2010).
25. Yu Keping, "Guanyu 'Zhongguo Moshi' De Sikao" (Thinking about the "China model"), *Hongqi (Red Flag)* 19 (2005): 13.

26. See Qiu Gengtian, "Zhongguo Moshi Yu Di Daijia Fazhan Daolu" (The China model and the path of low-cost development), *Zhonggong Zhongyang Dangxiao Xuebao (Journal of the Party School of the Central Committee of the CPC)* 12, no. 3 (2008): 35–36; Luo Jianbo, "Ruan Shili Yu Zhongguo Waijiao" (Soft power and China's diplomacy), *Xin Yuanjian (New Thinking)* 5 (2008): 48; Ma Zhengang, "Xifang Xuanran 'Zhongguo Moshi' Zhi Beihou" (On the West's exaggeration of the "China model"), *Renmin Luntan (People's Tribune)* 240 (2008): 29; Jiang Jinquan, "Jiexi 'Zhongguo Moshi'" (Understanding the "China model"), *Liaowang (Outlook)* 25 (2005): 42–43.
27. See Cai Tuo, "Tansuo Zhong De 'Zhongguo Moshi'" (The exploring "China model"), *Dangdai Shijie Yu Shehui Zhuyi (Contemporary World and Socialism)* 5 (2005): 13–14; Qiu, "Zhongguo Moshi Yu Di Daijia Fazhan Daolu," 35–39; Ma, "Xifang Xuanran 'Zhongguo Moshi' Zhi Beihou," 28–29.
28. Indian Prime Minister Manmohan Singh, for example, had been cited in China as saying that "India should view China as a model for economic growth and global trade." See Men Honghua, "Zhongguo Ruan Shili Pinggu Baogao" (An assessment report of China's soft power), *Guoji Guancha (International Review)* 3 (2007): 37–38; Tao Wenzhao, "Zhongguo Moshi De Shijie Yingxiang" (The global influence of the China model), *Renmin Luntan (People's Tribune)* 21 (2008): 50; "Zhongguo De Ruanshili Ziyuan" (The sources of China's soft power), *Dangzheng Luntan (Party and Government Forum)* 2 (2007): 79.
29. Tao, "Zhongguo Moshi De Shijie Yingxiang."
30. See, for example, Luo, "Ruan Shili Yu Zhongguo Waijiao," 47.
31. Interview with Chinese scholar, Shanghai, June 2011.
32. Zhang Youwen and Huang Renwei, ed., *2005 Zhongguo Guoji Diwei Baogao (China's International Status Report 2005)* (Shanghai: Shanghai Academy of Social Sciences, 2005), chap. 1.
33. Zhang Youwen and Huang Renwei, ed., *2009 Zhongguo Guoji Diwei Baogao (China's International Status Report 2009)* (Shanghai: Shanghai Academy of Social Sciences, 2009), 19.
34. Ibid., chaps. 1–3. See also the panel essay: Wang Yizhou, Yan Xuetong, Jin Canrong, Shen Dingli, Yu Wanli, and Zhang Guoqing, "Aoyun Zhihou: Zhongguo Diwei Bian Mei Bian" (After the Olympics: Change or no change in China's status), *Shijie Zhishi (World Affairs)* 18 (2008): 14–24; and Yan Xuetong, "The Rise of China and Its Power Status," *Chinese Journal of International Politics* 1, no. 1 (2006): 5–33. Regarding China's space activities, US deputy under secretary of defense Richard Lawless noted: "China's leaders view the development of space and counter-space capabilities as bolstering national prestige and, like nuclear weapons, demonstrating the attributes of a world power." See Lawless, "China: Recent Security Developments."
35. I have highlighted some of the more important dialogue mechanisms that were created during the second term of the Bush administration. Exceptions to this list are the Defense Consultative Talk (1997) and the Military Maritime Consultative Agreement meetings (1998). See Thomas Christensen, "Shaping China's Global Choices through Diplomacy," Statement before the US-China Economic

and Security Review Commission, March 18, 2008, https://2001-2009.state.gov/p/eap/rls/rm/2008/03/102327.htm; and Thomas Lum, "US-China Relations: Policy Issues," *Congressional Research Service Report for Congress*, March 12, 2010, 7–8. On an updated and fuller list of US-China dialogue mechanisms, see Bonnie S. Glaser, "The Diplomatic Relationship: Substance and Process," in *Tangled Titans: The United States and China*, ed. David Shambaugh (Lanham: Rowman & Littlefield, 2012), 175–76, textbox 7.1.

36. Christensen, "Shaping China's Global Choices through Diplomacy."
37. According to Fred Bergsten, around late 2004 he introduced to Zoellick the notion of holding a US-China "G2" meeting, and Zoellick subsequently discussed this idea with the Chinese. See Fred Bergsten, "A Partnership of Equals: How Washington Should Respond to China's Economic Challenge," *Foreign Affairs* 87, no. 4 (July–August 2008): 65–69. On the "Chimerica" neologism, see Niall Ferguson, "Team 'Chimerica,'" *Washington Post*, November 17, 2008.
38. See, for example, the panel essay by Fu Mengzi, Yuan Peng, Da Wei, Guo Yongjun, Niu Xinchun and Wang Wenfeng, "Zhanlue Duihua Yu Zhongmei Guanxi" (Strategic dialogue and Sino-American relations), *Xiandai Guoji Guanxi (Contemporary International Relations)* 8 (2005): 52–61.
39. Zoellick, Deputy Secretary Zoellick's Statement on Conclusion of the Second US-China Senior Dialogue.
40. Paulson, "Growth and Future of China's Financial Markets."
41. See Stephanie Kleine-Ahlbrandt and Andrew Small, "China's New Dictatorship Diplomacy: Is Beijing Parting with Pariahs?," *Foreign Affairs* 87, no. 1 (January–February 2008): 38–56; Thomas Christensen, "The Advantages of an Assertive China: Responding to Beijing's Abrasive Diplomacy," *Foreign Affairs* 90, no. 2 (March–April 2011): 56–57; Christensen, "Shaping China's Global Choices through Diplomacy"; Jonathan Holslag, "Embracing Chinese Global Security Ambitions," *Washington Quarterly* 32, no. 3 (2009): 105–18.
42. Christensen, "Advantages of an Assertive China," 56.
43. John Negroponte, "US-China Relations in the Era of Globalization," *Opening Statement before the Senate Foreign Relations Committee*, May 15, 2008, https://2001-2009.state.gov/s/d/2008/104932.htm.
44. According to a US Congressional Research Service report, the "purpose of that call was to ask for China's help to deal with this financial crisis by urging China to hold even more US Treasury bonds and US assets." See Wayne Morrison, "China and the Global Financial Crisis: Implications for the United States," *Congressional Service Report for Congress*, June 3, 2009, 8.
45. Henry Paulson, "China and the Global Economy," Remarks to the National Committee on US-China Relations, October 21, 2008, available at https://china.usc.edu/us-treasury-sec-paulson-%E2%80%9Cchina-and-global-economy%E2%80%9D-october-21-2008.
46. Clinton also stated that human rights issues should not be allowed to "interfere" with US-China cooperation on climate change and North Korea. See editorial, "Not So

Obvious," *Washington Post*, February 24, 2009. While in Beijing, Clinton expressed the US hope that China would continue to buy its debt. See Morrison, "China and the Global Financial Crisis," 8.

47. Zheng Yongnian and Lye Liang Fook, "The International Financial Crisis and China's External Response," *East Asian Institute Background Brief* no. 420 (December 2008): 1.
48. "Wang Qishan: Zhongguo Zhengfu Jiangtong Geguo Yiqi Yingdui Jinrong Weiji" (Wang Qishan: Chinese government will work together with the world on financial crisis), *Zhongguo Jinrong Jia (China Financial Analyst)* 10 (2008): 14. Wang's assurances also apparently convinced Paulson to remark to the National Committee on US-China Relations that "it is clear that China accepts its responsibility as a major economy that will work with the United States and other partners to ensure global economic stability." See Paulson, "China and the Global Economy."
49. "Wen Jiabao: Zhongguo You Xinxin Weihu Zhongguo Jinrong Shicang De Wending" (Wen Jiabao: China is confident of safeguarding the stability of its financial market), *Zhongguo Jinrong Jia (China Financial Analyst)* 10 (2008): 14. Vice-Premier Li Keqiang also made similar assurances, telling Robert Zoellick (who had become World Bank president) that China would adopt a "responsible attitude" in maintaining global financial stability. See "Li Keqiang Huijian Shijie Yinhang Hangzhang Zuolike" (Li Keqiang meets World Bank president Robert Zoellick), *Renmin Ribao (People's Daily)*, December 17, 2008. For an example of commentaries that mirrored the leadership rhetoric, see Hu Jian, "Miandui Jinrong Weiji, Zhongguo Buhui Gean Guanhuo" (Facing the financial crisis, China will not watch from the sidelines), *Shehui Guancha (Social Outlook)* 12 (2008): 8.
50. See ibid.; and "Wang Qishan: Zhongguo Zhengfu Jiangtong Geguo Yiqi Yingdui Jinrong Weiji," 14.
51. "Role of a Stakeholder," *China Daily*, November 14, 2008.
52. Zheng and Lye, "International Financial Crisis and China's External Response," 7–8.
53. Sarah Tong and Zhang Yang, "China's Responses to the Economic Crisis," *East Asian Institute Background Brief* no. 438 (March 2009): 1–15; William Overholt, "China in the Global Financial Crisis: Rising Influence, Rising Challenges," *Washington Quarterly* 33, no. 1 (2010): 28–30.
54. "Guowuyuan Zongli Wen Jiabao Huijian Zhongwai Jizhe" (Premier Wen Jiabao meets domestic and foreign reporters), Xinhua, March 13, 2009.
55. Interviews with Chinese scholars, Shanghai and Beijing, May–June 2011. See also Zhou Shijian's article in the party publication *Shishi Baogao* (published by the Central Committee Propaganda Department): "Shuishi Fuguo, Shuishi Qiongguo?" (Who is a rich country, who is a poor country?), *Shishi Baogao (Current Affairs Report)* 11 (2008): 55–56.
56. Liang Guodong, "Zhongguo Waijiao De Huimou Yu Zhanwang: Fang Waijiao Buzhang Yang Jiechi" (Looking back and ahead at China's diplomacy: Interviewing foreign minister Yang Jiechi), *Zhongguo Renda (The People's Congress of China)* 5 (2010): 32–33.

57. "FM: Hu's Proposals Play Important Role at G20," *China Daily*, April 4, 2009; Liu Rui and Xu Yiming, "Jinrong Weiji Zhihou Zhongguo Dui G20 Yingdang Chiyou De Jiben Lichang" (China's basic position on the G20 after the financial crisis), *Shehui Kexue Yanjiu (Social Sciences Research)* 2 (2010): 67–72.
58. One prominent call came from China's Central Bank governor, Zhou Xiaochuan. Zhou proposed the expansion of the currency basket in the IMF's special drawing right (SDR) and the use of this broadened SDR to replace the US dollar as the international reserve currency. The idea was to reduce the Chinese and international economy's vulnerability to a weakening US dollar, which accounted for around 60 percent of the reserves of global central banks. See Wang Xu, "Big Push for Global Reserve Currency," *China Daily*, March 31, 2009; Andrew Marble, "China, the Financial Crisis, and Sino-American Relations: An Interview with Pieter Bottelier," *Asia Policy* 9 (2010): 126–29.
59. See these examples: Li Jie, "Cong Jinrong Weiji Toushi Guoji Tixi Zhuanxing Dongxiang" (Perceiving trends in international system transition through the lens of the financial crisis), *Guoji Wenti Yanjiu (International Studies)* 3 (2009): 11–17; Yan Xuetong, "Dangqian Guoji Xingshi Yu Zhongguo Waijiao De Tiaozheng" (The current international situation and the adjustment of Chinese diplomacy), *Zhanlue Juece Yanjiu (Journal of Strategy and Decision-Making)* 2 (2010): 3–17. Meanwhile, Qin Yaqing assesses that in the wake of the financial crisis, China entered the "core of the international system" for the first time. See Qin Yaqing, "Guoji Tixi De Yanxu Yu Biange" (Change and continuity in the international system), *Waijiao Pinlun (Foreign Affairs Review)* 1 (2010): 9.
60. See the executive summary of the CASS-organized conference on the global financial crisis: Chen Yingchun, "Quanqiu Jinrong Weiji, Guoji Yingxiang Jiqi Duice: Yantao Hui Jianxun" (Conference on the international impact of and countermeasures toward the global financial crisis: Executive summary), *Shijie Jingji Yu Zhengzhi (World Economy and Politics)* 12 (2008): 2. See also Shao Feng, "Jinrong Weiji Dui Guoji Guanxi De Yingxiang Ji Zhongguo De Yingdui" (The financial crisis's impact on international relations and China's response), *Shijie Jingji Yu Zhengzhi (World Economy and Politics)* 12 (2008): 23–26; Xu Jin, "Jinrong Weiji Nanyi Dianfu 'Yichao Duoqiang' Geju" (Difficult for the financial crisis to overturn the "one superpower, many great powers" structure), *Shijie Jingji Yu Zhengzhi (World Economy and Politics)* 12 (2008): 26–27; Zhao Bin, "Jinrong Weiji Daozhi Meiguo Huayu Shishi Wo Baquan Zhongjie?" (Did the financial crisis lead to a weakening of America's voice or the conclusion of American hegemony?), *Dangshi Wenyuan (Literary Circles of CCP History)* 2 (2010): 24–25; and Qin, "Guoji Tixi De Yanxu Yu Biange," 8–11. For an alternative view that posits the possibility that the crisis might actually enhance the US's unipolar status, see Song Wei, "Guoji Jinrong Weiji Yu Meiguo De Danji Diwei" (The international financial crisis and America's unipolar position), *Shijie Jingji Yu Zhengzhi (World Economy and Politics)* 5 (2010): 25–48.
61. See, for example, Wu Xinbo, "Guoji Xingshi Jubian Xia Zhongguo De Guoji Quxiang" (China's international orientation amid changes in the global situation),

Guoji Wenti Yanjiu (International Studies) 1 (2010): 21–26; and Shao, "Jinrong Weiji Dui Guoji Guanxi De Yingxiang Ji Zhongguo De Yingdui," 23–26.

62. Liang, "Zhongguo Waijiao De Huimou Yu Zhanwang," 32.
63. "G20: Zhongguo Chengwei Fuzeren Daguo De 'Yuke Ban'" (G20: The "preparatory class" for China as a responsible great power), *Huanqiu Shibao (Global Times)*, June 23, 2010.
64. On acknowledgment of the global impact of China's policy responses, see "WB, US, Brazil Hail China's Economic Stimulus Plan," *China Daily*, November 10, 2008; "IMF Hails China's Policy Response in Financial Crisis," Xinhua, July 27, 2010. On critical assessments, see John Fox and Francois Godement, *A Power Audit of EU-China Relations* (London: European Council on Foreign Relations, 2009), 2.
65. "G20 Refuses to Back US Push on China's Currency," *China Daily*, November 12, 2010; "Hu Jintao Jieshou Faguo Feijia Luobao Putaoya Lusashe Caifang" (Hu Jintao interviewed by France's Le Figaro daily and Portugal's Lusa news agency), *Renmin Ribao (People's Daily)*, November 4, 2010.
66. Sun Jingxin, "Jingji Lingyu Zhong De 'Zhongguo Zeren Lun' Pouxi" (Dissecting the "China responsibility theory" in the economic arena), *Duiwai Chuanbo (International Communications)*, 10 (2010): 37–38; Zhao Changhui, "'Zhongguo Zeren Lun' De Daode Xianjing" (The moral trap of the "China responsibility theory"), *Zhongguo Baodao (China Report)* 3 (2009): 110.
67. North Korea had denied involvement in the *Cheonan* incident.
68. Christensen, "Advantages of an Assertive China," 57–58; David Shear, "China: Recent Security Developments," *Statement before the House Armed Services Committee*, January 13, 2010, available at https://china.usc.edu/david-shear-china-recent-security-developments-jan-13-2010; Daniel Kritenbrink, "US Policy toward the People's Republic of China (PRC)," Statement before the US-China Economic and Security Review Commission, April 13, 2011, https://2009-2017.state.gov/p/eap/rls/rm/2011/04/160652.htm.
69. "China Denounces US Arms Sales to Taiwan," *China Daily*, January 9, 2010; John Pomfret, "US Sells Weapons to Taiwan, Angering China," *Washington Post*, January 30, 2010.
70. "Waijiao Bu Fayanren Ma Chaoxu Jiu Meiguo Zongtong Huijian Dalai Fabiao Tanhua" (Ministry of foreign affairs spokesman Ma Chaoxu comments on the meeting between the US president and the Dalai Lama), The Central People's Government of the People's Republic of China Portal, February 19, 2010, http://www.gov.cn/gzdt/2010-02/19/content_1536646.htm.
71. Christensen, "Advantages of an Assertive China," 59; Edward Wong, "Beijing Warns US about South China Sea Disputes," *New York Times*, June 22, 2011.
72. Suisheng Zhao, "Shaping the Regional Context of China's Rise: How the Obama Administration Brought Back Hedge in Its Engagement with China," *Journal of Contemporary China* 21, no. 75 (2012): 373–74.
73. Although Clinton's November 2011 speech, "American's Pacific Century," is seen as representing the official announcement of the US strategy to "pivot" toward the

Asia-Pacific, documentary evidence suggests the outlines of this shift were first articulated around fall 2010. See Hillary Clinton, "America's Engagement in the Asia-Pacific," Remarks in Honolulu, October 28, 2010, https://2009-2017.state.gov/secretary/20092013clinton/rm/2010/10/150141.htm; Hillary Clinton, "Inaugural Richard C. Holbrooke Lecture on a Broad Vision of US-China Relations in the Twenty-First Century," Remarks in Washington, DC, January 14, 2011, https://2009-2017.state.gov/secretary/20092013clinton/rm/2011/01/154653.htm.

74. Ibid. See also William Burns, "Keynote Remarks at the Fifth Biennial US-China Relations Conference," Remarks at Texas A&M University, October 24, 2011, https://2009-2017.state.gov/s/d/former/burns/remarks/2011/176071.htm; Hillary Clinton, "America's Pacific Century," Remarks at the East-West Center, November 10, 2011, https://2009-2017.state.gov/secretary/20092013clinton/rm/2011/11/176999.htm.
75. Kritenbrink, "US Policy toward the People's Republic of China (PRC)."
76. As Zhu Feng, Zhao Kejin, and Yin Xiting argue, the American "strategic turn toward the East" is predicated on the idea of China as the "hypothetical enemy" (*jiaxiang di*). Liu Liming also writes that several Chinese observers saw the US policy adjustment as a means by which to "prevent China's rise" and a form of strategic "defense through attack." Not all Chinese analysts thought, however, that the US's Asia "pivot" amounts to a straightforward containment policy of China. See Zhu Feng, "Aobama Zhengfu 'Zhuansheng Yazhou' Zhanlue Yu Zhongmei Guanxi" (The Obama government's "pivot to Asia" strategy and Sino-US relations), *Xiandai Guoji Guanxi (Contemporary International Relations)* 4 (2012): 1–7, 50; Zhao Kejin and Yin Xiting, "Meiguo Zhanlue Tiaozheng Yu Zhongmei Xinxing Daguo Guanxi" (The US strategic adjustment and the new type of Sino-American big power relations), *Guoji Guanxi Xueyuan Xuebao (Journal of University of International Relations)* 6 (2012): 71–84; Lin Liming, "Yigong Weishou: Meiguo 'Zhanlue Dongyi' De Zhanlue Benzhi Pingxi" (Defense through attack: Assessing the basic character of the US "strategic turn" toward the East), *Dangdai Shijie (Contemporary World)* 9 (2012): 8–11. For other examples, see Liu Bo, "Meiguo Zhanlue Dongyi De Xingdong Tedian" (The characteristics of the American strategic action to turn toward the East), *Guoji Guanxi Xueyuan Xuebao (Journal of University of International Relations)* 5 (2012): 54–58; Han Zhaoying and Wang Shishan, "Meiguo De Yatai Zai Pingheng Zhanlue Jiqi Fumian Yingxiang" (On the US Asia-Pacific rebalancing strategy and its negative impacts), *Xueshu Qianyan (Academic Frontiers)* 12 (2012): 6–13. On the supposed realistic nature of US strategic thinking as asserted by some in China, see Wu Xinbo, "Forging Sino-US Partnership in the Twenty-First Century: Opportunities and Challenges," *Journal of Contemporary China* 21, no. 75 (2012): 392.
77. Zhao, "Shaping the Regional Context of China's Rise."
78. See, for example, Clinton, "Inaugural Richard C. Holbrooke Lecture on a Broad Vision of US-China Relations in the Twenty-First Century"; Robert Hormats, "The United States and China: The Next Five Years," Remarks at the Brookings-Caixin Conference, May 18, 2011, https://2009-2017.state.gov/e/rls/rmk/20092013/2011

/163815.htm; Robert Hormats, "Addressing the Challenges of the China Model," Remarks at AmCham-China's Annual DC Dialogue, May 3, 2011, https://2009-2017.state.gov/e/rls/rmk/20092013/2011/157205.htm.

79. See James Steinberg, "Administration's Vision of the US-China Relationship," Keynote Address at the Center for a New American Security, September 24, 2009, https://china.usc.edu/james-steinberg-obama-administrations-vision-us-china-relationship-september-24-2009; Transcript of Remarks at the Press Conference with President Obama and President Hu of the People's Republic of China, January 19, 2011, available at https://obamawhitehouse.archives.gov/the-press-office/2011/01/19/press-conference-president-obama-and-president-hu-peoples-republic-china.
80. See, for example, Transcript of News Conference by President Obama, November 14, 2011, https://obamawhitehouse.archives.gov/the-press-office/2011/11/14/news-conference-president-obama; Transcript of Remarks by President Obama and Prime Minister Gillard of Australia in Joint Press Conference, November 16, 2011, https://obamawhitehouse.archives.gov/the-press-office/2011/11/16/remarks-president-obama-and-prime-minister-gillard-australia-joint-press; Hormats, "United States and China." Indeed, the Chinese state capitalism model had been described as "a direct threat to US jobs and competitiveness." See Hormats, "Addressing the Challenges of the China Model."
81. Kritenbrink, "US Policy toward the People's Republic of China (PRC)"; Shear, "China: Recent Security Developments." Regarding climate change, some observers felt that China had played a spoiler role at the December 2009 Copenhagen Climate Summit. US deputy secretary Steinberg, however, saw things differently and went on the record with praise of China's contribution, noting: "I think we saw in the final outcome in Copenhagen a clear recognition of China taking at least positive steps, if not complete steps, on each of (the) elements (needed to address the issue)." See James Steinberg, "US-China Cooperation on Global Issues," Remarks at the Brookings Institution, May 11, 2010, https://2009-2017.state.gov/s/d/former/steinberg/remarks/2010/169324.htm.
82. Hillary Clinton, Remarks with Chinese Foreign Minister Yang Jiechi, September 5, 2012, https://2009-2017.state.gov/secretary/20092013clinton/rm/2012/09/197343.htm.
83. Steinberg, "US-China Cooperation on Global Issues."
84. Zhao, "Shaping the Regional Context of China's Rise," 377.
85. See, for example, Vice-Premier Li Keqiang's commentary, "The World Should Not Fear a Growing China," *Financial Times*, January 9, 2011; and "China, US Shoulder Important Responsibilities on Host of Major World Issues: Hu Jintao," Xinhua, July 27, 2009.
86. Yan Xuetong, "Dangqian Guoji Xingshi Yu Zhongguo Waijiao De Tiaozheng," 9.
87. "China's Roars Grow Louder," *Straits Times*, March 18, 2010.
88. It should be emphasized that these positions are not mutually exclusive. Very often Chinese scholars hold composite views that are a combination of aspects from the different positions.

89. Li Baojun and Xu Zhengyuan, "Lengzhan Hou Zhongguo Fuzeren Daguo Shenfen De Jiangou" (China's self-identity construction as a responsible power in the post–Cold War era), *Jiaoxue Yu Yanjiu (Teaching and Research)* 1 (2006): 51; Niu Haibin, "'Zhongguo Zeren Lun' Xilun" (Examining the "China responsibility theory"), *Xiandai Guoji Guanxi (Contemporary International Relations)* 3 (2007): 48; Xing Yue and Zhan Yijia, "Fuzeren Daguo: Lilun, Lishi Yu Xianshi" (Responsible great power: Theory, history, and reality), in *Guoji Zeren Yu Daguo Zhanlue (International Responsibility and Great Power Strategy)*, ed. Pan Zhongqi (Shanghai: Shanghai Renmin Chubanshe, 2008), 82–84.
90. Liu also opines that "objectively speaking," given China's rise in global economic power and influence, it should contribute a larger share to the United Nations budget. See Liu Jianfei, "'Zhongguo Zeren Lun' Kaoyan Heping Fazhan" ("China responsibility theory" a test of peaceful development), *Xiandai Guoji Guanxi (Contemporary International Relations)* 4 (2007): 22–23. Conversely, Xing Yue and Zhan Yijia argue that "one cannot expect small powers in the system to shoulder major responsibilities." See Xing and Zhan, "Fuzeren Daguo," 82.
91. Jin Canrong, *Daguo De Zeren (Big Power's Responsibility)* (Beijing: Zhongguo Renmin Daxue Chubanshe, 2010), 1.
92. Yan Xuetong, "How Assertive Should a Great Power Be?," *New York Times*, March 31, 2011.
93. For Li Baojun and Xu Zhengyuan, the maintenance of international order represents the "lowest common consensus" on great-power responsibility. See Li and Xu, "Lengzhan Hou Zhongguo Fuzeren Daguo Shenfen De Jiangou." See also Niu, "'Zhongguo Zeren Lun' Xilun," 48–49.
94. See Yan, "How Assertive Should a Great Power Be?" For a fuller exposition on Yan and his colleagues' ideas about the notion of China as a "humane authority" in international affairs, see *Wangba Tianxia Sixiang Qidi (Thoughts of World Leadership and Implications)*, ed. Yan Xuetong and Xu Jin (Beijing: Shijie Zhishi Chubanshe, 2009).
95. Ma Zhengang, "Zhongguo De Zeren Yu 'Zhongguo Zeren Lun'" (China's responsibility and the "China responsibility theory"), *Guoji Wenti Yanjiu (International Studies)* 3 (2007): 1; Zhang Xiaotong, "Hu Jintao Shidai Guan De Zhongguo Zhuzhang" (Hu Jintao's contemporary view on China's stand), *Liaowang (Outlook)* 47 (2009): 32–36; and interview with Chinese scholar, Beijing, May 2011.
96. See, for example, the Fudan University seminar report: "Zhidu Gonggei Yu Daguo Jueqi: Zhongguo De Shimin" (Order co-contributor and the rise of a great power: China's destiny) in *Dongtai Yu Zhengce Pinglun (Trends and Policy Review)* 14 (2011): 8.
97. Interviews with Chinese scholars, Shanghai and Beijing, May–June 2011; interviews with Chinese scholars, Shanghai, September–November 2011; Wang Cungang and Wang Ruoling, "Lun Zhongguo Fuzeren Daguo Shengfen De Jiangou" (Discussing the construction of China's identity as a responsible great power), *Shijie Jingji Yu Zhengzhi Luntan (Forum on World Economics and Politics)* 1 (2008): 21; Liu, "'Zhongguo Zeren Lun' Kaoyan Heping Fazhan."

98. Shi Yinhong, "Chengjiu Yu Tiaozhan: Zhongguo Heping Fazhan, Hexie Shijie Linian Yu Duiwai Zhengce Xingshi" (Achievements and challenges: China's peaceful development, harmonious world concept and the external policy situation), *Dangdai Shijie Yu Shehui Zhuyi (Contemporary World and Socialism)* 2 (2008): 83–84.
99. Wu, "Guoji Xingshi Jubian Xia Zhongguo De Guoji Quxiang," 24.
100. Fudan University, "Zhidu Gonggei Yu Daguo Jueqi," 8; Liu, "'Zhongguo Zeren Lun' Kaoyan Heping Fazhan," 26; Xu Zhengyuan, "Quanli Yu Zeren: Lengzhan Hou Zhongguo Fuzeren Daguo Shengfen De Jiangou" (Power and responsibility: The construction of China's identity as a responsible great power after the Cold War), in *Guoji Zeren Yu Daguo Zhanlue (International Responsibility and Great Power Strategy)*, ed. Pan Zhongqi (Shanghai: Shanghai Renmin Chubanshe, 2008), 47.
101. Interview with Chinese analyst, Shanghai, November 2011.
102. According to Liu, the idea of great power responsibility is "not uniform, encompassed contradictory elements, and [is] nebulous." In his view, thus far no "international authority" has been able to provide a definitive account of the concept. Liu Ming, "Zhongguo Guoji Zeren Lun Pingxi" (Appraising the China international responsibility theory), *Mao Zedong Deng Xiaoping Lilun Yanjiu (Studies on Mao Zedong and Deng Xiaoping Theories)* 1 (2008): 52–54.
103. Interviews with Chinese scholars, Shanghai and Beijing, May–June 2011; "China Not Second Strongest Economy: FM Official," *China Daily*, April 10, 2012; "Responsibilities of a Big Power," *Beijing Review* 44 (2007): 37; Li Jie, "Cong Zeren Lun Toushi Guoji Tixi Zhuanxing" (Viewing the transformation of the international system from the perspective of the responsibility theory), *Guoji Wenti Yanjiu (International Studies)* 1 (2008): 36–41, 47; Liu, "'Zhongguo Zeren Lun' Kaoyan Heping Fazhan," 24; Liu, "Zhongguo Guoji Zeren Lun Pingxi," 52–54; Xu, "Quanli Yu Zeren" 46–55.
104. Li, "Cong Zeren Lun Toushi Guoji Tixi Zhuanxing," 41.
105. Jin, *Daguo De Zeren*, 7.
106. Liu, "'Zhongguo Zeren Lun' Kaoyan Heping Fazhan," 26; Xu, "Quanli Yu Zeren," 46–47.
107. Interviews with Chinese scholars, Beijing and Shanghai, May-June 2011; "Experts Lash Out at 'China Responsibility' Theories," *China Daily*, August 20, 2010; "Beware Extolling China to Danger with World-Level 'Responsibilities,'" People's Daily Online, August 17, 2010, http://en.people.cn/90001/90776/90883/7107682.html; Zhao, "'Zhongguo Fuzeren Lun' De Daode Xianjin"; Zhang Shengjun, "'Zhongguo Fuzeren Lun' Keyi Xiuyi" ("China responsibility theory" can retire), *Renmin Luntan (People's Tribune)* 6 (2007): 50.
108. Ma, "Zhongguo De Zeren Yu 'Zhongguo Zeren Lun,'" 3.
109. Interview with Huo Jianguo, President of the International Economic and Trade Research Institute of the Ministry of Commerce, "Why Is China Supposed to Be Responsible for the World?," *Beijing Review* 35 (2010): 46–47.
110. Yan, "How Assertive Should a Great Power Be?"

111. I interviewed several Chinese scholars and a Chinese policymaker between April and June 2011 (in Shanghai and Beijing) and September–December 2011 (in Shanghai).
112. This is not to claim that China is becoming more "responsible"; this relates to a normative question that is not the focus of the book.

5

XI'S CHINA: POST-RESPONSIBILITY SINCE 2013?

Under Xi Jinping's stewardship China is seen as exercising a more assertive brand of foreign policy with the intent of renegotiating its relationship with the global order in greater favor of Chinese interests.[1] These shifts have led some to speak of the "fall" of the responsible power, with the assumption that China has now "abandoned" that role reference. Xi's China, one noted IR scholar writes in the *Washington Quarterly*, is a "post–responsible power."[2] "Without a self-identification that aligns China with the global status quo and [as] an anchor for Western engagement," he adds, "post-responsible China has become a lot more revisionist." A deconstruction of Chinese great-power identity in the Xi era suggests such arguments oversimplify the actual situation. Far from marginalizing or discarding the responsible-power identity, the Xi government and Chinese elites have continued to actively pursue this role imagination, even as they have tweaked its content in their envisioning of China's place within international society. Building on the genealogical tracing of the previous chapters, this chapter draws attention to some of the key ideas, debates, events, and developments that inform the process of identity construction in the Xi era.

Xi's Lesser-Known Pursuit and Continuing US Role Pressure

Contrary to assessments that perceive Beijing as repudiating the responsible-power identity, there is considerable evidence to indicate that the promulgation of this identity has in fact been *reinforced* under Xi. As the previous chapters show, the idea of a responsible power is a role notion that has been formalized at the highest political levels since the Jiang Zemin and Hu Jintao eras. By the time of

Hu's handover of power to Xi, the *Report of the Eighteenth Party Congress* avers that China will "exhibit the function of a responsible great power."[3]

The Xi government has continued where the previous regimes left off, not only in terms of engaging the RGP discourse but also in making ideational calibrations that further consolidate this role categorization. Notions such as the "China dream," the "great rejuvenation of the Chinese nation," and "a new type of international relations" have tended to occupy attention as the key political formulations of the Xi regime. However, it is often missed that the idea of China's global responsibility has been a nontrivial aspect in Xi's policy narratives. This was exemplified in June 2013 when, early in his presidency, Xi informed UN secretary general Ban Ki Moon that the PRC understood and would assume the "heavy responsibilities" of a Security Council permanent member.[4] The United Nations was again Xi's choice for projecting the country's responsible-power role when, addressing the General Assembly in September 2015, he declared the contribution of US$1 billion to support UN activities, as well as the provision of an eight-thousand-strong peacekeeping standby force and US$100 million to assist in crisis response in Africa.[5] These pledges came at the time of Xi's first state visit to the US. Ahead of that visit, in a written response to a *Wall Street Journal* interview, the Chinese president noted that "respond[ing] to various global problems and challenges . . . is what the international community expects of China and to do so is China's responsibility."[6] He added that the country "wishes to join hands with the US to tackle major regional and global issues." This willingness, Xi later claimed during the visit, related to the "deep" coupling of Chinese and American interests, which meant "greater responsibilities" for sustaining the international system.[7] But perhaps the clearest articulation of the RGP identity came during the reverse fixture a year earlier (Obama's state visit to China in 2014). When directly asked how Beijing sees its own position and role in international affairs during the presidents' joint press conference, Xi stated that today's China is more than just a participant in the global system; it is also a "*builder* of, and contributor to," that system.[8] Therefore, as "China continues to develop . . . [it] will shoulder more and more international responsibilities that are commensurate with [its] own strengths and position."

That Xi would continue to assert the RGP identity could be explained in part by the fact that in the Chinese political system this identity has become an established role narrative, denoting a degree of institutional continuity and "stickiness" to its evocation. At the same time, Beijing sees the category of responsible power as a socially desirable status within international society and is keenly aware that full American recognition of its great-power status is related to the extent China is willing to bear its share of global obligations. Xi himself alluded to this understanding during his 2015 stateside visit, where he acknowledged (or, in his words, "appreciated") that the United States would like China to do more and assume a bigger global role.[9]

On this US role pressure, as noted in chapter 4, there had been a subtle but discernible stiffening of the Obama administration's rhetoric on China by the latter half of its first term, which squared with Beijing's perceived rising foreign policy assertiveness from around 2010. The tougher American language initially appeared to be carried over to the second term of the Obama administration. In an August 2014 interview with the *New York Times*, the US president notably called China a "free rider," comments that drew indignant Chinese responses accusing Obama of "playing the card of international responsibility."[10] By November, however, Washington seemed to moderate its assessment of and tone on China. At the 2014 APEC Leaders Meeting, Obama publicly affirmed Chinese "contributions to international security." The following year Deputy National Security Adviser Ben Rhodes acknowledged that Beijing had provided "crucial support" on a number of global priorities.[11] The more approving American rhetoric did not mean that areas of disagreement or tension had necessarily lessened, but it did suggest some recognition of the Xi regime's efforts to address expectations of the country as a responsible stakeholder. By the end of 2014 some of these efforts were beginning to show tangible results, including: (i) the unprecedented climate change agreement by China to limit its emission levels by 2030; (ii) its role in the P5+1 negotiations, which eventually yielded the landmark 2015 Iran nuclear deal; and (iii) Chinese contributions in global public health, particularly in West Africa (which the White House expressed as being "very appreciative" of).[12]

From Washington's perspective these were positive signs for its long-standing strategy of coaxing China into a responsible global power, an identity that Obama has declared the US "[didn't] just welcome" but actively "support[ed]." There were certainly numerous occasions for the US president to directly communicate this role prescription to Xi. By the time of Xi's 2015 state visit to the US, it would be the sixth meeting between the two leaders in three years. At this sixth meeting Obama elaborated the US rationale for supporting a bigger Chinese role on the world stage. Despite its unique strengths, Obama noted, the United States could not resolve global problems alone. This is why, he argued, it is in American "interests" to see China grow stronger, to the extent that the latter "can then serve as an effective partner on a range of international challenges." In Obama's view, China has reached the point where it cannot be expected to be treated as the "poor developing country" that it was fifty years ago. China "is now a powerhouse," the US president stressed, "and that means it's got responsibilities and expectations in terms of helping to uphold international rules . . . part of the deal of being on the world stage when you're a big country, is you've got more to do."[13]

Great-Power Confidence

Obama's "powerhouse" remark did not raise eyebrows in China. As argued earlier, there had been an overall upward trajectory in Chinese estimations of their nation's comprehensive power status since around 2008, a belief further reinforced when China emerged from the global financial crisis in relatively healthier shape than most Western economies. In 2010 China overtook Japan to become the world's second-largest economy, a considerable boost to Chinese self-esteem, given the deep historical rivalry between the two.

In the Xi era, some notable events helped nourish Chinese and external perceptions of the country's rising global status, including the inauguration of the China-led Asian Infrastructure Investment Bank (AIIB) and its success in attracting fifty-seven prospective founding members, including American allies such as the United Kingdom, Israel, and Germany;[14] the milestone inclusion of the renminbi in the IMF's Special Drawing Rights basket, effectively marking the currency as one of the few world reserve currencies;[15] and China's hosting of the APEC (2014) and G20 (2016) global summits. In addition, by 2014 China had burgeoned into the world's largest economy, based on purchasing-power parity.[16] In the military dimension, the introduction of China's first aircraft carrier, the *Liaoning*, is seen as a potent emblem of the country's growing military strength and blue-water ambitions.

These circumstances, among other reasons, inform the reason Chinese big-power confidence has not only been sustained; there has been arguably greater willingness among Chinese elites to *emphasize* their nation's great-power identity. Xi's published work *The Governance of China* reflects this confidence: the tome devotes a specific section to China's "new model of great power relations" and recognizes only America, Russia, and the European Union as peer powers (excluding India and Japan).[17] Indeed, this notion of a new model of great-power relations (*xinxing daguo guanxi*) has become one of the key foreign policy narratives of the Xi regime. To be sure, the term itself has seen earlier usage. State Councillor Dai Bingguo advocated for a "new type of great power relations" between China and the US at the 2010 Strategic and Economic Dialogue (SED), while President Hu Jintao evoked similar terms at the 2012 SED.[18] Nevertheless, the concept assumed "new significance" when it was featured prominently in Xi's rhetoric during his first summit with President Obama (at Sunnylands in June 2013) as well as subsequent high-level Sino-American talks.[19] Its basic premise is that relations among modern great powers should be characterized by a modality of "no conflicts or confrontations, mutual respect, and win-win cooperation."[20]

Chinese enthusiasm over the concept contrasts with American perceptions of wariness and circumspection. To the Obama administration, embracing the framework, particularly the second principle of mutual respect, potentially implies an acceptance of Chinese "core interests" that might include disputed maritime territorial claims involving US allies in East Asia.[21] It was also not lost on the administration that such an endorsement could affect perceptions of US commitment to the region.[22] Within China, however, the idea has sparked considerable discussion. While Chinese analysts continue to debate over the framework's substantive content, a number of subtexts with implications for China's identity are discernible. First, the new model reflects the PRC's desire to be seen as America's "equal." Although the concept does not necessarily refer only to Sino-American relations, it implies China is among the top tier of powers in a self-imagined global hierarchy, signifying a "level playing field" with the US.[23] Second, as an organizing framework, the new model seeks to rise above the kind of clashes history suggests usually occur between a rising power and an incumbent power—the so-called Thucydides Trap. Xi himself referenced this historical metaphor during his 2015 US visit. The new model of great-power relations, Xi stressed, requires China and the US to "read each other's strategic intentions correctly" and avoid the "mistakes of strategic miscalculation" that might create self-fulfilling Thucydides Traps.[24] Third, in proposing the new model it signals greater Chinese ambition to shape the US-China strategic agenda and discourse. Chinese scholars note that under Jiang and Hu, China tended to be the more "passive" (*beidong*) party in its political intercourse with America; the responsible-stakeholder concept is one exemplar of a US-driven strategic narrative shaping bilateral relations.[25] Xi's China is showing greater initiative to push forward its own ideas to co-steer the US-China relationship.

Striving for Achievement

The stronger ideational activism on the global stage parallels developments in Chinese strategic thinking under Xi. One connects to the question of whether Deng Xiaoping's strategic guideline, *Tao Guang Yang Hui* (TGYH), is still relevant for China's present international context.[26] TGYH, or "hide brightness, cherish obscurity," is often referred to as China's putative foreign policy strategy of "keeping a low profile" in the post–Cold war era. The basic assumption is that a low global profile will help China's development priorities. While the concept has evolved to include the influential phrase "*yousuo zuowei*" (get some things done), it is the idea of maintaining a low profile that is most commonly associated with the TGYH principle.[27]

Chinese elites have continued to debate the wisdom of the TGYH strategy in the Xi era. Those who argue for the enduring relevance of TGYH cite, among other things, the following justifications: (i) the global strategic balance remains, fundamentally, "West strong, East weak"; (ii) as a latecomer to global society, China remains in the "sensitive" period of growth and should avoid "attracting the target onto itself"; and (iii) Chinese development still has several difficult challenges to address.[28] That said, the PRC's improving power conditions as well as a changing international environment have led several Chinese thinkers to question the applicability of TGYH, arguing that China should assume a more proactive role in international affairs, with strategic emphasis on the latter dictum of "getting some things done" (i.e., *yousuo zuowei,* or YSZW). While not necessarily jettisoning the TGYH principle completely, these thinkers argue that, depending on the "circumstance and emphasis of the time," Chinese foreign policy should concern itself with establishing an appropriate balance between TGYH and YSZW. In the current period this balance has shifted toward YSZW.[29]

In October 2013, at the CCP's first Central Foreign Affairs Work Conference held since 2006, Xi appeared to resolve the debate in favor of the YSZW argument when he added his own conceptual modification of "striving for achievement" (*fenfa youwei*), suggesting a less passive and more proactive approach toward Chinese diplomacy.[30] This proactivism was again emphasized at the 2014 Central Foreign Affairs Work Conference, where Xi urged the party to "proactively plan" and "forge ahead assiduously" (*nuli jinqu*) in foreign affairs.[31] It was recognized that "China's dependence on the world and its involvement in international affairs are deepening." And, because the world is able to affect

China more (and vice versa), it behooves China to be proactive and "foster a more enabling environment" for its continuing development. It also means that China must give "full consideration" to "both domestic and foreign resources, and both domestic and international rules, and use them in a coordinated way."[32] All of these are part of what Xi sees as the development of a "distinctive diplomacy befitting the role of a great power."[33] It is worth noting that, at both meetings, there was a conspicuous absence of the TGYH rhetoric in Xi's speeches.

Senior policymakers and scholars have drawn attention to the "striving for achievement" (SFA) approach in their speeches and writings. Foreign minister Wang Yi uses the term "*jiji jinqu*" (forge ahead actively) to describe the current phase of Chinese diplomacy, while State Councillor Yang Jiechi (who outranks Wang) notes that China has "vigorously" pursued its foreign affairs goals.[34] Several intellectuals agree with this assessment of an adjustment in Chinese foreign policy. Prominent Chinese scholar Wang Yizhou writes:

> In the past, although its growth is rapid, China emphasized [TGYH] more and won't voice out politically . . . today's Chinese foreign strategy emphasizes pro-activeness and displays greater ambition. It also encompasses a kind of global perspective.[35]

According to Tsinghua University's Zhao Kejin, the new proactiveness is a response to "growing internal and external pressures and demands" that require China to harness its rising influence in order to achieve foreign policy goals.[36] For Xu Jin of the Chinese Academy of Social Sciences, the shift in approach concerns the "new appraisal" of China's global position, that the country now does not have the "objective conditions" to justify a low-profile strategy. Ergo, striving for achievement has become the "new normal" of Chinese diplomacy.[37]

The SFA discourse also plugs into the discussion on China's responsible-power role. Foreign Minister Wang declared at the 2014 National People's Congress that as part of a more "striving" foreign strategy, the PRC would "proactively demonstrate the function of a responsible great power." It was claimed that, among other things, Beijing would more actively participate in global and regional affairs, offer more "Chinese solutions" (*zhongguo fangan*), and play a bigger role in helping address international problems.[38] The added significance of the RGP identity is not surprising to Fudan University scholar Chen Zhimin, who sees the "change in self-identity" as the result of a more achievement-oriented and "intense" period of Chinese diplomacy.[39] The leading Chinese scholar Yan Xuetong concurs. Providing a more detailed exposition, Yan argues that the SFA approach is differentiated by its greater emphasis on international morality. Yan believes that "a rising power will never have a favorable environment unless it can *initiatively* and morally shape the international environment." To this end it becomes important for China to act as a "humane" leader and be proactive in undertaking global responsibilities. Doing so, he contends, will help China enhance its "strategic credibility" and bolster its "political legitimacy and strength" in international society.[40]

Global Governance

The SFA narratives about Chinese leadership in the world engage with a related policy discourse that has seen more emphasis under Xi: the role of China in global governance. This was deliberated at the twenty-seventh study session of the Politburo, convened specifically on the issue, at which the party outlined its vision of global governance for the first time.[41] At that October 2015 meeting Xi affirmed that China would "resolutely safeguard" and consolidate the extant postwar order. This did not mean, however, that reforms were not needed. Some ostensibly essential reforms include "laying down rules for the international order and international mechanisms" and "deciding in which direction the world will head." Reforms also entail asking questions about China's global identity (as well as the identities of others); in Xi's words, "what roles and functions nations will play in the long-term systemic arrangement of international order."[42]

Of course, discussion of global governance and its related issues has been going on within Chinese policymaking and scholarly circles for some time. In the Xi era there remains considerable continuity in several of these perspectives. Antecedent arguments about reforming the global order's "unjust and improper" arrangements, addressing the interests of developing states and making the order more representative, enhancing China's global voice, and affirming the importance of state sovereignty and equality are some key ideas that continue to be perpetuated by the Xi regime.[43] That said, some calibrations in Chinese global governance thinking are discernible. While these adjustments are more of degree than kind, I suggest they are nontrivial, particularly in the context of the RGP identity.

First, as a policy interest, global governance has elevated in strategic priority for Beijing. This was made clear when the CCP officially laid out its "theory" of global governance and unprecedentedly spotlighted the subject in the October 2015 and September 2016 collective study sessions. In March 2016 China announced its Thirteenth Five-Year Plan, which also affirmed the country's intention to "actively participate in global economic governance and contribute to the provision of global public goods."[44] Chinese scholars note that until the Eighteenth Party Congress (2012), global governance tended to be broached in terms of the broad trends or background contexts through which Chinese foreign strategy was discussed; now it is depicted as an integral component of this strategy.[45]

Second, there has been a stronger emphasis on positioning China as one of the rule makers of global order. This ambition extends beyond existing regimes (e.g., the economic and financial arenas) to setting rules and agendas in new domains (e.g., cyberspace, outer space, deep sea, polar zones, and climate change). Beijing perceives a strategic opening to make inroads in this pursuit. Noting that "the international balance of power has shifted," Xi has called for China to "take the chance and ride the wave" of global reform to leave a "Chinese mark" on the evolving order.[46]

Third, there has been a more discernible effort to clarify China's aims in global governance. In pursuing global reform Chinese narratives stress that China does not seek to overturn the extant order and instead aims to modify the current architecture by working from within it. These narratives also emphasize continuing support for free trade and economic openness, two pillars of the existing world economic system. Further, Chinese analysts argue that China is a net beneficiary of the present system and therefore see little need of replacing it with a fundamentally different one. Indeed, Xi uses the term "safeguard" (*weihu*) to underline China's overall desire to maintain the current order, even as it also seeks to steer this order's evolution in ways that align with Chinese visions.[47]

Fourth, a discussion of global governance in terms of China's international responsibility has become more palpable, particularly at the official level. This particular rhetoric is not new, and since around the time of China's involvement in the G20 forum Chinese analysts have sought to link the country's global governance exertions to the RGP discourse.[48] This has continued and arguably intensified in the present era, a development undoubtedly aided by Xi's remarks at the September 2016 study session. Xi instructed:

> We should actively take part in global governance, proactively assume global responsibilities, and do the best to our abilities.[49]

As "proof" of the shouldering of greater responsibilities in global governance, Chinese narratives cite China's contribution in several areas, of which two are commonly mentioned. One is its so-called summit diplomacy, with prominent examples being the country's hosting of the 2014 APEC Beijing meeting and the 2016 G20 Summit in Hangzhou. More than just "important measures" of the country's performance in global governance, they bespeak the belief that major multilateral meetings, especially the ones that China hosts, can be leveraged to achieve strategic and foreign policy aims. Hosting such summits, it is being argued, not only helps China demonstrate its big-power credentials and showcase the country as a responsible actor, it also advances its global leadership ambitions through the promotion and inclusion of Chinese ideas. Moreover, as the host country China has "home ground" (*zhuchang*) advantage and can "set the theme and influence" the outcome of the meetings. Xinhua, for example, proudly noted that China's ideas were "widely" incorporated in the Hangzhou summit's outcome and leaders' communiqués.[50]

The G20 platform has particular pride of place in Chinese thinking on and exercise of global governance. In China, involvement in that forum is thought of as the first time that the country participated as a "builder, founding member, and core" of the global-governance system. This involvement came as part of a collective effort by the world's major economies to coordinate the global response to the 2008–2009 financial crisis, and as seen in the previous chapter it represented the most visible aspect of China's external crisis response. While the crisis has abated somewhat, Beijing continues to champion the G20's relevance, arguing that several of the world's problems can be addressed only through collaboration in that platform. Indeed, Chinese narratives speak of reinforcing the G20's "core" position in global governance, with the goal of evolving the institution to become a long-term governance mechanism.[51]

Beyond the G20, however, the other major platform often cited as China's "vessel" of global governance is its much talked-about "One Belt, One Road" (OBOR) initiative.[52] The signature policy of Chinese diplomacy under Xi, OBOR seeks to "revive" the historical overland and maritime silk trading routes that link China to Europe through a continental trail via West Asia, Central Asia, and the Middle East (the "Silk Road Economic Belt"), as well as a sea path along Southeast Asia, South Asia, and Africa (the "Maritime Silk Road"). The objective, with China as the focal point, is to better connect the economies and peoples along these transregional spaces by strengthening infrastructure building; capital, technology, goods, and resource flows; people-to-people exchanges and development; policy coordination; communication linkages; and trade liberalization and integration. To facilitate this goal, in 2014 China established the US$40 billion Silk Road Fund and the complementary US$100 billion Asian Infrastructure Investment Bank to provide financing for related OBOR regional and country projects. The seriousness with which Beijing treats its OBOR initiative is evinced by the specific creation of a supraministerial committee, the Leading Group for the Construction of the One Belt, One Road, to oversee implementation.[53] Beijing has claimed that as of August 2016, over one hundred countries and international organizations have agreed to participate, with formal agreements established with thirty periphery countries and production cooperation started with twenty others.[54]

This apparent support sits uncomfortably with the more mixed assessments of the OBOR scheme outside of China. Questions remain about what the plan portends specifically and whether it amounts to nothing more than a political sloganizing of existing trading networks. But it is its potential and the implications of that potential that have generated the most misgivings. Economically there are fears that the initiative could mean greater Chinese leverage over regional and transregional economies, giving rise to a potentially more coercive economic statecraft (especially if and when the "feelings" of 1.4 billion Chinese are perceived to be hurt). Security-wise there are concerns that some of the OBOR's nodes—typically ports, transshipment facilities, and coastal industrial zones—may evolve into a network of "overseas strategic support bases" with secondary military utility or may draw greater Chinese military presence in protection of these overseas economic interests.[55] Both scenarios continue to shape contingency thinking in Washington and other regional capitals. On a broader geostrategic level, the OBOR has been likened to China's version of the Marshall Plan, which, if successful, could extend its "strategic and political influence at America's expense." This reflects the view that the OBOR represents a threat to the US-shaped order in Asia through its alternative China-centric arrangements and vision.[56]

These reservations have not gone unnoticed in Beijing, and, unsurprisingly, Beijing dismisses them. Beijing particularly rejects the Marshall Plan metaphor, arguing that the American postwar scheme was "hegemonic" in design and exclusionary, while the OBOR stresses equality and is "open to all." The

OBOR is "not a solo but a symphony" of all relevant countries, Chinese leaders assert.[57] Chinese narratives on the subject further depict a number of international objectives where this initiative is concerned. For one, the OBOR provides a structure for spreading the benefits of China's growth to its periphery regions. It amounts to, in the words of the OBOR Action Plan unveiled in March 2015, an "invitation" to others to hitchhike on China's growth train. Two, the initiative represents China's answer for lifting the sluggish global economy, showing the way toward a more inclusive form of globalization. This answer is also, three, a unique Chinese "design" of global governance participation that will see the country provide more global public goods in the form of driving international development, particularly regarding infrastructure. In emphasizing development, it is hoped that, four, deepening economic interdependence will create "a solid foundation for enhancing political and security cooperation," making for a "safer" Asia. Ideally all of this should lead to a process of collective identity change and remake Asia into what Xi calls "a community of common destiny."[58]

At the same time, Chinese writings do not deny that the initiative should serve national interests. Indeed, economic imperatives are among some of the key motivations. These would include: (i) better securing the supply of natural resources needed to fuel the country's continuing development; (ii) opening up new foreign markets and production bases; (iii) promoting the globalization of Chinese enterprises and human resources; (iv) better utilizing China's massive reserves and diversifying its capital outflow destinations; (v) addressing the issue of Chinese economic overcapacity; (vi) spurring the further development of China's less-developed western regions; and (vii) promoting the greater internationalization of the yuan.[59] Taken together these rationales speak to Xi's broader goal of "comprehensively" reforming the Chinese economy, which, among other things, strives to move the country up the global production chain and focus on more technologically advanced and higher-wage economic activities. The OBOR is vital to this ambition, and China believes it will help "consolidate its position" as the focal point of an evolving global supply and production system that is increasingly centered on Asia. [60]

Economics is not the only facet, however (although it is arguably the most important). While Beijing is wary that OBOR is seen as having a politico-strategic agenda, a number of Chinese writings point to a number of non-economic interests. There are, for example, the arguments that the initiative would help bolster China's soft power, operationalize its new more "striving" diplomacy, and showcase the "wisdom" of Chinese ways. Other narratives depict the OBOR as a product of strategic necessity in that China has had to look westward because of a more threatening strategic environment in Asia in light of the US rebalance policy. In pursuing its own "rebalance" to the West via the OBOR, the logic is to "avoid confrontation with the US while at the same time expanding the number of opportunities that exist for cooperation." This westward shift would also support the broader Chinese ambition to assert a bigger role and voice on the world stage, particularly in regions where the strategic room for maneuver is perceived to be greater. For these reasons and more the OBOR has been described as a key conduit through which China will "express" its identity as a responsible power.[61]

Shifting Debate on China's Responsibility

The allusion to the responsible-power identity in the OBOR discourse (and other strategic discussions) speaks to the growing prominence of the RGP narrative under Xi. As we have seen, this role narrative is not an infrequent feature of Xi's policy statements, and its assertion and diffusion within Chinese public discourse have arguably intensified during his leadership. Data from the CCP's main newspaper, the *People's Daily* (Fig. 5.1), show a general and steady increase in the public usage of the identity term "responsible great power" from 2003 to 2016, with a clear upward spike beginning in 2013 (the start of the Xi era). This trend is also largely mirrored in the People's Liberation Army news media, the *PLA Daily*, which typically focuses more on military issues as opposed to the broader ambit of Chinese diplomacy (Fig. 5.2).

The "rise" of the RGP identity in public discourse is paralleled by a stronger policy focus on the questions of China's obligations within international society, embodied in the introduction of the "morality-interest view" (*yili guan*) as the official guiding concept on such issues. First raised by Xi during his March 2013 visit to Africa, the morality-interest concept proposes that in the course of its peaceful rise, China must "correctly handle the relationship between morality (*yi*) and interests (*li*)" and not neglect ethics and responsibilities in international affairs. This relates to the Confucian view that "a country must treat morality as its interests too." In a subsequent September 2013 *People's Daily* commentary, Foreign Minister Wang further echoed the concept, arguing that China needs to "sometimes emphasize morality over interests;" it cannot treat "self-interest as its only motivation" or be "over-calculative."[62]

Figure 5.1 Frequency of articles that use the term "responsible great power" (负责任大国) in the *People's Daily*, 2003–2016. Source: *People's Daily* database, China National Knowledge Infrastructure (CNKI).

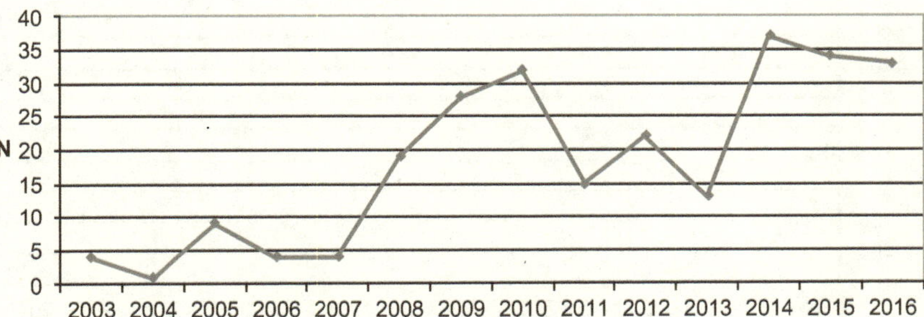

Figure 5.2 Frequency of articles that use the term "responsible great power" (负责任大国) in the *People's Liberation Army (PLA) Daily*, 2003–2016. Source: *PLA Daily* database, China National Knowledge Infrastructure (CNKI).

Such arguments shape the equally proliferating but richer discussions among Chinese intellectuals (see Figs. 5.3 and 5.4).[63] As the previous chapter shows, there had been essentially three schools of "responsibility" thought in the evolving RGP debate: what I have termed the internationalist, developmental, and skeptics' positions. In the Xi era, even as these positions are still discernible, Chinese sources are suggesting a shift in narrative toward the internationalist perspective. Chinese writings suggest scholars in the state-affiliated university/think-tank system are increasingly receptive and evocative of the broad argument that China should assume more global responsibilities, and are moving away from limited responsibility and suspicion that the developmental and skeptics' positions espouse respectively. There appears to be broad intellectual agreement that international responsibility is a positive notion that should be further embraced, and that undertaking such obligations is the necessary quality of being a great

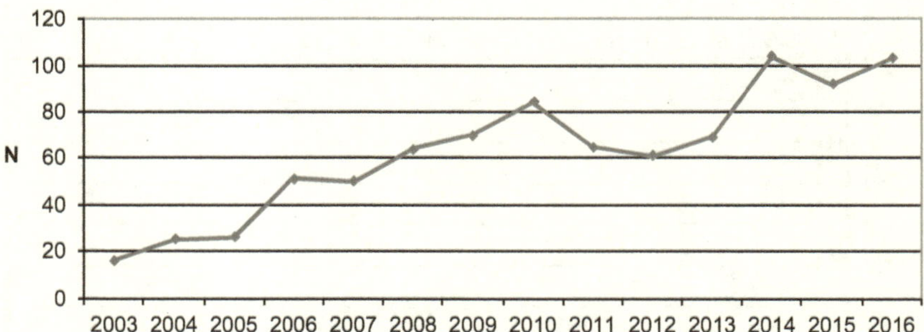

Figure 5.3 Frequency of journal articles that focus on the topic of the "responsible great power" (负责任大国), 2003–2016. Source: China Social Sciences Journals database, China National Knowledge Infrastructure (CNKI).

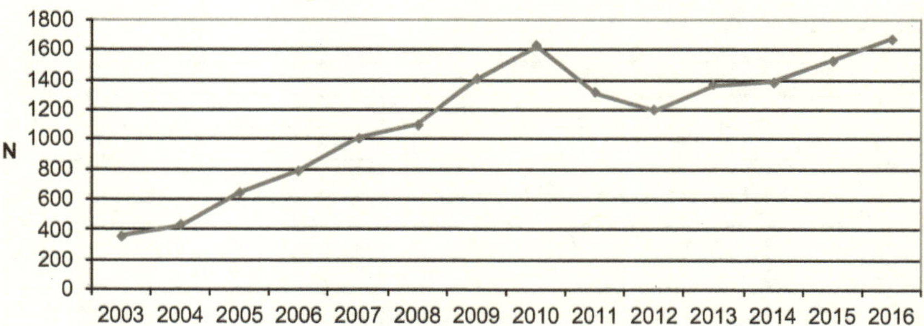

Figure 5.4 Frequency of journal articles with the term "responsible great power" (负责任大国) in the main text, 2003–2016. Source: China Social Sciences Journals database, China National Knowledge Infrastructure (CNKI).

power. Indeed, the term "dandang" (担当) is frequently used to express the notion of a China that "boldly" addresses its global obligations as opposed to merely "fulfilling" them.[64] This emerging consensus toward international responsibility does not mean, however, that the *content* of Chinese views is necessarily altruistic or in agreement with American perspectives. In this section I examine some key narratives informing adjustments in the Chinese RGP debate.

Unity of Interests, Rights, and Responsibilities

One set of conversations over the RGP debate deals with the nexus between China's responsibility and its "morality-interest view." Here, there are two interrelated arguments. The more humanist version, as exemplified by the writings of Qin Yaqing and others, advises that China should reject the "primacy of national interests" that supposedly underpins traditional international relations and instead develop a broad-minded mentality that meshes its interests with the pursuit of morality in its diplomacy. This means taking on more responsibilities for international society so as to occupy the high ground of international morality and order. Without a sufficient moral base for Chinese power, it is noted, it will be difficult for the PRC to attain "comprehensive" recognition of its great-power position.[65]

The more utilitarian view argues that while there have been increasing external calls for China to assume more responsibilities within the global system, these calls have not been matched by a corresponding increase in the country's rights or decision power in the system. This is particularly vexing to the Chinese, given that China now holds court as the world's second-largest economy and contributes almost 30 percent to global economic growth. In this context the launch of the OBOR initiative as well as co-establishment of the BRICS Development Bank and the Asian Infrastructure Investment Bank are presented as China's way of taking "proactive" responsibility over the global economic system so as to better exercise its "directional function" as a great power.[66] This proactivity is preferred, proponents argue, because a more self-initiatory mind-set toward its global responsibilities will enable China to better meet its national interests through: (i) having a greater "choice" in determining or prioritizing the kinds of obligations it should assume; (ii) acquiring a greater voice and influence in international society; and (iii) pushing the global order in a more reasonable and fairer direction. The broader goal is to help China condition an external environment that is more favorable to (or at least not hampering) its interests.[67] In essence, global responsibility is conceived as a means by which Beijing can better address the perceived imbalance of its rights and interests in a global society that, while acknowledging its power, purportedly denies those elements. Hence, China Institutes of Contemporary International Relations scholar Wang Honggang avers that the greater American clamor for China to assume more responsibilities should be embraced. "Regardless of the motivations," Wang notes, "China can use this trend."[68]

Coordination of Great Power Responsibility

Citing A. F. K. Organski's power transition theory or Graham Allison's more recent political analogy of the Thucydides Trap, Chinese scholars are not unaware of assessments postulating that China's rise increases the potential for conflict with other great powers (particularly the US). Responses have varied from rejection and criticism of such arguments to policy and intellectual proposals for mitigating the possibility of conflict scenarios. Among the latter group, some suggest that "responsibility coordination" between great powers is one viable way of moderating the dangers of power shifts between them. According to this view, the problem lies not in power transition per se but in differing structural objectives: the hegemon seeks to minimize "power transition" and maximize "responsibility transition," while the rising power seeks the converse—that is, maximizing the power transition and minimizing the responsibility transition. Thus, to avert conflict it behooves both the hegemon and the rising power to come to a "non-optimal" compromise of balancing their respective responsibilities and power positions in international society. In reference to Sino-American relations, it is suggested that the two powers share and coordinate their global responsibilities in a way that assures US primacy status while ensuring China's commensurate global status.[69] As CASS scholar Wang Wei notes, "The hegemon and the rising power cannot escape the fact that shifts in power relations will lead to shifts in responsibility burdens, and vice versa"; ergo, China and the US will have to jointly manage the spoils and burdens of power transition.[70]

A related, less ambitious narrative similarly calls for greater big-power coordination but focuses on the idea of "competition management" as opposed to obligation coordination. There are two aspects to this narrative. One strand hews toward a Bullian conception of great-power responsibility, noting that it is imperative for great powers to "properly manage great-power relations." Only when these "special" relations are handled well, proponents argue, would forward progress be made in the international system. It therefore becomes critical for, as well as the responsibility of, great powers to strengthen coordination, in particular in preventing new areas of contention from developing while keeping existing differences under control.[71] The second strand, while not an entirely new argument, holds that the "responsibility discourse" is the flipside of the "China threat discourse." Recognizing China's structural and ideological tensions with the US—as both a rising and a communist power—the suggestion is that Beijing should take on more responsibilities and provide more global public goods as a way of offsetting these competitive perceptions and elements.[72]

A Matter of Opportunity

Concurring with a generally more strategic view of responsibility, there are those who believe that the RGP identity represents a major "historic opportunity of the times" for the country.[73] The language of opportunity is not unusual in Chinese political discourse, as scholars and policymakers frequently evoke the phrase "strategic window of opportunity" (*zhanlue jiyuqi*) to describe how critical it is for China to maximize its rise prospects while circumstances (both internal and external) are favorable. Indeed, the *Sixteenth Party Congress Report* had employed the concept to describe the first twenty years of the twenty-first century as that opportune window of time.[74]

In relation to the international system, it is claimed that "the time has come for China to undertake the responsibility" for spurring the latest round of evolution. Given Europe's continuing economic doldrums, America's political and societal fissures, and Russia's stalled rejuvenation, it is not lost on some Chinese scholars that "China is widely seen as the most likely engine and force for driving the latest round of development of the global system."[75] This is an expectation and opportunity that China should grasp, they argue. "Just as how eighteenth- and nineteenth-century Europe and twentieth-century America were influential in shaping the then-international system," writes one scholar, "today's China fully has the conditions to play a similar role."[76] Proponents further argue that the core objective of China's grand strategy is the rejuvenation of the Chinese nation, and a key factor is the country's relationship with the outside world, particularly the developing world. If the coevolution of this relationship goes well, it will provide China with "deeper strategic resources and broader strategic space" to realize its national rejuvenation.[77] Some analysts are more circumspect, though. They note that, historically, Great Britain and the United States spent a long time "learning how to be a great power," while other states, such as Russia and Japan, "wasted their chance[s] to be one."[78] Connecting to its role ambitions, the lesson is that China may not be able to avoid the potentially arduous learning journey of a great power.[79]

Chinese Actions

There have been behavioral indications of a China keen to showcase itself as a responsible power. Beijing's inauguration of the OBOR initiative and the AIIB, as well as its burgeoning role in the G20 Forum, are activities cited by the Chinese as demonstrating the country's more proactive disposition toward its international obligations.

Another such effort relates to the global response to tackling climate change, described by Obama as a "special responsibility" of China and the US.[80] The centerpiece undertaking here is the milestone agreement between both countries to cap their emissions growth, with Beijing pledging to do so by 2030. The Chinese commitment not only caught much of the international community by surprise but also drew particular plaudits from Washington, which "commended" the Xi government and lauded the deal as an example of "what's possible when [both powers] work together on an urgent global challenge."[81] This agreement also added much-needed momentum to the negotiations to conclude a world climate pact by the 2015 Paris Conference. Unlike the 2009 Copenhagen meeting, when the PRC delegation was perceived in some quarters as obstructionist, at the 2015 round of talks Chinese negotiators were generally seen as playing a constructive role in driving the global endeavor to forge a climate change accord. Beijing was certainly keen to trumpet its contribution when the landmark pact was reached, claiming that the deal showed its "sense of responsibility as a major country tackling climate change."[82] Ahead of the Hangzhou G20 summit in September 2016, China, along with the US, announced its formal accession to the Paris climate agreement.[83]

Climate change is not the only international domain that saw greater Sino-American leadership. One understated collaboration has been the first formal partnership between the two powers to drive global development. This encompasses: (i) widening cooperation to improve food security, agricultural development, energy access, and disaster assistance in regions such as Africa and Asia; (ii) establishing a coordination mechanism for realizing the UN's post-2015 development agenda; and (iii) working together to promote sustainable development. This partnership on international development built on earlier bilateral efforts to cooperate on global public health, an area in which Chinese assistance on fighting Ebola in West Africa had proved critical.[84]

The two countries also managed to achieve some degree of progress on the contentious issue of cybersecurity. In 2015 Beijing and Washington reached a common "understanding" that they would not knowingly support or engage in cybertheft or cyberespionage that might profit commercial entities. Such alleged activities from China had vexed the Obama administration, and the 2015 consensus on the issue was seen as an attempt by both powers to work together to co-develop the "rules of the road" for the global cyberregime, even as considerable American skepticism remained.[85]

On other aspects of international security, a number of developments are notable in Chinese diplomacy. Peacekeeping work has been a key arena in which China's involvement continues to expand. Chinese officials are wont to remind others that their country remains the largest contributor of personnel to UN peacekeeping operations among Security Council permanent members. By August 2016 this contribution had burgeoned to around twenty-six hundred Chinese peacekeepers, a fourfold increase from 2004. China's financial support of the UN peacekeeping budget has also grown, overtaking Japan as the second-largest contributor (10.3 percent) after the United States. As of 2016, Chinese blue helmets are spread across more than half of UN peacekeeping operations, of which PLA troops are directly involved in several assignments, including those in Congo (MONUSCO), Mali (MINUSMA), Darfur (UNAMID), Liberia (UNMIL), Lebanon (UNIFIL), and South Sudan (UNMISS).[86] What is interesting here is that this military involvement has started to entail, for the first time, combat troops. In 2013 a Chinese "guard detachment" was dispatched to Mali. The following year the first Chinese infantry battalion undertook "protection" work for UN forces in South Sudan, a deployment that has been maintained on an annual rotational basis.[87] The changing character of Chinese military involvement in UN missions is also reflected in the establishment of a permanent PLA "facility" in Djibouti, which, outside of China, was described as its first overseas military base. Beijing has framed the installation as a way to better support its peacekeeping operations in the surrounding regions.[88]

These recalibrations speak to a more flexible interpretation of the "non-intervention" principle in the Xi era, changes that have meant a less reticent Chinese engagement in a number of global hotspots. For example, Beijing has started to take a more visible role in the Syrian civil war: it appointed its first special envoy to Syria; it dispatched a senior PLA representative to Damascus to meet senior Syrian officials, where an agreement was made to expand Chinese aid and personnel training; and it has continued to host on-off talks between the Syrian government and opposition forces.[89] In Afghanistan, growing evidence of a Chinese hand in the reconstruction process is also discernible. These attempts include seeking to (quietly) mediate between Kabul and the Taliban, instigating subregional dialogue mechanisms in the form of "trilaterals" (China-Afghanistan-Pakistan) or "quadrilaterals" (China-Afghanistan-Pakistan-Tajikistan), and stepping up assistance to the Afghan military. On the last point, notably, Beijing has begun conducting "joint counterterrorism operations" with Kabul, even as it is careful to deny the presence of the PLA.[90] It should be pointed out that China's overall approach is still to avoid unnecessary entanglement in foreign conflicts, especially overt military involvement. Hence it has not always escaped scrutiny, particularly from Washington, over the perceived inadequacy of its responses to some of these conflicts; indeed, this sort of purported inaction had been the basis of Obama's "free rider" charge of China.[91]

Beijing's part in another major Middle Eastern political hotspot, the Iran nuclear issue, would be appreciated more by Washington. Working with the US as part of the P5+1, China was seen to be integral to the diplomatic process that culminated in the historic July 2015 agreement committing Tehran to restrictions on nuclear weapons development in exchange for sanctions relief. China's importance to the nuclear deal related to more than solely its traditional influence with Tehran. Among other things, the Chinese played a role in redesigning Iran's Arak reactor to prevent its potential use for nuclear militarization and was among a number of countries that "voluntarily" eased their purchases of Iranian oil to chime with American pressure. The "China factor" was also cited as a key consideration in Russia's eventual willingness to back the nuclear pact.[92]

China's record in the East Asian security theater presents a more complicated picture. Regarding North Korea, there has been broad alignment between Beijing and Washington on the denuclearization of the Korean peninsula. Since Xi's ascension to power this convergence has inched closer in some respects, while China–North Korea relations have frayed.[93] The strains with Pyongyang can be seen in a number of situations. For instance, in unusually strong comments following Pyongyang's 2013 nuclear test, Xi pointedly warned that "no one should be allowed to throw . . . the whole world into chaos for selfish gains."[94] That year saw the once "special" Sino–North Korean relationship downgraded to "normal" state-to-state relations.[95] China also continued to back UN sanctions, which have become increasingly tougher as Pyongyang persists in conducting nuclear and missile tests. In early 2017, in what Beijing described as an effort to support existing sanctions and "strictly carry out [its] international obligations," China stopped all coal imports from North Korea.[96] While these measures are undoubtedly welcomed by Washington, the US would have liked Beijing to do more. Beijing is seen as being reluctant to pressure Pyongyang more, even if it shared American concerns of the latter's destabilizing conduct. In some areas, moreover—such as the expanding Sino–North Korean bilateral trade and perceived Chinese attempts to water down UN sanctions—China is thought to be shortchanging the global effort to rein in Pyongyang.[97]

But if North Korea has seen limited cooperation between China and the US, another regional flashpoint may prove to be far more contentious: the East and

South China Seas territorial disputes. Aspects of China's conduct, such as the growing repression of domestic civil and political liberties, the perpetuation of perceived "unfair" trading practices, and Chinese cyberhacking activities, have concerned (and grated on) Washington.[98] Yet, even as Washington continues to put a spotlight on these issues, the question of China's rising assertiveness in Asia's maritime spaces has come increasingly to the fore in the relationship between the two countries. Often-cited examples of this maritime assertiveness include: Beijing's unilateral declaration of a Chinese air defense identification zone in the East China Sea; its continuing occupation of several disputed South China Sea islets; the stepping up of the use of armed naval vessels to enforce its maritime claims and interests; and its expansionary activities in the South China Sea, entailing installation of military weapons and infrastructure. These actions have led American policymakers to believe that the PRC is actively undermining the "rules-based" regional maritime order, a perception reinforced in the wake of an international tribunal ruling declaring the illegality of these activities.[99]

From China's perspective, however, such behavior is not only legitimate; it is also "reasonable" since Beijing is only doing what it should do to better protect the country's sovereignty and territorial integrity. The Chinese foreign ministry is quick to remind international audiences that the country is merely catching up on activities that had long been practiced by other claimants or that other claimants had first acted in ways that are equally, if not more, unconstructive (e.g., the unilateral referral by the Philippines of its maritime claims to a UN tribunal).[100] Equally noteworthy is the linkage that China has sought to draw between its East and South China Seas actions and the RGP identity. In response to criticism of Chinese construction activities on disputed islets, for example, the foreign ministry has come out to claim that such work is being carried out "at a pace and on a scale befitting China's international responsibilities and obligations." This work, it is claimed, is about addressing China's maritime responsibilities in "search and rescue, disaster mitigation, meteorological observation, ecological conservation, navigation safety, and fishery services" as well as about providing public goods for the global maritime community.[101] Similar arguments have also been made by Chinese scholars. Su Hao of China Foreign Affairs University suggests that the fact that a rising China has yet to fully recover its legitimate maritime rights in the South China Sea testifies to its "self-restraint." This restraint is comparable to its principled actions during the Asian financial crisis, Su argues, and demonstrates that the country is a "responsible power that values [regional] peace and stability."[102]

The RGP Identity under Xi

The evidence discussed in this chapter suggests a more intricate picture of China's identity evolution under Xi than is commonly presented in existing literature. Most analyses tend to underestimate or discount the degree to which the Xi regime has engaged the responsible-power concept in Chinese diplomacy. The findings here show that the pursuit of the RGP identity has not only continued in the Xi era; it has discernibly intensified. At the same time, the content of this identity has evolved in a way that not only attests to continuing American role pressure but also reflects particular Chinese ideational shifts. These shifts speak to calibrations in Chinese strategic thinking that have meant a less passive and more proactive foreign policy approach as well as a greater emphasis on China's role in global governance. They also speak to movements in the domestic RGP debate that suggest that while there is an emerging consensus that China should take on more global responsibilities, this notion is intertwined with the growing discussion of interests in Chinese ideas of responsibility.

Coupled with the behavioral evidence thus far, we are led to a layered picture of Xi's China that defies simplistic categorization. To a considerable extent, today's China is still very much a status quo power that has acted to support or reinforce aspects of the extant global order. Yet, in several areas it is evidently more revisionist, has sought to effect change, and is less reticent to assert its perceived rights. This revisionism reflects a greater desire to shape and cultivate a more "enabling" external environment for China's development. It does not imply a wholesale overturning of the existing order, but it does suggest asserting a stronger role *within* this order to calibrate the global rules of the game to better suit the country's overriding objective of rising peacefully. For the Xi leadership, that "shaping" role is increasingly expressed through China's pursuit of its great-power identity and global responsibilities.

Notes

1. Hoo Tiang Boon, ed., *Chinese Foreign Policy under Xi* (London and New York: Routledge, 2017), chap. 1.
2. Yong Deng, "China: The Post-Responsible Power," *Washington Quarterly* 37, no. 4 (2015): 117–32.

3. *Hu Jintao Zai Zhongguo Gongchan Dang Di Shiba Ci Quanguo Daibiao Da Huishang De Baogao* (*Report of Hu Jintao to the Eighteenth National Congress of the Communist Party of China*), available at http://cpc.people.com.cn/n/2012/1118/c64094-19612151-1.html.
4. Teddy Ng and Kim Wall, "President Xi Hints at More Assertive Foreign Policy," *South China Morning Post*, June 21, 2013.
5. "Working Together to Forge a New Partnership of Win-Win Cooperation and Create a Community of Shared Future for Mankind," Statement by HE Xi Jinping at the General Debate of the Seventieth Session of the UN General Assembly, New York, September 28, 2015.
6. "Interview with Chinese President Xi Jinping," *Wall Street Journal*, September 22, 2015.
7. Transcript of Remarks by President Obama and President Xi of the People's Republic of China, Washington, September 25, 2015, https://obamawhitehouse.archives.gov/the-press-office/2015/09/25/remarks-president-obama-and-president-xi-peoples-republic-china-joint.
8. Transcript of the Joint Press Conference of President Obama and President Xi of the People's Republic of China, Beijing, November 12, 2014, https://obamawhitehouse.archives.gov/the-press-office/2014/11/12/remarks-president-obama-and-president-xi-jinping-joint-press-conference.
9. Transcript of Remarks by Obama and Xi, September 25, 2015.
10. Bree Feng, "Obama's 'Free Rider' Comment Draws Chinese Criticism," *New York Times*, August 13, 2014.
11. David Nakamura, "Obama and China: Trying to Play Well with a Close Frenemy," *Washington Post*, September 15, 2015.
12. Transcript of Remarks by Obama and Xi, September 25, 2015.
13. Ibid.; and Transcript of Joint Press Conference of Obama and Xi, November 12, 2014.
14. Swaminathan Anklesaria Aiyar, "Why US Allies Are Happy to Join China's AIIB," *Diplomat*, June 30, 2015.
15. Nathaniel Taplin and Ben Blanchard, "China's Yuan Joins Elite Club of IMF Reserve Currencies," Reuters, October 1, 2016.
16. Keith Fray, "China's Leap Forward: Overtaking the US as World's Biggest Economy," *Financial Times*, October 8, 2014.
17. Xi Jinping, *The Governance of China* (Beijing: Foreign Languages Press, 2014).
18. Qi Hao, "China Debates the 'New Type of Great Power Relations,'" *Chinese Journal of International Politics* 8, no. 4 (2015): 350.
19. Jane Perlez, "China's 'New Type' of Ties Fails to Sway Obama," *New York Times*, November 9, 2014.
20. "Xi Jinping Gaikuo Zhongmei Xinxing Daguo Guanxi, Bu Chongtu, Bu Duikang, Xianghu Zunzhong, Hezuo Gongying" (Xi Jinping sums up China-US new type of great power relations as no conflict, no confrontation, mutual respect, win-win cooperation), Xinhua, June 10, 2013.

21. Perlez, "China's 'New Type' of Ties Fails to Sway Obama."
22. Cheng Li and Lucy Xu, "Chinese Enthusiasm and American Cynicism over the 'New Type of Great Power Relations,'" *Brookings Institution Commentary*, December 4, 2014.
23. Ibid.
24. "Full Text of Xi Jinping's Speech on China-U.S. Relations in Seattle," Xinhua, September 24, 2015.
25. Discussions with Chinese foreign policy experts, Beijing, March 2014.
26. Parts of the TGYH debate described here are adapted from my article: Hoo Tiang Boon, "Hardening the Hard, Softening the Soft: Assertiveness and China's Regional Strategy," *Journal of Strategic Studies* 40, no. 5 (2017): 645–46.
27. Dingding Chen and Jianwei Wang, "Lying Low No More? China's New Thinking on the Tao Guang Yang Hui Strategy," *China: An International Journal* 9, no. 2 (September 2011): 195–216.
28. See, for example, Guan Li, "Deng Xiaoping Yu Taoguang Yanghui, Yousuo Zuowei De Zhanlue Fangzhen" (Deng Xiaoping and the strategic guideline of hide brightness, cherish obscurity, and do some things), *Zhonggong Zhongyang Dangxiao Xuebao (Journal of the Party School of the Central Committee of the CPC)* 4 (2014): 18–22.
29. Cheng Zhijie and Wang Wan, "Waijiao Dingwei, Waijiao Siwei Yu Zhongguo De Waijiao Zuowei Guan" (Diplomatic role, diplomatic thought, and China's foreign policy view), *Xin Shi Ye (New Horizon)* 4 (2014): 36–41.
30. Xu Jin, "Zhongguo Waijiao Jinru 'Fenfa Youwei Xin Changtai'" (China's diplomacy enters the "new normal of striving to achieve"), Zhongguo Ribao Zhongwen Wang (China Daily Chinese online), December 16, 2013, http://column.chinadaily.com.cn/article.php?pid=3264.
31. "Xi Jinping Chuxi Zhongyang Waishi Gongzuo Huiyi Bing Fabiao Zhongyao Jianghua" (Xi Jinping attends the central conference on work relating to foreign affairs and gives important speech), Xinhua, November 29, 2014.
32. "Xi Eyes More Enabling International Environment for China's Peaceful Development," Xinhua, November 30, 2014.
33. Ibid.
34. Yu Zhengliang, "Jiji Jinqu, Yinling Yazhou, Quanqiu Zai Pingheng" (Forge ahead actively, lead Asia, rebalancing the world), *Guoji Guancha (International Review)* 1 (2015): 1; "Yang Jiechi Chen Yuan Canjia Dui Waiyou Haojie Bie Weiyuan Taolun" (Yang Jiechi and Chen Yuan participate in committee discussion on treating foreign friends well), CPC News Network, March 12, 2015, http://cpc.people.com.cn/n/2015/0312/c64094-26683237.html.
35. Wang Yizhou, "Xin Yijie Lingdao Ren Waijiao Zhanlue Qige Guanjian Ci" (Seven key phrases of the new leadership's foreign strategy), CPC News Network, February 18, 2014, http://theory.people.com.cn/n/2014/0218/c367550-24393662-2.html.
36. Li Ying, "Zhongguo Waijiao: Cong Taoguang Yanghui Dao Fenfa Youwei" (China's foreign policy: From keeping a low profile to striving for achievement), *Cankao*

Xiaoxi (Reference Information), January 14, 2014, http://ihl.cankaoxiaoxi.com/2014/0114/331003.shtml.

37. Xu, "Zhongguo Waijiao Jinru 'Fenfa Youwei Xin Changtai.'"
38. "Waijiao Bu Buzhang Wang Yi Huida Zhongwai Jizhe Tiwen" (Foreign minister Wang Yi answers questions from foreign and domestic press), Xinhua, March 8, 2014.
39. Chen Zhimin, "Zhongguo De Waijiao Chuangxin Shifou Xuyao Waijiao Gemin?" (Will China's diplomatic innovation lead to a diplomatic revolution?), *Shijie Jingji Yu Zhengzhi (World Economics and Politics)* 12 (2014): 37–51.
40. Yan Xuetong, "From Keeping a Low Profile to Striving for Achievement," *Chinese Journal of International Politics* 7, no. 2 (2014): 153–84.
41. "Spotlight: China Continues to Champion Global Governance in International Forums," Xinhua, November 23, 2016.
42. "Xi Stresses Urgency to Reform Global Governance," Xinhua, October 13, 2015.
43. Michael Swaine, "Chinese Views on Global Governance since 2008–9: Not Much New," *China Leadership Monitor* 49 (2016): 1–13.
44. "Xinhua Insight: China Embraces Summit Diplomacy in Addressing Global Challenges," Xinhua, September 17, 2016.
45. Cai Tuo, "Zhongguo Canyu Quanqiu Zhili De Xin Wenti Yu Xin Guanqie" (China's new challenges and concerns in global governance), *Xueshu Jie (Academics)* 9 (2016): 5–14.
46. "Xi Calls for Reforms on Global Governance," Xinhua, September 28, 2016.
47. "Xi Dismisses 'Rearranging Architecture of Global Governance toward China,'" Xinhua, September 22, 2015; "Chinese Expert Calls for Negotiated Global Governance in Apolar World," Xinhua, September 26, 2016.
48. See, for example, Cai, "Zhongguo Canyu Quanqiu Zhili De Xin Wenti Yu Xin Guanqie."
49. "Zhongguo Ruhe Tuijin Quanqiu Zhili, Xi Jinping Zheyang Shuo" (How China can advance global governance, Xi Jinping has this to say), Zhongguo Ribao Zhongwen Wang (China Daily Chinese Online), September 29, 2016. http://www.chinadaily.com.cn/interface/yidian/1138561/2016-09-29/cd_26939720.html.
50. "Yang Jiechi Gives Interview on G20 Hangzhou Summit," Ministry of Foreign Affairs of the People's Republic of China, September 7, 2016, http://www.fmprc.gov.cn/mfa_eng/zxxx_662805/t1396161.shtml; "From Beijing APEC to Hangzhou G20: China's rise as a responsible power," Xinhua, September 5, 2016; "Xinhua Insight."
51. "Zhe Sannian, Xi Jinping Quanqiu Zhili Shida Chengjiu" (Xi Jinping's ten major accomplishments on global governance for the past three years), Zhongguo Ribao Zhongwen Wang (China Daily Chinese Online), January 18, 2016, http://www.chinadaily.com.cn/interface/yidian/1120783/2016-01-18/cd_23128427.html.
52. Part of this segment is adapted from Hoo, "Hardening the Hard, Softening the Soft," 654–55.
53. "Yidai Yilu Lingdao Banzi: 'Yizheng Sifu' Mingdan Shou Baoguang" (The one belt one road leading group: "One leader and four members" revealed for the first time), Xinhua, April 6, 2015.

54. "Xi Calls for Advancing Belt and Road Initiative," Xinhua, August 18, 2016.
55. India, for example, has been disquieted by the OBOR's South Asia footprints. See Hoo Tiang Boon, "The Hedging Prong in India's Evolving China Strategy," *Journal of Contemporary China* 25, no. 101 (2016): 797–98.
56. Jean-Marc Blanchard, "Probing China's Twenty-First Century Maritime Silk Road Initiative (MSRI): An Examination of MSRI Narratives," *Geopolitics* 22, no. 2 (2017): 246–68; Abhijit Singh, "A 'PLA-N' for Chinese Maritime Bases in the Indian Ocean," *Pacific Forum CSIS PacNet* 7, January 26, 2015; Katrina Manson, "China Military to Set Up First Overseas Base in Horn of Africa," *Financial Times*, March 31, 2016; Hugh White, "China's Belt and Road Initiative to Challenge US-Led Order," *East Asia Forum*, May 8, 2017.
57. Wang Shang, "Chinese Marshall Plan Analogy Reveals Ignorance, Ulterior Intentions," Xinhua, March 11, 2015; Chen Boyuan, "'Belt and Road' Opens to All," China Internet Information Center Portal, October 19, 2015, http://china.org.cn/china/2015-10/19/content_36836016.htm.
58. Lu Yingxu, "Yidai Yilu Guantong Yazhou Meng, Shijie Meng" (The one belt one road links up with the Asia dream, world dream), Xinhua, March 31, 2015; Wang Yiwei, "'Yidai Yilu' Chengguo Weihe Haoyu Yuqi?" (Why "one belt, one road" exceeds expectations ahead of time), *Renda Chongyang Chuanlan (Commentary of the Chongyang Instiute of Renmin University)*, September 6, 2016; Zhang Pengfei, "One Belt, One Road Initiatives Key for Building a Safer Asia: Experts," Xinhua, September 25, 2014; Yu Yang, Shi Pengfei, Hu Zexi, and Wang Fahong, "G20 Yongdong 'Yidai Yilu' Re" (G20 stirs "one belt, one road" fever), *Renmin Ribao (People's Daily)*, September 5, 2016.
59. Hoo, "Hardening the Hard, Softening the Soft," 655–56.
60. "Belt and Road Initiative Strives to Reflect 'Globalization 2.0,'" *China Daily*, March 26, 2017; White, "China's Belt and Road Initiative to Challenge US-Led Order."
61. Blanchard, "Probing China's Twenty-First Century Maritime Silk Road Initiative"; Lu, "Yidai Yilu Guantong Yazhou Meng, Shijie Meng"; Yu et al., "G20 Yongdong 'Yidai Yilu' Re."
62. Chai Yifei, "Xi Jinping Tichu Zhengque Yili Guan: Zhongguo Waijiao De Yimian Qizhi" (Xi Jinping proposes correct morality-interest view: One banner of Chinese foreign policy), China Internet Information Center portal, August 11, 2016, http://news.china.com.cn/2016-08/11/content_39065875.htm; Wang Yi, "Jianchi Zhengque Yili Guan Jiji Fahui Fuzeren Daguo Zuoyong" (Uphold the correct morality-interest view and actively play the role of a responsible great power), *Renmin Ribao (People's Daily)*, September 10, 2013.
63. The data search for figures 3 and 4 is confined to journals of the following subject categories: literature/history/philosophy, politics / military affairs / law, education and social sciences, and economics and management.
64. Wang Yiwei, "Kaifang Xing Shijie Jingji De Zhongguo Dandang" (China's pursuit of the responsibility of promoting an open world economy), *Renda Chongyang*

Chuanlan (Commentary of the Chongyang Instiute of Renmin University), September 6, 2016.

65. Qin Yaqing, "Zhengque Yili Guan: Xinshi Qi Zhongguo Waijiao De Linian Chuangxin He Shijian Yuanze" (Correct morality-interest view: Ideational innovation and practice principles of China's diplomacy in the new era), *Qiushi (Seeking Truth)* 12 (2014): 55–57; Yan, "From Keeping a Low Profile to Striving for Achievement."
66. Cheng and Wan, "Waijiao Dingwei, Waijiao Siwei Yu Zhongguo De Waijiao Zuowei Guan," 39–40. See also Men Honghua, "Goujian Xinxing Guoji Guanxi: Zhongguo De Zeren Yu Dandang" (Building a new type of international relations: China's responsibility and undertakings), *Shijie Jingji Yu Zhengzhi (World Economics and Politics)* 3 (2016): 24–25.
67. Wang Honggang, "Xiandai Guoji Zhixu De Yanjin Yu Zhongguo De Shidai Zeren" (The evolution of modern international order and China's responsibility of the times), *Xiandai Guoji Guanxi (Contemporary International Relations)* 12 (2016): 13–14; Wu Bing, "Cong Tianxia Zeren Dao Fuzeren Daguo" (From heavenly responsibility to the responsible great power), *Dangdai Yatai (Journal of Contemporary Asia-Pacific Studies)* 4 (2015): 122–23; Cheng and Wan, "Waijiao Dingwei, Waijiao Siwei Yu Zhongguo De Waijiao Zuowei Guan."
68. Wang, "Xiandai Guoji Zhixu De Yanjin Yu Zhongguo De Shidai Zeren," 13.
69. Wang Wei, "Quanli Bianqian, Quanli Xietiao Yu Zhongmei Guanxi De Weilai" (Power shift, responsibility coordination, and the future of China-US relations), *Shijie Jingji Yu Zhengzhi (World Economics and Politics)* 5 (2015): 58–78.
70. Ibid., 66, 78.
71. Wang, "Xiandai Guoji Zhixu De Yanjin Yu Zhongguo De Shidai Zeren," 9–10; Men, "Goujian Xinxing Guoji Guanxi Zhongguo De Zeren Yu Dantang," 25.
72. Men, "Goujian Xinxing Guoji Guanxi Zhongguo De Zeren Yu Dantang," 25; Cai, "Zhongguo Canyu Quanqiu Zhili De Xin Wenti Yu Xin Guanqie," 9; Chen Xiaoding, "Quyu Gonggong Chanpin Yu Zhongguo Zhoubian Waijiao Xin Linian De Zhanlue Neihan" (Regional public goods and the new strategic meaning of China's peripheral diplomacy), *Shijie Jingji Yu Zhengzhi (World Economics and Politics)* 8 (2016): 52–53.
73. See, for example, Wang, "Xiandai Guoji Zhixu De Yanjin Yu Zhongguo De Shidai Zeren," 12–14.
74. Cui Shixin, "Zhuazhu Zhongyao Zhanlue Jiyu Qi: Fangdang De Shiliu Da Daibiao, Liaoyang Shi Weishu Ji Chen Shinan" (Grasp the important strategic window of opportunity: Interview with the sixteenth party congress representative, Liaoyang city party secretary Chen Shinan), *Renmin Ribao (People's Daily)*, November 14, 2002.
75. Wang, "Xiandai Guoji Zhixu De Yanjin Yu Zhongguo De Shidai Zeren," 11–13.
76. Ibid., 12. See also Wu Bing, "Cong Tianxia Zeren Dao Fuzeren Daguo," 122. Wu suggests that the RGP identity is about China "following the historical trend."

77. Cheng and Wan, "Waijiao Dingwei, Waijiao Siwei Yu Zhongguo De Waijiao Zuowei Guan," 39. See also Chen Xiang, "Fuzeren Daguo: Zhongguo De Xin Shenfen Dingwei" (Responsible great power: China's new identity position), *Shijie Jingji Yu Zhengzhi Luntan (Forum of World Economics and Politics)* 6 (2016): 44–45. Chen notes the importance of "positive mutual interactions" between China and the outside world for the RGP identity.
78. Zheng Yongnian, "Zhongmei Guanxi He Guoji Zhixu De Weilai" (Sino-American relations and the future of the global order), *Guoji Zhengzhi Yanjiu (International Politics Quarterly)* 1 (2014): 44.
79. Ibid.
80. Mark Landler and Coral Davenport, "Obama Presses Chinese on Global Warming," *New York Times*, September 23, 2014.
81. Transcript of Joint Press Conference of Obama and Xi, November 12, 2014.
82. Li Jing, "Paris Climate Talks: China Goes from Back Foot to Big Leap Forward in Negotiations," *South China Morning Post*, December 13, 2015; "Foreign Ministry Spokesperson Hong Lei's Remarks on the Outcomes of the Paris Climate Conference," Ministry of Foreign Affairs of the People's Republic of China Portal, December 13, 2015, http://www.fmprc.gov.cn/mfa_eng/xwfw_665399/s2510_665401/t1323918.shtml.
83. Mark Landler and Jane Perlez, "Rare Harmony as China and US Commit to Climate Deal," *New York Times*, September 3, 2016.
84. "China, US Sign MOU on Development Cooperation," State Council of the People's Republic of China Portal, September 7, 2015, http://english.gov.cn/news/international_exchanges/2015/09/27/content_281475199366744.htm; Transcript of Remarks by Obama and Xi, September 25, 2015.
85. Everett Rosenfeld, "US-China Agree to Not Conduct Cyber Theft of Intellectual Property," *CNBC News*, September 25, 2015.
86. "Foreign Ministry Spokesperson Hua Chunying's Regular Press Conference," Ministry of Foreign Affairs of the People's Republic of China Portal, September 10, 2014, http://www.fmprc.gov.cn/mfa_eng/xwfw_665399/s2510_665401/t1189900.shtml; Dennis Blasko, "China's Contribution to Peacekeeping Operations: Understanding the Numbers," *China Brief* 16, no. 18 (2016); Barbara Crossette, "As China Becomes a Major Player in UN Peacekeeping, Will It Respond to Crises?," *Huffington Post*, August 19, 2016, http://www.huffingtonpost.com/barbara-crossette/as-china-becomes-a-major _b_11582954.html.
87. Editorial, "China's Role as Peacekeeper Shows It Is a Responsible Power," *South China Morning Post*, June 5, 2014; Blasko, "China's Contribution to Peacekeeping Operations."
88. "Waijiao Bu: Zhongguo He Jibuti Zheng Jiuzai Ji Jianshe Baozhang Sheshi Jinxing Xieshang" (Foreign ministry: China and Djibouti are discussing the construction of a support facility), Xinhua, November 26, 2015; Manson, "China Military to Set Up First Overseas Base in Horn of Africa"; Hoo Tiang Boon and Charles Ardy,

"China and Lilliputians: Small States in a Big Power's Evolving Foreign Policy," *Asian Security* 13, no. 2 (2017): 10.

89. Ben Blanchard, "China Appoints First Special Envoy for Syria Crisis," Reuters, March 29, 2016; Christopher Bodeen, "Chinese Admiral Visits Syria in Show of Support," Associated Press News, August 18, 2016; Laura Zhou, "China's Role in Syria's Endless Civil War," *South China Morning Post*, April 7, 2017.
90. "First Round of China–Afghanistan–Pakistan Trilateral Strategic Dialogue Held in Kabul," Ministry of Foreign Affairs of the People's Republic of China Portal, February 10, 2015, http://www.fmprc.gov.cn/mfa_eng/wjbxw/t1236606.shtml; Javed Hamim Kakar, "China Pledges Hike in Assistance to Afghan Military," Pajhwok Afghan News, May 25, 2017, https://www.pajhwok.com/en/2017/05/25/china-pledges-hike-assistance-afghan-military; Shannon Tiezzi, "China Hosted Afghan Taliban for Talks: Report," *Diplomat*, January 7, 2015; Charles Clover, "Mystery Deepens over Chinese Forces in Afghanistan," *Financial Times*, February 27, 2017.
91. Feng, "Obama's 'Free Rider' Comment Draws Chinese Criticism."
92. Readout of the President's Call with Chinese President Xi Jinping, July 21, 2015, https://obamawhitehouse.archives.gov/the-press-office/2015/07/21/readout-president%E2%80%99s-call-chinese-president-xi-jinping; Li Jing, "The Leading Power: China to Take Charge in Iran's Nuclear Plant Revamp," *South China Morning Post*, August 28, 2015; Pavel Baev, "The China Factor in Russian Support for the Iran Deal," *Brookings Institution Commentary*, July 21, 2015.
93. The relationship appears to be improving in light of developments in 2018 that have led to Xi's unprecedented meeting with Kim Jong-un.
94. Celia Hatton, "Is China Ready to Abandon North Korea?," *BBC News*, April 12, 2013.
95. Scott Snyder, "Will China Change Its North Korea Policy?," *Council on Foreign Relations Brief*, March 31, 2016. See also Adam Cathcart and Christopher Green, "Xi's Belt: Chinese-North Korean relations," in *Chinese Foreign Policy under Xi*, ed. Hoo Tiang Boon (London and New York: Routledge, 2017), 131.
96. Choe Sang-Hun, "China Suspends All Coal Imports from North Korea," *New York Times*, February 18, 2017.
97. Jane Perlez and Yufan Huang, "China Says Its Trade with North Korea Has Increased," *New York Times*, April 13, 2017.
98. Nakamura, "Obama and China."
99. Patrick Cronin, Ely Ratner, Elbridge Colby, Zachary Hosford, and Alexander Sullivan, *Tailored Coercion: Competition and Risk in Maritime Asia* (Washington, DC: Center for a New American Security, 2014); Linda Jakobson, *China's Unpredictable Maritime Security Actors* (Sydney, Australia: Lowy Institute for International Policy, 2014).
100. "Chinese FM Rejects Philippine, Japanese, US Claims on South China Sea Issue," Xinhua, August 7, 2015.

101. Zhang Yunbi, "Nansha Islands Construction to Benefit Shipping," *China Daily (Asia Weekly)*, May 29–June 4, 2015.
102. Su Hao, "Zhongguo Shi Weihu Nan Zhongguo Hai He Heping Wending De Fuzeren Daguo" (China is a responsible power that upholds the peace and stability of the South China Sea), *Taiping Yang Xuebao (Pacific Journal)* 7 (2016): 44–47.

CONCLUSION

"The new Davos man," proclaimed the *Economist* when Xi Jinping became the first Chinese president to attend the World Economic Forum in January 2017.[1] Addressing the meeting of the global elite in Davos, Xi took the occasion to affirm China's support of the extant economic order. "Protectionism," he argued, is akin to "locking oneself in a dark room." Moreover, when the world faces difficulties, one should not "run away from responsibilities," Xi urged, who in the same speech highlighted Chinese contributions that included outward investments of over US$1.2 trillion and provision of over ¥400 billion of foreign aid.[2] Standing in contrast with the seemingly more protectionist sentiments of Donald Trump's America, Xi's advocacy of free trade sought to project China's responsible-power identity and underline its global leadership credentials.

It was a moment that captured headlines around the world. Analysts and pundits were quick to describe the development as "surreal." The irony was not lost on many that China was positioning itself as a champion of the US-led liberal economic order that America now appears keen to pull back from. "For [Xi] to stand up in Davos as an advocate of globalization and free trade is insanity," said Winston Lord, a former US ambassador to China.[3]

Hyperbole notwithstanding, such astonishment reveals gaps in common understandings of China. Seen in the context of this book's examination of the evolution of the RGP identity, Xi's Davos declaration should not be surprising. It is consistent with, and reflective of, a development that is often underappreciated in analyses of China: that since the early 1990s a rich discursive space has emerged domestically regarding the idea of China as a responsible power. What is more, this is a role understanding curated by American attempts to shape China's course in the world.

This role perception is also more than a convenient propagandistic tool, one often dismissed by scholars (including myself, I confess, prior to this study). It is true that image concerns play a role in China's pursuit of the responsible-power narrative. Indeed, in chapter 2 I suggest that the RGP narrative was first made with a view toward improving China's external image at a time when the country was just breaking out of its post-Tiananmen isolation. Yet the overall evidence uncovered in this book tells a larger and more complex story. The production and reproduction of the RGP identity is animated by a blend of factors that go beyond just addressing image concerns. Other than the shaping role played by the United States, elements such as contingent events, strategic rationales, domestic ideational influences, and social aspirations within international society have informed China's pursuit of the responsible-power identity.

The aim of the book, therefore, is to hopefully furnish a more nuanced and complete portrait of China as a great power. Its aim, I *emphatically reiterate*, is not to "prove" China is becoming more responsible in international society or suggest it is essentially a benevolent power. Nor should this study be seen as some sort of "defense" of Chinese foreign policy. This book is motivated by a different focus: telling the story of how and why China has come to pursue a self-identity as a responsible great power. The contention here is not that China is a responsible power but rather that Beijing has been increasingly imagining itself as one, in ways that suggest the Chinese have been thinking about big-power responsibility far longer and more seriously than commonly assumed. This development has profound consequences for international society, whose implications I will address in the later part of the conclusion.

Key Findings

It is useful to take stock of some of the key findings of the book. In the following sections, I address these findings.

Identity Evolution

The start of China's identification as a responsible great power can be basically traced to the period between the early and mid-1990s, when Chinese leaders began to draw linkages between China's responsibility and its global-power role. However, the RGP narrative did not emerge out of a temporal and ideational vacuum. It was prefaced by "cognitive priors" that preceded the reform era and that encompassed the earlier political beliefs of Chinese elites.[4]

In the premodern era the Central Kingdom complex was the embodiment of traditional China's sense of its great-power status. This perspective conceived the Chinese polity in terms of a "world empire," a perception that conflated China with the idea of "all that existed" and imagined it as the principal hegemon. Nevertheless, by the mid-nineteenth century such an outlook was dramatically turned on its head. Chastening encounters with more advanced foreign powers led to a deep sense of Chinese self-doubt and insecurity, as Chinese belief in the superiority of its own model was profoundly shaken. Subsequently, a "weak" and "victimized" China complex developed, but it was one that resided in considerable tension with suppressed residual beliefs of China's national greatness. It would take the advent of communist China for perceptions of national greatness to be more substantively revived. In the Maoist period, developments such as the outcome of the 1950–53 Korean War, China's development of nuclear weapons capability, Beijing's pursuit of leadership in the Third World and the socialist bloc, the Sino-American rapprochement, and the PRC's formal entry into the UN and UN Security Council, among others, were conditions that helped strengthen China's sense of itself as a global power. The Maoist leadership was not unaware of its nation's patent material inadequacies, however, and did not hesitate to play up the PRC's status as an impoverished state when it suited.

On early Chinese ideas of responsibility (until the end of the Maoist era), the book finds limited evocation of the concept in Chinese political narratives. In premodern China, discussions of responsibility were informed by the Confucian concept of *yiwu* (duty), in which obligations were framed in terms of socially defined duties within a communitarian setting and were primarily domestic in scope. The discourse assumed a more political character during the republican and Maoist periods. The writings of Sun Yatsen, Chiang Kai-shek, and Mao Zedong show that leading Chinese political figures did seek to connect the notion of international responsibility with China's big-power aspirations. Sun, for example, spoke of China's obligation to "aid the weaker nations and oppose the imperialist powers of the world" when it "becomes strong again;" Chiang referred to China's "world" duty to "stand shoulder to shoulder" with other nations to share "the responsibilities for the maintenance of permanent world peace and the liberation of mankind."[5] Mao's references were more indirect and mainly couched in the language of China's "contribution to humanity" or its international "revolutionary" duties.[6] Nevertheless, in republican and Maoist China, the level of discussion on the responsibility concept could hardly be described as extensive or deep. While there was some limited discussion, the notion of global responsibility was not among the key themes that then concerned Chinese elites.

Deng Xiaoping's elevation to paramount leadership in the late 1970s marked the end of the Maoist era and the start of China's reform and opening up. It was evident that Deng's China was a substantially different actor from the earlier Maoist version. No longer seeking to be a disruptive international influence, the PRC strove to "link up with the international track," with the general trend suggesting a country keen to further its integration with global society.[7] Economically, the 1980s was a period of tremendous revitalization for China, which helped bolster Chinese big-power perceptions. Nevertheless, the end of the 1980s came as a severe testing period for Beijing, as forces unleashed by the 1989 Tiananmen violence threatened to unravel the communist regime and China was deemed a pariah by several Western countries, with sanctions imposed against it. Along with the end of the Cold War and its attendant implications, this was clearly perceived in Beijing as a time of major threat to China's great-power identity. Against this backdrop, involvement in UN diplomacy vis-à-vis the 1990 Gulf War was an opportunity for Beijing to repair its image and mitigate the diplomatic isolation and it used the occasion to position itself as a responsible member of international society. This later culminated in official declarations of the country as a responsible great power in 1992–1993.

From 1993 to 1996 Chinese leaders continued to promulgate the narrative of the PRC as a responsible power. In Beijing there was rising confidence regarding the country's capacity to play a global power role, in part because of a self-awareness that China was becoming more influential in the world economy. Significantly, this was accompanied by claims that China was aware of its big-power obligations and that it would continue to advance "world peace and development."[8] Such rhetoric came at a time when American policymakers were beginning to take greater interest in China's emergence as a global actor. The view from Washington was that the PRC had arrived at the "great power table" and that this status required it to assume corresponding responsibilities.

The period from 1997 to 2004 can be interpreted as the second distinctive phase of China's self-identification as a responsible power. The early years of this period marked the onset of the Asian financial crisis, an event followed by a discernible expansion of the RGP discourse in China. At the official level, Chinese leaders were keen to evoke the RGP identity, but qualitatively this did not go beyond general assertions. At the broader, subofficial level of the Chinese academic/think-tank community, however, there was greater depth and diversity to the discursive terrain. As chapter 3 shows, Chinese scholars became increasingly engaged in a wide-ranging discussion about the questions of China's great power role and responsibilities. There appeared to be some level of intellectual receptivity to the idea of China as a responsible power, although this is not to suggest that there were no critical opinions or that Chinese interpretations necessarily aligned with those held in Washington. For its part, the US continued a policy of pushing China to act more "responsibly" within international society. Though there were American calls for US-China relations to go beyond shared interests to incorporate a sense of shared values, in general the message to Beijing remained a consistent one: the US welcomed China's rise, but its ascendancy needed to be matched by a willingness to shoulder the concomitant global responsibilities.

The 2005–2012 years were characterized by a growing level of dialogue and policy engagement between Washington and Beijing, which reinforced perceptions of China's great-power identity but also created additional opportunities for the US to spotlight and apply pressure on questions of China's obligations to international society. Alongside the shift in American strategic focus toward the Asia-Pacific region, this pressure appeared to become more pronounced from around late 2010, as Washington ratcheted up the tone of its rhetoric and was more critical of some of China's policies. As for Beijing, it did not deviate from its RGP role script. Chinese leaders continued to rely on assertions that "China, as a major country, does not shirk its responsibilities" or that they understood that the great-power role brought "important responsibilities on a host of major issues."[9] Indeed, the RGP narrative gained further traction at both official and intellectual levels during this time. Notably, over this period the key positions in the Chinese RGP debate became further delineated and were more perceptible, with at least three general schools of thought emerging. The next section summarizes this debate.

The Domestic Debate on China's Responsibility

While external role pressures had been considerable, equally important in the construction of the RGP identity was the internal contestation and debate over its direction and content. As mentioned, there have been at least three key angles in the national conversation over China's responsibility—what I have classified as the internationalist, developmental, and skeptics' position (see Table C.1 for a simplified overview).

The internationalist standpoint broadly aligns with the idea that China should take on more global responsibilities. This perspective is informed by a number of interrelated narratives and rationales. The first speaks to the concept of noblesse oblige; that is, great powers, by virtue of their stronger capacities and special status, have larger obligations toward international society. It acknowledges that China needs to redefine or expand its international obligations to better match its growing strength. The second narrative, which draws on Chinese ideas such as *tianxia* (all under heaven) and the harmonious world theory, conceives China as being morally and normatively responsible to the shared and common world of which it is a part. It perceives China's future and interests as being inescapably linked to this world society. The third narrative speaks to a logic of consequences. Here the argument is that it is in China's interests to contribute to the international system because: (i) it would not benefit China if this system floundered; (ii) it would improve China's socio-moral standing in international society and reduce the likelihood of a hostile external environment that might be deleterious to China's development; and (iii) it would improve China's bargaining power for a larger share of rights within international society. An important caveat is that even as the internationalist discourse argues for the shouldering of more global responsibilities, it is qualified by the insistence from its interlocutors that these responsibilities reflect Chinese choices.

The developmental position advocates a more circumspect and inward-looking perspective toward China's responsibilities. Promoting a view of China that highlights its developing status, this position counsels against assuming excessive global responsibilities, arguing that the country should prioritize its domestic obligations and focus on "helping itself first." It perceives international responsibilities as unnecessary burdens to national development and argues that Beijing should take on only external responsibilities that are believed commensurate with China's level of development and capacity. Proponents are wont to point to, among other limiting conditions, the PRC's still relatively modest national income per capita; the considerable number of poor people among its population; and the ongoing domestic problems posed by its development.

But while the developmental perspective accepts that China could take on some international responsibilities (albeit in accordance with national

Table C.1: General Positions in the Chinese RGP Debate

	Internationalist	Developmental	Skeptics'
Broad Argument	Assume more global responsibilities	Assume global responsibilities in accordance with the perceived level of national development	Dismissive of global responsibilities
Rationale	1. Great powers have greater responsibilities because of their stronger capacities and special status 2. Morally and normatively accountable to the world society 3. Strategic incentives 4. Choice of responsibilities should be self-determined	1. China is still a developing country 2. Excessive external obligations risk national overextension 3. Focus on "helping oneself first"; priority is on domestic responsibilities 4. Choice of responsibilities should be self-determined	View global responsibilities as a veiled attempt to: 1. Overburden China and check its rise 2. Pass the buck on world's major problems 3. Exploit China's strength to maintain American hegemony

conditions), the skeptics' position is dismissive and distrustful of the responsibility concept. Suspicious of talk of China's responsibility, in particular those coming from the West, it views the RGP discourse through the lens of a hidden agenda to: (i) constrain China through international burdens; (ii) pass the buck on global problems to China; and (iii) exploit China's rising strength to perpetuate the American-dominated global order. The skeptics' position believes the RGP concept is an anti-China "moral trap" akin to a softer version of the "China threat" or "China collapse" theories.

In the Xi era, elements of the internationalist, developmental, and skeptics' arguments are still visible in the domestic debate. However, as chapter 5 shows, Chinese narratives have increasingly taken on an internationalist hue and appear to be departing from the logics espoused by the developmental and skeptics' standpoints. Chinese elites are increasingly rationalizing that their country should "pursue" more responsibilities within the international system as it rises. On that account, the conversation has become less a question of whether China should behave responsibly and more a question of *how* it should behave responsibly.

The emerging convergence toward the internationalist perspective is, in part, greased by a number of ideational movements on the official front. Xi's engagement of the concept of global responsibility in his speeches, the advocacy of the "morality-interest view" that calls on the country to pay more attention to the moral dimensions of foreign affairs, and the heightened policy focus on global governance—these are some notable kinetics that have interfaced with the RGP discussion and drawn focus on the ways by which China could address its obligations in international society. Incidentally, there has been a notable lack of reference to the traditional "keep a low profile" strategy under Xi (even if this debate still persists in the scholarly sphere). Instead, there is an increasing emphasis on the notion of "striving for achievement" in foreign policy, which calls for a more proactive and engaged China in global affairs.

Narratives at the intellectual level have reflected this internationalist convergence, and discussion has increasingly centered on how the pursuit of global obligations will help address China's national interests. For instance, it is ventured that a more proactive "responsibility" approach would help China gain first-mover advantage in its choice of obligations. Another rationalization sees this as a means by which China could mitigate the dangers of power transition or at least soften the competitive dynamics between itself and the US. This pursuit has also been framed in terms of an "opportunity" for China to better position itself as one of the rule-makers in the next evolution of the international system.

Explaining China's Responsible Great-Power Identity

It is not wrong to say that Chinese elites promoted and perpetuated the RGP narrative to improve China's global image. It is inaccurate, however, to suggest this is the sole reason for the pursuit of the responsible-power role. Optics had been (and still is) an important consideration. But the RGP identity is the sum of a number of interwoven domestic and external factors. Beyond image, five other drivers can be inferred. These factors are not mutually exclusive and can overlap, but for analytical purposes they are taken as separate categories here.

The Role of America and Other Others

As the key external source of role ideas—the significant other—the United States plays a central role in the construction of the RGP identity in China. Its impact can be observed in three ways. First and foremost, the US is China's primary interlocutor in the RGP discourse. Since around the time of the Clinton administration, the key thrust of Washington's China policy has been to push Beijing to take greater ownership over global challenges and act more "responsibly" in international society. As is evident, American beliefs, ideas, and practices have had a bearing on Chinese RGP discussions. This influence is most visible at the intellectual discursive level, where Chinese writings frequently evoke American arguments and policies as: (i) a starting point, (ii) a foil, or (iii) as "analytical fodder" for domestic debate on China's great-power role and responsibilities. The conspicuous example is former US deputy secretary of state Robert Zoellick's introduction of the "responsible stakeholder" concept, which provoked debate in China and added new impetus to evolving Chinese identity discussions. Chinese leaders, too, have referenced the US in their statements on the RGP identity. Xi Jinping, for example, publicly acknowledged American expectations for the country to play a bigger global role and shoulder more system responsibilities.

Second, as the preponderant power in international society, the US is effectively the doorkeeper to China's aspirations for great-power status. Whether Washington recognizes China's big-power role has a concomitant impact in Beijing and other capitals, a social reality that the Chinese understand. Indeed, American appreciation of China's power has a perceptible influence on Chinese estimations of their nation's great-power status. But full American recognition also encompasses a normative dimension, and Washington made it known to Beijing that the latter has to act "responsibly" for the US to fully recognize it as a great power.

Third, from a geopolitical perspective the US is perceived in Beijing as the key "constraint" or "enabler" of China's rise.[10] Chinese policymakers and analysts see the US as the external actor with the most potential to make or break the rise of China. This perception shapes the calculus of Chinese deliberations vis-à-vis the great-power role and responsibilities.

The dominant role of the United States does not mean that other external actors have no part in the RGP story. During the Cold War not a few newly decolonized states saw Beijing as a supportive world power, which affirmed Maoist China's big-power identity to the extent that it had aspirations to lead the Third World and socialist bloc. In more contemporary times, international responses to a number of Chinese actions had reinforced the PRC's sense of itself as a responsible global player. In the 1990 Gulf crisis, for example, China's decision to exercise limited diplomacy and send foreign minister Qian Qichen to meet Saddam Hussein was met with appreciation by the countries concerned. And when Beijing opted not to devalue its currency in the wake of the 1997–1998 Asian financial crisis, several regional countries viewed it as having acted "responsibly." On both occasions the positive external perceptions facilitated the development of the RGP self-identity.

External Events

The preceding mention of the two crises calls attention to another nontrivial variable: events. As observed, a number of external circumstances had a catalytic effect on the discussion of the RGP identity in China. The financial crisis in Asia led to a marked expansion of Chinese RGP narratives, as scholars and policymakers linked China's crisis responses to its responsible-power identity. The various US-China presidential summits culminated in several statements by Chinese leaders asserting their country's RGP identity. Beijing's contributions to counterterrorism efforts in the aftermath of the 9/11 terrorist attacks, to global trade after its formal ascension to the World Trade Organization, and to the Six-Party Talks on the North Korea nuclear issue, among others, prompted discussion of the RGP role in China. The 2008–2009 global financial crisis and Beijing's ensuing actions sparked spirited internal conversations on China's responsibility vis-à-vis the global economic order. These are some examples of how particular events have played a precipitating or conditioning role in the production and reproduction of Chinese RGP perceptions. In many respects these events highlight the role of contingency in identity development.

Instrumentalism

As noted in the introduction, global identity construction can involve purposive aspects, where role imagination is informed on the basis of interests as determined by the state. Relating to China, the book finds considerable evidence that the responsible-power identity has been pursued in part because it is perceived to be in China's interests to position itself as one. Indeed, the notion that the RGP identity can and should benefit China has been evident in the writings of several Chinese scholars who have discussed the subject. Many see it as a useful identity that embodies a viable strategic path for navigating international politics. For instance, it is seen as a useful conceptual tool to address the perception that China's rise will be a threat to others in the international system. It has been argued that it would profit Beijing to be characterized as a benign and beneficent power so as to lessen the prospect that other powers, in particular the United States, consider it a threat to be opposed. This reflects the Chinese assessment that the country requires a relatively peaceful external environment to advance its goals of economic development. This objective is still salient in the Xi era, but the strategic bar has become more ambitious: going beyond the goal of fostering a "benign" milieu to the active cultivation of "enabling" external conditions in order to realize China's great rejuvenation. As we have seen, this has meant a conceptualization of global responsibility as a vehicle through which China can revise and "improve" its terms of engagement with international society.

Social Aspirations

There is a sociological dimension to the pursuit of the RGP identity in that the identity portends social rewards in international society. The role category of a responsible power will be helpful for deepening China's membership and role in international society. But, more than that, it will be helpful for gaining greater American acceptance of an emerging Chinese big-power identity that became more pronounced by the mid-1990s. To be sure, explicit arguments on the social rationale have not been particularly obvious in Chinese writings. What is more palpable in these writings are two related points: One, the PRC strongly desires to be seen and treated as a great power in international society—that is, as a "legitimate great power."

Two, the Chinese acknowledge the linkage and importance of the responsibility issue to attaining fuller great-power recognition from the US and other states.[11] The suggestion is, therefore, that Chinese elites strove to identify their country as a responsible global actor, at least partly because of perceived benefits to China's great-power status. In some ways this connotes an element of instrumentalism, albeit on a social basis.

Domestic Ideational Influences

A process of ideational "localization" interplays with American ideas and influence in the construction of China's RGP identity. Much of the perspectives informing the responsible-power identity are essentially endogenous conceptions and include some of the major Chinese political and strategic narratives over the years. Concepts such as the peaceful development thesis, the harmonious worldview, and the "striving for achievement" approach all square with and lubricate the discussion of the RGP identity in China. The peaceful development discourse connects to claims that the enactment of such a strategy represents the fulfillment of China's obligation and role as a responsible power. Beijing's advocacy of the harmonious worldview supposedly signals its commitment to shouldering global responsibilities. The shift to the "strive for achievement" strategy intermeshes with arguments that call for China to be more proactive in pursuing its global obligations. These examples and more point to what should be a commonsensical notion: inasmuch as a state's identity is about social learning from other states about its role in international society, the internal collective cognition that shapes its self-perception is equally if not more important. As with identity instrumentalism, this facet reflects the agency of the actor in identity formation.

So What?

Why should anyone care about China's pursuit of the responsible great-power identity? I suggest the findings here unveil some important insights into a number of real-world issues and theoretical puzzles of international politics.

The Question of Behavior

The dependent variable of this book is China's global identity, specifically its role identification as a responsible power. In other words, the book situates the RGP identity and its evolution as the outcome to be analyzed and explained. Nevertheless, in telling this story the task has necessitated drawing attention to China's behavior as a big power. This discussion has come in two contexts.

One relates to the issue of how China's conduct impacts its identity. Identity studies suggest that perceived behavioral consistency with identity "standards" helps strengthen an actor's identity, while perceived behavioral discrepancies will weaken it.[12] In other words, a state's behavior can have implications for its identity. This has proved to be the case with China's responsible-power identity. Beijing's responses to both the Asian and global financial crises, its support for global anti-terror efforts, its growing activism and leadership in global organizations, its deepening involvement in UN peacekeeping activities, its role in the North Korean nuclear issue, and its engagement with the global climate regime are examples of behaviors that have reinforced the RGP identity insofar as these practices strengthen Chinese perceptions, or stimulate domestic discussion, of China as a responsible global actor. To the extent that these actions have resulted in social recognition from others (especially the US), Chinese RGP beliefs have been further accentuated.

The second involves assessing the extent to which China's behavior connects to its RGP identity. I do not claim in the book that there is necessarily a causal relationship between the RGP identity and Chinese conduct. I suggest, however, that the responsible-power identity provides a useful ideational context to augment our understanding of China and its actions. Take China's engagement with the global economic order, for example. A range of economic considerations—including securing resources, markets and production bases needed to power the country's further development, and its own domestic economic reforms—inform why Beijing is stepping up efforts in regionalism and is positioning itself as a champion of free trade and globalization. Yet those efforts are not unrelated to China's great-power aspirations and its perspectives on global responsibility. Chinese writings and sources describe the initiation of the Belt-Road plan and the Asian Infrastructure Investment Bank in terms of exercising greater leadership and responsibility over the global economic system. They cite Xi's repudiation of protectionism at Davos as exemplifying the country's "responsible global role." Indeed, Chinese RGP perspectives point to an increasingly strategic view of international responsibility whereby the pursuit of responsibility is conceived as a conduit for Beijing to shape the trajectory of the global economic system in a way that makes it more conducive for China's continued growth.

Even in a counterintuitive case of China's maritime assertiveness in Asia, the RGP identity can tell us something. As chapter 5 shows, the idea of responsibility has become a basis for legitimizing Chinese actions in the South China Sea. To defend Chinese sovereignty and territorial integrity, it has been argued, the assertion of "reasonable maritime rights is a responsibility the Chinese government must take on."[13] Meanwhile, Chinese construction activities on disputed islets have been justified on the grounds that such work represents the fulfillment of China's responsibility to provide maritime public goods as a rising sea power. The point here is not whether such arguments are valid; in fact, they have predictably little traction among other claimant states. Rather, it is that a self-imagined moral belief, as expressed through the RGP narrative, has become part of the dynamic reinforcing Chinese assertiveness in the South China Sea—a point often overlooked in analyses of China's behavior there.

America's China Strategy

A key observation of the study is that Washington has played a substantive role in fostering the development of China's responsible-power identity. The ways in which the US role has mattered have been earlier elaborated, so I turn to its attendant implications here.

From an identity perspective, one could argue that America's China strategy has been more successful than given credit for. The crux of this strategy is to shape the arc of China's ascendancy, and since the mid-1990s this has centered on "encouraging" Beijing to shoulder the global responsibilities commensurating with its rising power. Washington has never explicitly spelled out what it thought these obligations should be or the level of contribution. This ambiguity notwithstanding, China's actions have been seen as making progress on a number of issue-areas. Of course, this does not mean that Washington considers the PRC a responsible actor; as the "free rider" charge indicates, Chinese behavior still has much ground to make up to fully address American expectations. Nevertheless, on a number of global challenges—such as the North Korean and Iranian nuclear issues, counterterrorism, nuclear nonproliferation and arms control, climate change, and global public health—Chinese involvement is viewed as crucial. But perhaps the more direct imprint of the US influence relates to its impact on Chinese thinking of their country's great-power role and responsibilities. As Chinese writings show, American ideas and policies have prompted and shaped domestic discussions of the RGP identity.

Taken together, the conclusion drawn is that China can be "socialized"—to an extent—by the United States. This socialization does not necessarily involve physical interaction between state agents of both countries. It is "the relationship between the knowledge each has of the other, not physical co-location, that drives the construction of the [RGP] identity."[14] Counterfactually, therefore, it is plausible to argue that had the US used an alternative but similarly moral role prescription to engage Beijing (say, China as a "peaceful" power), the odds are that this concept would have become part of the identity debate in China. From a policy standpoint, the implication is that the long-standing American strategy of engaging China is not as misguided as what some critics assert. More than that, the evidence suggests Washington should continue and indeed do more to encourage China's pursuit of the RGP identity. Former US deputy assistant secretary of state Susan Shirk would welcome this approach. As she puts it:

> When I see Xi Jinping at Davos defending the open global order, I feel very good about that—and even a small measure of personal satisfaction as somebody who worked in the government on China policy. I believe the US actually has sponsored China's emergence as a constructive global power—not just allowed it but really actively encouraged it.[15]

What Kind of Great-Power Politics?

The aforementioned implication lends itself to the larger question on the trajectory of China's relationship with the US and, more broadly, the global order. Some scholars believe that as China rises, its growing power is likely to lead to conflict with the United States. John Mearsheimer sees a future Sino-American great power "tragedy."[16] Ted Carpenter speaks of a "coming war" between the two powers.[17] Graham Allison warns of a Thucydidean quandary wherein the potential for war between China and the US is high.[18] At the heart of these arguments is the idea that power transitions within the international system are inherently dangerous and that when a rising power threatens to displace the incumbent hegemon, "war is more likely than not."[19]

I suggest such fatalism is overdrawn. In addition to two compelling mitigating factors of nuclear mutual assured destruction and growing economic interdependence, left out of this conversation is a consideration of how identity impacts great-power politics. State identities are not static, nor are states "faceless" atomistic actors in the international system. As China's RGP identity shows, state identities can evolve in ways that have meaning and implications for its behavior. They can also be shaped by external forces, in particular by other influential states. In relation to the RGP identity and its evolution, the outcome is a Chinese frame of self that firmly situates the country within the extant global order even as it also seeks greater leadership and say over this order. The RGP identity does not portend an absence of competition or increasing strains between China and America. The imperatives of national interest also imply limits on how far Beijing will behave as a global actor to address

American expectations. Meanwhile, China continues to grapple with a sense of historical victimhood that complicates its global ambitions as a great power. Yet the overall story of the RGP identity is essentially a shared one between the rising power and the incumbent power. It tells of a China that is changed in part by American ideas and whose own ideas of global leadership and responsibility are evolving and becoming increasingly internationalist. It tells of a China that has worked with the US in a number of global domains even if this cooperation might not equate to a "G2" concert or what Washington expects of a "responsible stakeholder." It tells of a China that recognizes the dangers of great-power conflict and places the stability of Sino-American relations as its key strategic priority. The larger point is that the US-China chessboard is not as rigid as what its supposed structural constraints make it out to be. Both powers have shown a capacity to make adjustments that—while they may not be enough to avert great-power frictions—could temper the insecurity dynamics that lead to a Sino-American war.

Theoretical Implications

This book is not concerned with theory-building, nor is it situated within the paradigmatic debates of international relations theory. Its focus is on unraveling the real-world puzzle of China's responsible great-power identity, a task that has entailed tracking the history, politics, and ideas behind this identity's evolution. To that extent, this study is an idiographic approach toward understanding change in world politics. That being said, its empirical findings can have implications for a number of theoretical issues in IR.

For one, the findings contribute to our knowledge of state identity formation. In general, IR scholarship can be said to have established the idea that identity "matters" in international politics. Yet, concerning *how* identity has come to matter—in particular, how state identities emerge and then persist or change—is a subject that is less well understood. This is an important issue because before we can fully grasp the significance of the relationship between state identities and foreign policy, we must first understand what these identities are, where they come from, and how they get produced or change.

While this study does not set out to specifically address the issue of state-identity formation, the RGP identity comes as a rich case for shedding more light on its intricacies. Here I spotlight some notable works on identity formation in

IR as foils to situate the theoretical relevance of the book's findings. One such work is Ted Hopf's masterful mapping of Soviet (point A) and Russian (point B) identities in 1955 and 1999, respectively. Setting aside the difference—that his focus is on a state's domestic identity as opposed to its global identity (this book's concern)—Hopf shows how to develop an informed snapshot of a state's identity at a particular time and space. Hopf, however, does not say much about how and why identities evolve, and makes little attempt to explain how Moscow moved from point A to point B in its identity trajectory.[20]

Jeffrey Legro's work on the elasticity of a state's international identity provides more of an examination of identity change. Exploring the cases of nineteenth-century Japan and twentieth-century Soviet Union, Legro argues that state identities become amenable to change when the old "orthodoxies" that constitute these identities become discredited by real-world events. Whether an old identity gives way to a new one and whether a new identity eventually consolidates depends on: one, the availability of a "leading replacement" concept; and two, the ability of the new identity narrative to bring about sustained and "desirable" real-world results for the country. While Legro's account throws invaluable light on identity change, the change he envisions is one that involves a dramatic transformation of a state's global orientation and priorities. Yet, such seismic shifts are atypical in world affairs and, as empirical evidence shows, state identities do not *normally* change drastically. They do change, of course, but permutations are usually more glacial than dramatic. In other words, Legro's account tells little of how identity change appears to function most of the time: incremental movements that do not amount to momentous change but nonetheless result in non-trivial identity consolidation or weakening over time.[21]

Such gradual changes, or what might be called the "everyday" aspects of identity formation, are given more scrutiny in this book. This account of identity situates change as part of an evolutionary process and argues that part of the new identity that a state may come to adopt is connected to its past or its old self. As demonstrated, Beijing's sense of itself as a global power did not emerge tabula rasa; it has a deep foundation and is intimately tied to how premodern China conceived itself as the center of the world's social and political universe. Equally, Chinese debates on global responsibility did not emerge solely as a response to Washington's 2005 call for Beijing to be a responsible stakeholder (even if this call was influential). Instead, it evolved from a nascent discussion of China as a responsible power since the early 1990s, a conversation sparked in part by Beijing's desire to break out of its post-Tiananmen political isolation.

The other account to mention is Alex Wendt's treatment of identity formation in the canonical *Social Theory of International Politics*. My book draws on the same symbolic interactionist framework of the self and other as theorized by Wendt. While my discussion of the self-other dialectic here may fall short of what some scholars might have liked for "theory work," the more relevant point is how this book employs its basic idea—that a state's identity is an evolving product of its self-perception and social learning from other states about its global role—in order to flesh out the erstwhile untold story of China's responsible-power identity. This is where the book builds on Wendt's work by offering an account of operationalizing the self-other framework. Unlike the Hopf and Legro accounts, Wendt adduces little empirical evidence to substantiate his thought experiments (although, to be sure, his aim is to do "pure theory").[22] While not claiming to corroborate Wendt's arguments on identity formation, this study represents one of the few sustained empirical works to apply the self-other framework to a study of political developments in Asia.

Beyond the question of state identity formation, the findings of this book also hold implications for constructivist IR theory. This study adopts an approach that combines both sociological and rationalist elements, a position that references Ernst Haas and Peter Haas's *pragmatic constructivism*.[23] Such an approach may not sit well with traditional constructivist scholarship, which has tended to emphasize the "social" element (be it external norms or ideas) in shaping actor preferences, and frowns on the "conflation" of the logic of consequences with the logic of appropriateness.[24] My view is that we should not be held back by theoretical straitjackets in making sense of a messy and complex world. For some real-world issues, an analytically eclectic approach may well be profitable.[25] In the case of China's RGP identity, a social logic has been evidently important; a recurrent theme is the extent to which the US has been central in socializing China to the idea that its rising power brings growing responsibilities. However, how these external ideas are filtered or interpreted by Chinese elites themselves is also crucial.[26] Far from being passive recipients of American ideas, Chinese elites actively debated what it means for China to be a responsible power. It is a conversation that spans different schools of "responsibility" thought, including arguments that seek to construe China's obligations through functional or strategic lenses. This account highlights the volition and rationality in identity construction that strict sociological understandings tend to take for granted without ignoring the socializing forces that clearly make a difference too.

Last but not least, the findings also connect with the broader theoretical literature on how ideas shape and lend particular meaning to global politics. One such idea is the responsibility of power: the notion that the "allocation" of responsibility in international society is linked to its material distribution. This is rooted in the view that states are not only actors in that society but also "bearers of responsibilities." Here the pioneering work of Mlada Bukovansky and her coauthors goes some way to addressing a subject that has received inadequate attention. They notably focus on the role of the US in framing, propagating, and giving expression to the idea of responsibility as is played out in world politics.[27] My book does not advance any generalizable claims on global responsibility, but it offers a first look at the involvement of another key actor, China, in this discussion. The findings suggest, at best, a mixed impact by China on the broader cosmopolitan dialogue on responsibility, which remains largely US-driven. In some policy domains such as climate change, this impact has been more visible: for instance, Chinese understandings were influential in shaping how the Paris climate accord eventually defined "common and differentiated responsibilities."[28] Elsewhere, on issues such as the East and South China Seas territorial disputes, Chinese arguments have gained little, if any, international traction.

The Future of Chinese Global Leadership

It has been said that musing over China's future is "an exercise in frustration."[29] Indeed, there is no lack of examples in modern Chinese history where the country took turns that confounded even the most seasoned China watchers. Yet the challenges of prognosis should not stop us from at least exploring some *possibilities* of how China's arc might unfold. More often than not there are sufficient clues in its evolving story for patterns to be discerned and informed judgments to be drawn. In this section I conclude by considering a number of scenarios in which China's trajectory as a great power could develop in the next ten to twenty years.

At a more fundamental level, Chinese sense of national greatness will persist. In fact, this particular belief is likely to strengthen further as its economic and military modernization continues apace. This is not to preclude the possibility of economic decline or political upheaval in China in the future. Domestic challenges such as the "three divides" (i.e., the urban-rural divide, the income gap divide, and the coastal-interior divide) continue to pose destabilizing risks, while China's ongoing economic reforms have proved more tenuous than expected. But it is worth remembering that even when the country was at its weakest during its so-called century of humiliation, collective perceptions of China's latent greatness endured. As this book has shown, Chinese self-awareness as a great power is deeply rooted and is part of a much longer journey that ties to the nation's memory of itself as the center of the global political universe. This is why for many Chinese elites, China's current rise is essentially a restorative event: it is about reclaiming its lost glory as opposed to "obtaining something new."[30] The identity of a great power is seen as something natural for China to assume. Such beliefs have been reaffirmed at the latest party congress in 2017. In Xi's report to the meeting, he pointedly characterized China as a "strong power" or "great power" twenty-six times.[31] A time line of China's ascent was also given: by 2050 it would become a leading great power with a "world-class" military.[32] All of these indications do not imply that the country will now shed its "historical victim" or "developing country" sides, but they do point to a future where its great-power identity will become an increasingly, if not the, dominant face of China going forward.

Less straightforward is the question of how Beijing will use its growing power as it internalizes a great-power mind-set. Connected to the evolving internal debate on China's global responsibilities, at least three pictures of the future can be posited here.

At one extreme, the PRC could turn inward and resist playing a more active and larger role in global society. This is not to suggest that the country will opt out of globalization (à la North Korea) but rather to depict an isolationist shift that reflects a course more in line with the developmental and in particular the skeptics' logics in the Chinese RGP debate. In this scenario China would: dial back its involvement in maintaining international peace and security (for example, reducing participation in UN peacekeeping activities or nonproliferation regimes); assume a more passive profile in global governance institutions such as the United Nations, the G20, and the BRICS; cut back on foreign aid and investment; and diminish its role in addressing global problems such as climate change, terrorism, and public health. Considering that in recent years the world has witnessed a general rise in the forces of anti-globalism and pro-insularity, the idea of a more withdrawn China is not as far-fetched as it sounds. Yet, this future remains unlikely for a number of reasons. First, as a political concept, the responsible-power narrative has become relatively established, with its promulgation within the Chinese system intensifying over time. At the Nineteenth Party Congress, for example, it was again stressed that China would "continue to play the role of a responsible great power."[33] These signs point to increasing institutional entrenchment of the RGP identity and express a continuity of the globalized outlook in Beijing's orientation toward the world. Meshing with this factor is the growing Chinese belief that in order to sustain China's rise, the country cannot ignore the politics of morality in international society. It calls for China to "compete" for the moral high ground in international affairs. Incidentally, Beijing now sees fit to preach to the United States on its global obligations. When the Trump administration unilaterally pulled the US out of the global climate accord, for instance, Beijing lost no time in telling Washington that "there is an international responsibility to act over climate change."[34] Finally, while China remains dissatisfied with several aspects of the global order, it recognizes that many of its interests cannot be easily divorced from this order. This was indicated as much at the 2014 Central Foreign Affairs Work Conference, which noted that the country's "dependence on the world" has grown.[35] Therefore, China is unlikely to want to retreat from or be too disruptive to the extant order, as doing so would invariably mean harming its own interests. If anything, it seeks to deepen its linkages with the world, as Xi has signaled.

This speaks to a second vision of the future: China integrating into global society in the direction of the responsible stakeholder role as envisioned by the US. Notwithstanding the lack of specificity in this stakeholder prescription, such a future would see China essentially uphold the US- and Western-led postwar order and adhere to its norms. One could imagine this to include, among other things, eschewing state intervention in its trading and currency policies (what Washington terms "unfair" competition), bringing to bear its full weight on the North Korea nuclear issue, and acting to alleviate anxieties about its behavior in cyberspace and East Asia's maritime spaces. Domestically China might move toward a degree of liberalization that introduces greater civic and political freedoms. The previously described scenario is not beyond implausibility. As the book has shown, in several areas of international political life Beijing has made relative strides and is increasingly playing a bigger global role. That said, I do not assess this "stakeholder" trajectory to be any more likely than the "isolationist China" scenario. Such a path would have been most closely associated with the internationalist school in the Chinese RGP debate, which calls for the country to take on more global responsibilities. But even the more liberal internationalist position has its limits. For one, it is qualified by the overarching Chinese insistence that the choice of China's obligations should be self-decided. At the same time, the internationalist position is not monolithic. It has several evolving strands, of which the instrumentalist logic—the notion that the pursuit of global obligations should help China's national interests—has gained growing currency. In the Xi era this language of interest has become even more palpable in Chinese arguments on global responsibility, which asks questions of China's obligations when these interests differ from those of others in international society.[36] Taken together, the parameters of Chinese thinking on the RGP identity suggest an inevitable threshold to how far Beijing's actions will fully converge with American expectations.

Thus, the future that is likely to emerge is one with a more nuanced storyline: China will seek to embed further in the extant order but on its own terms. Within China there is an emerging policy and intellectual consensus that the country can and should take on more global responsibilities. And, in line with the turn to a more ambitious "strive for achievement" diplomacy, Beijing has become less reticent of staking its global leadership claims and has started taking a more proactive approach toward its international obligations. Yet the motivations behind these changes are not always unselfish. The pursuit of global obligations is increasingly seen in terms of how this endeavor will help advance China's objectives—economic, political, and strategic. The goal, ultimately, is to take greater *initiative* in engendering what Xi calls a more "enabling" external environment for China's continued rise.[37] Beijing is therefore likely to seek a larger role in global governance in the road ahead, not necessarily to reinforce the existing international order but to put itself in the driver's seat to shape the rules of this order in a way that maximizes the prospects of its rise. As its great-power consciousness grows, China will want to be more of a change-maker than a change-taker in global politics.

The *Guardian* wryly writes that the future edition of Xi's tome, *The Governance of China*, will be called *The Governance of the World*.[38] Perhaps this book will give some inkling of how that imaginary edition might look.

Notes

1. "Xi Jinping Portrays China as a Rock of Stability," *Economist*, January 21, 2017.
2. "Jointly Shoulder Responsibilities of Our Times, Promote Global Growth," Keynote Speech by HE Xi Jinping, President of the People's Republic of China, at the Opening Session of the World Economic Forum Annual Meeting, January 17, 2017.

3. See, among others, Tom Phillips, "How Xi Jinping's Global Ambitions Could Thrive as Trump Turns Inward," *Guardian*, February 10, 2017; Mark Magnier, "Xi to Stress China's Responsible Global Role in Davos," *Wall Street Journal*, January 11, 2017.
4. Amitav Acharya, *Whose Ideas Matter? Agency and Power in Asian Regionalism* (Ithaca, NY: Cornell University Press, 2009).
5. Sun Yatsen, *Sanmin Zhuyi (Three Principles of the People, 1924)* (Hunan: Yuelu Shushe, 2000), 68; Chiang Kai-shek, *China's Destiny*, trans. Philip Jaffe (London: Dennis Dobson, 1947), 107, 148–50, 157, 202–38.
6. Mao Zedong, "Patriotism and Internationalism," in *Quotations from Chairman Mao Zedong* (Beijing: Foreign Languages Press, 1966), 178–80.
7. Hongying Wang, "Linking Up with the International Track: What's in a Slogan?," *China Quarterly* 189 (2007): 1–23.
8. See, for example, Chinese President Jiang Zemin's Speech at a Luncheon Hosted in His Honor by Several US Organizations in New York, including the America-China Society, the National Committee on US-China Relations, the US-China Business Council, the Foreign Policy Association, the Council on Foreign Relations, and the Asia Society, October 23, 1995.
9. Li Keqiang, "The World Should Not Fear a Growing China," *Financial Times*, January 9, 2011; Hu Jintao, "Message from President Hu Jintao at the Opening Session of the First Round of China-US Strategic and Economic Dialogues," July 27, 2009, http://www.mfa.gov.cn/ce/ceie/eng/NewsPress/t577369.htm.
10. Rosemary Foot and Andrew Walter, *China, the United States, and Global Order* (Cambridge, UK: Cambridge University Press, 2011), 19.
11. Shogo Suzuki, "Seeking 'Legitimate' Great Power Status in Post–Cold War International Society: China's and Japan's Participation in UNPKO," *International Relations* 22, no. 1 (2008): 45–63.
12. Peter J. Burke, "Identity Change," *Social Psychology Quarterly* 69, no. 1 (2006): 86. See also Peter J. Burke and Jan E. Stets, *Identity Theory* (Oxford, UK: Oxford University Press, 2009), 27–32; Teresa Tsushima and Peter J. Burke, "Levels, Agency, and Control in the Parent Identity," *Social Psychology Quarterly* 62, no. 2 (1999): 173–89.
13. Rujun Shen, "China's Xi Says Wants South China Sea Issue Resolved Peacefully," Reuters, November 7, 2015.
14. Ted Hopf, *The Social Construction of International Politics: Identities and Foreign Policies, Moscow, 1955 and 1999* (Ithaca, NY: Cornell University Press, 2002), 290.
15. Susan Shirk, cited in Phillips, "How Xi Jinping's Global Ambitions Could Thrive."
16. John Mearsheimer, *The Tragedy of Great Power Politics* (New York: W. W. Norton, 2001).
17. Ted Galen Carpenter, *America's Coming War with China* (New York: St. Martin's, 2005).
18. Graham Allison, *Destined for War: Can America and China Escape Thucydides's Trap?* (Boston: Houghton Mifflin Harcourt, 2017).
19. "Will America and China Go to War?," *Economist*, July 6, 2017.

20. Hopf, *Social Construction of International Politics.*
21. Jeffrey Legro, "The Plasticity of Identity under Anarchy," *European Journal of International Relations* 15, no. 1 (2009): 37–65.
22. Alexander Wendt, *Social Theory of International Politics* (Cambridge, UK: Cambridge University Press, 2008 edition).
23. Ernst B. Haas and Peter M. Haas, "Pragmatic Constructivism and the Study of International Institutions," *Millennium* 31, no. 3 (2002): 573–601.
24. Hopf, *Social Construction of International Politics,* 281.
25. For more on "analytical eclecticism," an intellectual position that espouses the "selectively recombin(ing) of analytic components . . . from explanatory theories, models, and narratives embedded in competing research traditions," see Rudra Sil and Peter Katzenstein, "Analytic Eclecticism in the Study of World Politics: Reconfiguring Problems and Mechanisms across Research Traditions," *Perspectives on Politics* 8, no. 2 (2010): 411–31.
26. For more on the ideational agency of local actors, see Acharya, *Whose Ideas Matter?*
27. Mlada Bukovansky, Ian Clark, Robyn Eckersley, Richard Price, Christian Reus-Smit, and Nicholas J. Wheeler, *Special Responsibilities: Global Problems and American Power* (Cambridge, UK: Cambridge University Press, 2012).
28. "Is China Challenging the United States for Global Leadership?," *Economist*, April 1, 2017.
29. Harvey Nelson, "The Future of the Chinese State," in *The Modern Chinese State*, ed. David Shambaugh (Cambridge, UK: Cambridge University Press, 2000), 216.
30. Yan Xuetong, "The Rise of China in Chinese Eyes," *Journal of Contemporary China* 10, no. 26 (2001): 34.
31. Chris Buckley and Keith Bradsher, "Xi Jinping's Marathon Speech: Five Takeaways," *New York Times*, October 18, 2017.
32. Xi Jinping, "Secure a Decisive Victory in Building a Moderately Prosperous Society in All Respects and Strive for the Great Success of Socialism with Chinese Characteristics for a New Era," *Report of the Nineteenth National Congress of the Communist Party of China*, October 18, 2017.
33. Ibid.
34. Ian Johnston, "China Tells Donald Trump There Is an International Responsibility to Act over Climate Change," *Independent*, June 1, 2017.
35. "Xi Eyes More Enabling International Environment for China's Peaceful Development," Xinhua, November 30, 2014.
36. The emphasis on national interests can also be seen in the continuing promulgation of the "core interests" discourse under Xi. See Hoo Tiang Boon, "Hardening the Hard, Softening the Soft: Assertiveness and China's Regional Strategy," *Journal of Strategic Studies* 40, no. 5 (2017): 648–52.
37. For more on China's more proactive diplomacy, see Hoo Tiang Boon, ed., *Chinese Foreign Policy under Xi* (London and New York: Routledge, 2017).
38. Phillips, "How Xi Jinping's Global Ambitions Could Thrive." Note: vol. 2 of Xi's *The Governance of China* was published in November 2017.

A NOTE ON SOURCES

This note provides additional information on the types of primary Chinese data sources that have been consulted in research on the RGP identity. It is not intended to be a bibliography of the Chinese sources. The primary data consulted in this book are categorized as follows:

Leadership Accounts

Publications such as *Xi Jinping Tan Zhiguo Lizheng* (Xi Jinping: The Governance of China) (published in 2014); *Deng Xiaoping Wenxuan* (Selected Works of Deng Xiaoping), vols. 2–3 (1993–1994); and *Jiang Zemin Wenxuan* (Selected Writings of Jiang Zemin), vols. 1–3 (2006) are rich collections of statements by current and former leaders. Equally valuable are the personal accounts of former diplomats or policymakers, which offer interesting insights into China's diplomatic positions and the thinking behind them. A good example is Qian Qichen's *Waijiao Shiji (Ten Episodes in China's Diplomacy)* (2003). Other useful readings include Chen Youwei's *Tiananmen Shijian Hou Zhonggong Yu Meiguo Waijiao Neimu (After Tiananmen: The Inside Stories of Sino-US Diplomacy)* (1999); Zeng Jianhui's *Yihui Waijiao (Congress Diplomacy)* (2005); and Wu Jianmin's *Waijiao Anlie (Case Studies in Diplomacy)* (2007).

Party Publications, Textbooks, and Government Reports

State and party documentary sources represent one window to Beijing's thinking. They include: (i) state or party periodicals, such as *Liaowang (Outlook), Qiushi (Seeking Truth), Renmin Luntan (People's Tribune), Shishi Baogao (Current Affairs), Dangdai Shijie (Contemporary World), Dangjian (Party Construction), Dangzheng Luntan (Party and Government Forum), Dangdai Shijie Yu*

Shehui Zhuyi (Contemporary World and Socialism), and *Zhonggong Zhongyang Dangxiao Xuebao (Journal of the Party School of the Central Committee of the CPC)*; (ii) party-affiliated books or textbooks on international relations and history, such as *Zhongguo Gong Chandang Yu Dangdai Zhongguo Waijiao (Chinese Communist Party and Contemporary China's Diplomacy)* (2010); *Zhongmei Guanxi Shi (A History of China-US Relations)* (2009) and *Guoji Zhengzhi Xue Gailun (Introduction to the Study of International Politics)* (2006); and (iii) government reports, such as the state council white papers (*Baipi Shu*).

Newspapers and Websites

Newspapers and news networks, such as *Renmin Ribao (People's Daily)*, *China Daily*, and Xinhua, are other useful sources of information. They are considered to be Beijing's "mouthpieces," although occasionally commentaries can hint of differences in opinion among the Chinese leadership. Considerable information on leaders' statements and government positions can also be obtained from websites such as www.china.org.cn (under the State Council Information Office); www.fmprc.gov.cn (under the Ministry of Foreign Affairs); www.mod.gov.cn (under the Ministry of National Defense); and cpc.people.com.cn (the main CCP portal).

Academic and Policy Periodicals

While Chinese intellectuals (working in mostly state-funded or state-affiliated universities or think tanks) do not represent the Chinese state per se, their views and writings are often reflective of the spectrum of opinions that can be found in Beijing. Rana Mitter describes these perspectives as a "microcosm of wider thinking in the Chinese leadership."[1] Moreover, Chinese intellectuals are becoming increasingly influential in their own right, giving rise to what Xuanli Liao calls "pluralistic elitism" in China.[2] Many Chinese scholars directly influence policy when they are asked to collaborate with or provide inputs to the Chinese government. For instance, Zheng Bijian, the former vice president of the Central Party School, is credited with being the intellectual thrust behind China's peaceful rise doctrine.[3] Another example is Gao Fei, a China Foreign Affairs University professor, who has the notable distinction of lecturing on the subject of global governance reform to leaders in the CCP Politburo.[4]

One valuable trove of such scholarly writings is Chinese journals. Some relevant "core" (*hexin*) or influential publications include: (i) *Shijie Jingji Yu Zhengzhi (World Economics and Politics)* by the Chinese Academy of Social Sciences; (ii) *Guoji Wenti Yanjiu (International Studies)* by the China Institute of International Studies; (iii) *Xiandai Guoji Guanxi (Contemporary International Relations)* by the China Institutes of Contemporary International Relations; (iv) *Guoji Zhengzhi Yanjiu (International Politics Quarterly)* by Peking University; (v) *Waijiao Pinglun (Foreign Affairs Review)* by China Foreign Affairs University; (vi) *Dangdai Yatai (Contemporary Asia-Pacific Studies)* by the Chinese Academy of Social Sciences; (vii) *Shijie Zhishi (World Affairs)* by the World Affairs Press under the Ministry of Foreign Affairs; (viii) *Guoji Guancha (International Review)* by the Shanghai International Studies University; (ix) *Jiaoxue Yu Yanjiu (Teaching and Research)* by Renmin University; and (x) *Guoji Zhanwang (Global Review)* by the Shanghai Institutes for International Studies. The journals published by think tanks naturally tend to be more policy oriented and can occasionally include articles by senior government officials. Indeed, David Shambaugh notes that they are often important "early warning indicators of policies to come."[5]

Books

There are growing numbers of full-length Chinese works that explore themes related to the RGP identity. Books that explicitly discuss the questions of China's big-power responsibility include Jin Canrong's *Daguo De Zeren (Great Power's Responsibility)* (published in 2011); Hu Jian's *Jiaose Zeren Chengzhang Lujing (Role, Responsibility and Growing Path)* (2010); and Pan Zhongqi's *Guoji Zeren Yu Daguo Zhanlue (International Responsibility and Great Power Strategy)* (2008). For books that probe the related themes of China's global role and leadership, there are a plethora of works. They include, inter alia, Wang Yizhou's *Chuang Zaoxing Jieru: Zhongguo Zhi Quanqiu Jiaose De Shengcheng (Creative Involvement: The Evolution of China's Global Role)* (2013); Wang Yu's *Daguo Siwei (Great Power Thinking)* (2010); Yan Xuetong and Xu Jin's *Wangba Tianxia Sixiang Ji Qidi (Thoughts on World Leadership and Implications)* (2009); and the book series *Zhongguo Xuezhe Kan Shijie (World Politics: Views from China)*

(2007) and *Daguo Ce (Great Power Policy)* (2009). The ones highlighted here are some representative works in what is becoming an increasingly vibrant intellectual terrain.

Fieldwork

To supplement existing documentary evidence, fieldwork in China was conducted on several occasions between 2011 and 2015. This work included interviews and/or discussions with Chinese analysts and scholars based at, among others, Peking University, Renmin University, Fudan University, Tsinghua University, Communication University of China, China Foreign Affairs University, the Shanghai Academy of Social Sciences, the Shanghai Institutes for International Studies, the China Institutes of Contemporary International Relations, and the China Institute of International Strategic Studies. Many of those interviewed are contributors to the domestic debate on the RGP identity.

As part of (and facilitating) this fieldwork, visiting fellowships were held at the Shanghai Institutes for International Studies and the Shanghai Academy of Social Sciences in 2011 and the China Foreign Affairs University (affiliated with the Ministry of Foreign Affairs) in 2014.

Notes

1. Rana Mitter, "An Uneasy Engagement: Chinese Ideas of Global Order and Justice in Historical Perspective," in *Order and Justice in International Relations*, ed. Rosemary Foot, John Lewis Gaddis, Andrew Hurrell (Oxford, UK: Oxford University Press, 2004), 225.
2. Xuanli Liao, *Chinese Foreign Policy Think Tanks and China's Policy towards Japan* (Hong Kong: Chinese University Press, 2006), 15–52.
3. Bonnie S. Glaser and Evan S. Medeiros, "The Changing Ecology of Foreign Policy-Making in China: The Ascension and Demise of the Theory of 'Peaceful Rise,'" *China Quarterly* 190 (2007): 291–310.
4. "Xi Calls for Reforms on Global Governance," Xinhua, September 28, 2016.
5. David Shambaugh, "China's International Relations Think Tanks: Evolving Structures and Process," *China Quarterly* 171 (2002): 575–96.

INDEX

Figures and tables are indicated by f *and* t *following the page number.*

ABOUT THE AUTHOR

Hoo Tiang Boon is assistant professor at the S. Rajaratnam School of International Studies, Nanyang Technological University. He holds a PhD in international relations from the University of Oxford. He is the editor of *Chinese Foreign Policy under Xi*.

www.ingramcontent.com/pod-product-compliance
Lightning Source LLC
LaVergne TN
LVHW050151080826
844660LV00002B/170
* 9 7 8 1 6 2 6 1 6 6 1 3 4 *